25

VEGETABLES

ANYONE CAN GROW

by

ANN ROE ROBBINS

ILLUSTRATED BY LEONARD J. ROBBINS

DOVER PUBLICATIONS, INC.
NEW YORK

This Dover edition, first published in 1974, is a republication of the work originally published by the Thomas Y. Crowell Company in 1942.

International Standard Book Number: 0-486-23029-5
Library of Congress Catalog Card Number: 73-93783

Manufactured in the United States of America
Dover Publications, Inc.
180 Varick Street
New York, N. Y. 10014

Preface

This is not a technical book. It treats vegetable gardening strictly from the amateur's point of view. No attempt has been made to describe the culture of vegetables in general. On the contrary, twenty-five of the most popular and useful vegetables have been selected, and the steps to be taken in growing and using them are dealt with individually for each vegetable.

There are many detailed books on vegetable gardening for truck farmers. There are few that reduce the science of successful vegetable production to the limits of a back yard. Therefore I hope this book will be of some use to you if your zeal is ardent but your knowledge limited as to just how to go about converting a barren strip of land into neat rows of flourishing vitamins and minerals. I have tried to make the treatment of each vegetable fully complete so that your task will be simplified. If I haven't stressed sufficiently how much pleasure and deep satisfaction are to be found in planning your own vegetable garden and planting it with your own hands, I hope you will soon find out for yourself.

ANN ROE ROBBINS

New Canaan, Connecticut

Acknowledgments

LIKE MOST GARDENERS who have the temerity to write about their absorbing craft, I have consulted many books on many points. In particular, I wish to acknowledge my indebtedness to *The Farm Garden* (U. S. Department of Agriculture: Farmers' Bulletin No. 1673) for planting dates throughout the country; *The Principles of Vegetable Farming* (L. H. Bailey) for information on classification of vegetables; and *Sturtevant's Notes on Edible Plants* (U. P. Hedrick) for some of the historical material.

I also wish to thank my friend, Andrew S. Wing, Editorial Director of *Garden Digest*, for reading the manuscript and contributing valuable suggestions.

A. R. R.

Contents

Note

EACH VEGETABLE CHAPTER contains detailed information under the following headings, which are arranged in the same order for ready reference:

HISTORY: High lights on the earliest known references to the vegetable, and its cultivation in the United States.

FOOD VALUE: The value of the vegetable in your diet as a source of vitamins and essential minerals.

CULTURE: What parts of the country the vegetable can be successfully grown in; its climate requirements; whether it is easy or more difficult to grow; whether it is quick or slow maturing.

HABITS OF GROWTH: How the plant develops and grows; the size and appearance of the edible portion or portions.

TYPES AND VARIETIES: Classification of the main types of the vegetable and a list of the recommended varieties for each type.

How MUCH TO BUY: The approximate number of feet of row or number of plants you can get from a given amount of seed, as a buying guide.

PLANTING: Specific information on the germination time of the seed, depth for seed or seedlings, spacing of plants and rows.

WHEN TO PLANT: Planting dates for early and late crops for zones throughout the country; how to select the proper dates for planting the vegetable for your own locality by reference to the maps on pages 194–196.

How TO PLANT: What to do when you are ready to put the seed in the ground; whether to sow thickly or thinly; whether to start the seed indoors or outdoors; whether the seedlings need transplanting.

WHERE TO PLANT: The best location in the garden for the vegetable for ease in cultivation and pest control; whether the vegetable can be used as a succession crop—that is, to precede or follow other vegetables in the same ground.

SOIL: The type of soil the vegetable thrives in; what fertilizer is advisable for best results.

CULTIVATION AND CARE: What attention the vegetable requires in the way of thinning, hoeing, weeding, and watering; what to do if the vegetable is susceptible to special pests.

HARVESTING: The size and appearance of the vegetable when it is ready to be pulled up or picked; how to avoid injuring your crops when harvesting.

STORING: If the vegetable is storable, how to prepare it, what to do, and the storage conditions required; how long the vegetable can be safely stored.

CANNING: If the vegetable is suitable for canning, you are referred to the special chapter on "Canning."

USES: Unusual recipes to make eating the vegetable a pleasure as well as a duty.

Introduction

"THE NUMEROUS BENEFITS resulting to every family from the production of a well-cultivated garden are too evident to need any remarks by way of illustration. The health they afford to the family, not only in the luxuries which they furnish for the table; but, in the exercise, amusement and enjoyment they impart in the cultivation, exceed all description. In fact, the fruits and vegetables of a garden are the life of the family, upon every principle of enjoyment and economy."

These words, written in 1826, ring singularly true today, more than a hundred years later. Vegetable gardening has always been an important factor in the home production of food for two reasons: home-grown vegetables are usually fresher and taste better than the ones you buy, and they cost less.

The desirability of having your own supply rather than of being dependent upon the markets is reiterated so often in newspapers and magazines today that we are probably all familiar with the underlying reasons. Briefly they are: railroad facilities will be needed for transportation in connection with many branches of defense; labor will be scarce; the United States will send millions of dollars' worth of food abroad; and it is vital in days of severe stress that every man, woman, and child be not only adequately fed but properly fed. Vegetables are one of the richest sources of life-giving vitamins and minerals.

So everyone who has suitable land should grow at least part of his family's total yearly vegetable requirements. Any properly located piece of ground that grows weeds will, with the right preparation and fertilization, grow vegetables. Even the smallest-size garden can produce a large supply of vegetables if the crops are chosen with care. About a quarter of an acre will supply a family of five or six with all the vegetables it requires for the summer and leave a surplus for storing and canning. A small plot, twenty by fifty feet, will go a long way toward taking a family out of the market for the summer. Small gardens, intensively cropped, are easier to weed, cultivate, and spray, and are often relatively more productive than large ones.

If you are growing vegetables for the first time, you should proceed carefully and take each step slowly, only after you know what you need to do. The site for the garden should be chosen with forethought. Vegetables need five or six hours of midday sun. If a location doesn't afford that vital condition, don't use it for vegetables. Also vegetables can't compete with tree roots for moisture and plant food, so don't expect to harvest a good crop if your land is near large trees and packed with their roots. These are the two most important conditions—land that gets full sun and is free of tree roots.

What to grow is the next consideration. I would suggest that you consult the list of twenty-five vegetables in this book and have a family conference, checking the list for preferences. It is important to grow vegetables that the family favors because then they will be eaten. If you have a large garden, you can grow an abundance of all the vegetables you like. In a small plot you will need to make some selection. The most economical planting will include large quantities of the crops that require little space and that can be either canned or stored or both, crops such as carrots, beets, turnips, parsnips, and onions. The space-consumers, such crops as peas and corn, that supply only a small harvest, should be limited. Tomatoes, however, are such an important nutritive food that they should be included in every garden, with enough plants, if possible, both for supplying the table and for canning whole and as juice.

The following list for the twenty-five vegetables is compiled from various agricultural experiment station bulletins, and gives the average amount of row required per person for a year's supply of each crop. It is interesting as a rough guide.

Crop	Feet of Row
Asparagus	20
Beans—dwarf	15 per planting (2-4 plantings)
" —pole	10
Beets	15 per planting (2 plantings)
Broccoli	10
Brussels sprouts	10
Cabbage	20 per planting (2 plantings)
Carrots	25

CROP	FEET OF ROW	
Cauliflower	10	
Celery	20	
Chard	5–10	
Corn (sweet)	25	per planting (4 plantings)
Cucumbers	10–20	
Eggplant	10	
Lettuce	10–20	per planting (2 plantings)
Onions	25	per planting (2 plantings)
Parsley	2–3	
Parsnips	10–20	
Peas	25–50	per planting (2-4 plantings)
Peppers	10–20	
Potatoes	50	early
	100	late
Radishes	10–20	per planting (as many plantings as possible
Spinach	20–30	per planting (2 plantings)
Spinach, New Zealand	5–10	
Squash	5–10	summer
	20–25	winter
Tomatoes	15	individual plants
Turnips and rutabagas	20	

Plan your garden carefully, particularly if it is small, so that the space will be in continual use. Figure out your seed list so that you will have a sufficient supply, but without waste. Seed isn't plentiful enough to throw any away. If you are in doubt about where to purchase your seed, consult your state agricultural experimental station for the names of some first-class seed houses.

Follow the steps outlined in the sections on each individual vegetable. If your land is limited, and you are not counting on having a regular flower garden, put some flowers in with your vegetables. The garden can easily be surrounded with a border of flowers, or you can have an occasional row to keep your house supplied with cutting flowers. Flowers are an important contribution to morale, and every garden should have some. Herbs are also useful and fun to grow, and one corner of the vegetable plot might well include a small herb bed. This doesn't mean that the vegetable patch should not be neat, with even corners, straight rows, and a well-ordered regularity.

Buying Seeds: Your entire success or failure in gardening is dependent upon the seeds you purchase. That is why it is foolish just to go into some general store, notice a stand of assorted seeds for five cents a package, buy a package or two of carrots or beets, for example, and plant these seeds in your garden. Something will probably come up. But the chances are that that something will be of poor quality and taste, and the variety may be one unsuited for the time you have chosen to plant it. This is one of those minor economies which does not pay.

Good seed grown by reliable seed houses is fairly expensive because of the care necessary in producing and selecting it. But it is true to type, fresh, weed free, and from sound stock. You should purchase your seeds only from a first-class seed house that publishes a detailed catalogue. And you should study your purchases carefully, buying not just carrots, for example, but a specific variety of carrots, suitable for your climate and planting season. Seed catalogues give you full information about each variety, but there are sometimes so many varieties of a given vegetable that a choice may be difficult. As an aid in making that choice, recommended varieties are mentioned in the following chapters. There are such wide differences in size, taste, period of growth, and planting time among varieties, that in fairness to yourself you should know just what you are planting and why.

Plant hybridizers are constantly at work improving various crops. They have produced, for example, rust-proof asparagus, coreless carrots, blight-resistant spinach, stringless snap beans. Many of the old standard varieties are still good today, but many have been surpassed by new varieties. So don't ask some old-time gardener about varieties because he may be devoted to an old favorite that is outdated now. On the other hand, don't go overboard for a brand-new variety until its worth has been tested. The cost of producing, advertising, and launching a new variety is great, and seedsmen usually tread warily and don't waste their money on a dubious product. But until the strains are well established, there are sometimes variations, and I would suggest that a small trial planting of a brand-new variety is sufficient for the first year.

There are many good seed houses all over the country, and the inexperienced gardener had best get a catalogue from one of them, spend many evenings studying all the possible choices, and make the final selection with as much care as though he were buying a hat or a pair of shoes. The problem is the same—something that fits and can be used at the right season and is suitable for the particular need for which it was bought.

This book describes only twenty-five vegetables. These are the ones that the average gardener will most probably want, and until you know your way around it's best not to be overambitious. But there are many more vegetables available, and it's a good plan to try at least one vegetable that you've never grown before, and maybe never even heard of, every year. There are at least fifty vegetables that can be grown in any garden, more if you include the obscure ones. It's surprising how much more interesting both gardening and eating are if you do a little experimenting. Don't forsake the old stand-bys, but add a few novelties from time to time.

Planting Seeds: The importance of planting at the right time cannot be emphasized too strongly. Crops are variable in their demands and you must satisfy them if you're to be successful.

Crops are usually divided into four classifications—hardy, half hardy, tender, and very tender. In general, hardy crops can stand hard frosts and can therefore be planted before the date of the last killing frost, while half-hardy crops can stand only light frosts and so should be planted just after the last killing frost. However the dividing line is somewhat nebulous. Tender crops cannot stand even a light frost, while very tender crops must have warm days and warm nights to flourish. Your plantings of various crops will begin in the spring about a month before the last killing-frost date, with the hardy crops, and planting can continue practically all summer off and on if you use your space to the best advantage.

The hardy crops in this book are asparagus, broccoli, Brussels sprouts, cabbage, onions, parsley, radishes, turnips and rutabaga, peas, spinach, lettuce, and potatoes. The half-hardy are beets, carrots, cauliflower, celery, chard, and parsnips. The tender are New Zealand spinach, snap beans, sweet corn, and tomatoes. The very tender are cucumbers, eggplant, lima beans, peppers, and squash.

The rows that you plant in the garden should be straight. The only way to make sure they are is to use a line. A ball of stout cord and two heavy stakes will do. Stretch the cord between the stakes, make a furrow the right depth with the handle of your hoe, drop the seeds in the furrow, and replace the soil with the hoe. If your garden is small and the soil dry, watering the furrow well after you replace the soil will speed germination. Seeds don't sprout without moisture.

Sometimes if the soil is very dry, it's a good idea to cover the row with burlap, and water it well. This covering will help retain the moisture in the soil. It must be removed, though, as soon as the seeds sprout.

Certain crops, such as tomatoes, eggplant, peppers, early cabbage, celery, and cauliflower, for various reasons require special seeding, inside the house or in a hotbed, if you wish to produce your own plants. A completely inexperienced gardener had better buy plants his first year or, if he is very ambitious, try to produce plants for only one or two crops (for example, tomatoes and cabbage) that are comparatively easy to raise and for which he can probably provide adequate indoor facilities.

It's all very well to talk glibly of raising plants for five or six crops—and it is feasible if you have a greenhouse or hotbed. But five or six seed flats sown indoors in a sunny window produce dozens of plants, and each one usually has to be transplanted at least once before being set in the garden. Few houses have enough sunny windows for large numbers of small growing plants, many of which have to be in individual pots or containers. Quite apart from that, the growing conditions in most heated houses are not ideal for young plants.

This is the discouraging side of the picture. It is intended to be a timely word of warning before you find your house swamped with pots and potting soil. Now that you've heard the worst, we shall proceed to examine in some detail the methods of raising plants indoors, and you may want to try your luck.

A greenhouse is perfect for seeds that require heat. If you have no greenhouse, you may be able to rent greenhouse space, which will provide you with an ideal testing ground. Hotbeds are difficult unless you have had years of experience with them. The construction is a technical business, and they are hard to manage, unless they are electrically heated with thermostatic control. The plants are likely to die from either too much or too little heat, and the temperature requirements vary with different crops. Hotbeds are not, as a rule, advisable for the novice to work with. However, if you are interested, write to your own state agricultural experiment station for details, or write to the U. S. Department of Agriculture for Bulletin No. 1743, *Hotbeds and Coldframes*.

For seeding indoors, sunlight, plenty of ventilation, and the right temperature are needed. Growing plants indoors is considered a difficult business. Beginners usually sin on two counts: having too high temperatures and not enough sun. When seeds are planted directly in the garden they are not coddled. They have to withstand cold weather and indifferent climate. And it is that fight against odds which makes them strong and sturdy. But with seeds planted indoors the tendency is to pamper them by putting them in excessively warm rooms, with the emphasis on the heat rather than on the sun. And the results are usually disastrous. Either the plants are lost entirely from "damping-off"; or they grow into tall, spindly, weak plants which are ill equipped to withstand average garden conditions outdoors.

Damping-off is the name of a fungus disease that can cause untold damage. The fungus lives near the surface of the soil and attacks the seedlings either as they sprout out of the ground or after they have begun to grow. Whole plantings can be laid waste overnight. It is discouraging and a difficult disease to combat indoors. The best defense is treating your seeds before planting with one of the special preparations which can be obtained easily from seed houses, with directions for correct use. These preparations come in either dust or liquid form and are applied either to the seeds before planting or to the soil after planting.

The temperature demands of different crops vary. Cool-season crops, as lettuce and cabbage, do best when the temperature during the day is about 55°–60° F.; while the tender crops, such as eggplant, tomatoes, and peppers, do best with a temperature of 70°–75° F. During the night the temperature should be 10 degrees or so less. Be firm, and don't keep them any warmer. Place them in a southern exposure, if possible, where they will get plenty of sunlight. You can't get good plants without sunlight.

Seed flats are best for sowing seeds, although clay pots will do, and shallow clay bulb pans are excellent though more expensive. Because seedlings require only an inch or two of soil, are soon transplanted, and have shallow root systems when they are small, the flats need be only 2 to 3 inches deep. A common size is about 12 by 18 inches, but if you are making your own, make them smaller for ease of handling. Many people use old cigar boxes. The regular flats have cracks about ⅛ inch wide between the bottom boards. Some such allowance should be made for drainage. If you are using other boxes, bore a few holes in the bottom.

Place a layer of some drainage material, either peat moss, sand, or gravel, at the bottom of the flat, one inch deep. Then put your potting soil on top of that. For the few flats that the average gardener uses, the easiest way to get good potting soil is to buy it from a seed house or florist. It will be sterilized (and save you the trouble of doing your own sterilizing), weed free, and properly mixed. If you mix your own soil, 2 parts garden soil, 1 part well-rotted manure or compost, and 1 part sand is a good mixture. The soil should be screened and sterilized. For the home gardener the best method of sterilization is the use of a formaldehyde preparation, which can be bought from a supply house with full directions for use.

Fill the flat with soil; tamp it down with your fingers around the edges and corners; and be certain that the surface is level and about half an inch below the surface of the flat. Water the soil well and let it stand a few hours before you sow your seeds. When the soil is sodden, you are encouraging damping-off. Sow the seeds at the depths given in the individual chapters; put a piece of brown paper over the flat; and over that put a piece of glass. Place the flat in the sun. Turn the glass every day or oftener if moisture collects very much. To keep the seedlings from getting too hot, you may have to lift the glass several times a day. It gets like a Turkish bath under the glass, and the steamy atmosphere tends to start damping-off.

As soon as the seeds sprout, remove the cover. When it is necessary to water the soil—and the soil must not under any circumstances dry out—do it with extreme care. A rush of water from an ordinary watering can may wash all the seeds together or ruin young seedlings. Either you can get a small bulb watering apparatus that squirts the water out like mist: or, better still, you can water from the bottom. Get a pan that is large enough to hold your flat readily. Put some water, room temperature, in the pan; set the flat in the pan; and leave it there until the water has seeped up from the bottom and the surface of the soil is damp.

The seedlings should be transplanted as soon as they show the first pair of true leaves, that is, the second pair to appear. Crowded seedlings do not get proper nourishment, and you want a strong root system. The distances required for the seedlings are given in the individual chapters. The transplanted seedlings can be either left in the original flats or put into individual pots, so-called fertile pots, or paper containers. Two-inch cardboard boxes which fit into flats are useful. If the plants get too big for these containers, they will need a further shift into a larger home.

Before the plants are put in the garden, they should be hardened off. This means gradually subjecting them to adverse growing conditions so that, instead of using their food for growing, they store it. Water is gradually withheld, and the plants are placed outdoors in the sun for longer and longer periods each day. Thus, by the time they are actually set in the garden, they will be entirely used to outdoor conditions.

A few hours before you finally set the plants in the garden, water them well. Do your transplanting, if possible, either on a cloudy day or late in the afternoon. If the plants are in a flat, dig them up gently (a small wooden garden label is a convenient tool) and disturb the roots just as little as possible. Scoop out a hole in the ground large enough to hold the roots; pour some water into the bottom of it (unless the soil is very damp); set the plants; and firm the earth well around them. The plants are usually set a little deeper than they were in the flat or container. That's all, except that they should be kept well watered until thoroughly established.

Seed houses sell various liquid chemical mixtures which, diluted with water, furnish a complete food supply for seedlings. You can sow your seeds in sand (regular builder's sand strained through a coarse mesh); water according to the directions of the manufacturer; and, with no fussing over sterilized soil, produce excellent seedlings with extremely strong root systems. In sand there is less danger of damping-off; the seedlings are easier to transplant because the roots slip out of sand without any injury; the same sand can be used countless times; and the seedlings are, in my opinion, usually superior to those grown in soil. It is definitely worth a try.

Soil and Fertilizers: You can't have a good vegetable garden if you don't give the soil thorough preparation. Just raking off the trash, scratching up the surface, and planting seeds won't give you very valuable results.

As the essential first step, the ground must be dug to a depth of at least 8 inches, preferably more, and the soil loosened so that it is in condition to permit proper growth and nourishment of the plant roots. The best time to dig is in the fall with a garden fork, if the soil has been turned before, or with a spade or mattock if it is sod. Better still, it might be plowed. The soil is then exposed to the breaking-up action of frost in the winter; underground insects are turned up to the surface where it is earnestly hoped they will die; and any coarse matter that is turned under has a chance to decay.

If the ground wasn't turned over in the fall, this can be done very early in the spring as soon as the soil is sufficiently soft to work. Coarse matter should not be turned under at this season.

In the spring the soil must be pulverized as soon as it is ready (a good test to determine when it is ready is to pick up a handful; if it crumbles easily, it's ready; if it forms a sticky mass, it isn't). You shouldn't attempt to sow seeds in lumpy ground. Turn the soil over again if there is time; that is the ideal preparation. But, at any rate, go over the ground with an iron rake, removing any big stones and root masses and leaving the surface smooth and porous.

The question of soil feeding is a complicated one. The ideal way to handle this problem is to send samples of your soil to your state agricultural experiment station to be analyzed, indicating the crops that you intend to grow, and follow the recommendations you will receive. Every soil has different requirements, and it takes an expert to diagnose them. On the other hand, the home gardener can produce good crops without soil analysis if he prepares his soil thoroughly and gives it some additional feeding.

Manure is the standard fertilizer, and until the advent of the automobile it was used in most gardens. However, it is usually expensive now and often difficult to obtain. It is not actually a balanced fertilizer, and it usually contains plenty of weed seeds. But if it happens to be available in your region at a reasonable price, it can be used when digging or plowing in the fall. Use it at the rate of one pound per square foot and turn it in well. Since many crops react badly to fresh manure, do not use it in the spring. Getting manure to the exact stage for best use in the garden is an art. Fresh manure is so strong that it burns young plants. It can be used for only very few crops. If you leave manure in a pile to get well rotted, much of the valuable minerals leach away, and you have mainly pure humus left. Manure is by no means essential to garden success, however, since the nutritive elements necessary for soil feeding can be obtained in quickly available form in commercial fertilizers.

The main essential nutritive elements needed for plant growth are nitrogen, phosphorus, and potassium. Commercial fertilizers supply these elements in the form of chemical compounds. A "complete" fertilizer contains all three. The three numbers used in complete commercial fertilizers indicate the percentages of available nitrogen, phosphorus as phosphate, and potassium as potash. A 10–20–10 complete fertilizer, for example, contains 10 per cent nitrogen, 20 per cent phosphoric acid, and 10 per cent potash. These fertilizers supply the soil with the additional nutrients required for proper plant growth. For the home gardener they are probably preferable to manure, and in any event they can be used to supplement manure feeding.

In the following chapters there are specific fertilizer recommendations for many of the vegetables. These fertilizers are ones that have proved to be the best for that particular crop. Many home gardeners, however, are not going to trouble themselves to give one crop one fertilizer and another crop something different. So the easiest practice, and one that will give good results, is to fertilize the whole garden with a complete fertilizer before the soil is raked down in the spring (if manure has not been used in the fall) and give special supplementary feedings when specified (some crops, for example, respond well to special doses of nitrate of soda). The exact fertilizer that you should use is hard to recommend because it depends entirely upon the type of soil and the degree of fertility. However, it has been found that 4–8–4 or 5–8–7 complete fertilizers are suitable for general use in many gardens. They should be applied at the rate of about 2–3 pounds per 100 square feet.

Soil also needs humus, which is organic matter in an advanced stage of decay. This can be supplied by (a) green manure, which is formed by plowing under a growing crop so that it decays in the ground (certain special crops such as rye, soybeans, cowpeas, or clover are often sown in the fall in vegetable gardens, after the ground is cleared, and plowed under in the spring, to provide green manure and also add nitrogen to the soil, to break up the subsoil with their roots, and to check erosion); (b) vegetative matter from certain garden crops, such as pea vines, which are turned under the ground after harvesting and allowed to decay; or (c) compost, which is formed by allowing dead leaves and plants to decay in a pile.

Some soils also need lime, but this should not be added unless you know your soil is too acid and needs neutralizing. Here again your state agricultural experiment station can assist you or if you're really enterprising you can do a little soil testing on your own with one of the kits sold for this purpose.

Cultivation:

> "The more we hoe,
> The more we grow."

And as Candide said, "We must cultivate our gardens." Cultivation is the care given to the ground after the seeds are sown. There are two reasons that the ground must be cultivated—one is to keep weeds down and the other to keep the soil loosened up.

In practically all garden operations weeds must not get a foothold. They use valuable soil moisture and minerals as well as light and air that are needed for your crops, and in many instances their growth is so vigorous that they will completely crowd out tender young seedlings. All soil has weeds, and every gardener must diligently pursue them. When weeds are tiny, it is an easy matter to dispose of them. In fact, there is no reason why weeds should ever get a start. Try to make it a practice to go over every row at least once a week, oftener if it rains a lot.

Keeping the surface of the soil loosened up also enables your garden to take proper advantage of rainfall. The rain will penetrate deeply, and your plants will not have to struggle with a hard crust of earth.

The secret of cultivation is to be conscientious at the beginning of the growing season for each crop to give the young plants a good start in life.

Three tools are generally used for cultivating. The best of all is a wheel hoe. This tool should be part of the standard equipment of every gardener. A wheel hoe is really a small hand plow. It can be operated easily and has various attachments which make it useful for many garden operations. The hoe attachment enables you to run down a row in a few minutes. It is important not to disturb the roots of some plants, so don't run your wheel hoe too close to the plants themselves. A little hand hoeing can be done close to and between the plants. And if the seedlings are small, hand weeding is best, although it does take time.

If you haven't a wheel hoe, either a hand hoe or an iron rake will do. If you rake between your rows every few days, the weeds won't have any opportunity of getting a start. The point to remember is that you don't need to dig the soil, all you need to do is to keep the upper inch or two of soil stirred up so that you'll eliminate the weeds. A little care every few days takes much less time in the long run than trying to rid the garden of weeds in one fell swoop when they have grown large and tough.

Thinning: All the seeds you sow won't germinate. Hence, you must plant more seeds than you need for the intended space. This is particularly important with crops like carrots and squash which do not transplant well because if you are niggardly and your rate of germination happens to be poor, you won't have enough plants. But a surprising percentage of seeds do come up for most crops, and then the gardener is faced with the heartbreaking task of pulling some of them out. I hate to do it; it always seems criminal to throw lusty young plants on a pile of refuse and see them wither and die. All seedlings don't have to be thrown away, of course. Some can be eaten, such as beets and turnips; some transplanted. But inevitably some will have to go, and it's a job that has to be done. Let someone else do it if you are weak, but definitely thin as soon as the plants are up, and give each remaining plant the space it requires for proper growth. Extra seedlings are as bad as weeds when it comes to robbing the soil of plant nutrients and moisture. Crowding will make all the plants weak and spindly and may seriously interfere with their development.

Diseases and Insects

YOUR vegetables will have many enemies. But two old truisms hold good—prevention is better than cure, and attack is the best method of defense. If you take the trouble to grow vegetables at all, you should certainly make the extra effort to get healthy results. Commercial growers have difficult problems in protecting large acreages, but there is absolutely no excuse for the average home vegetable garden to be pest ridden. Naturally you will be invaded by diseases and insects, depending, to a greater or less extent, on weather conditions, the season of the year, and your geographical location. But by regularly following a few simple rules and gardening habits you should easily be able to keep the marauders at bay.

Diseases and insects can be broadly, if loosely, classified as follows:

Bacteria and viruses. Particularly tend to cause root injuries and distorted growth.

Fungi. Very prevalent; generally affect leaf growth, causing blight, mildew, rust, and smut.

Chewing insects. These bite out pieces of plant tissues; some attack leaves and buds; others, the roots and stalks. Such injuries can readily be seen. Typical chewing insects are cutworms, grasshoppers, flea beetles, and various caterpillars.

Sucking insects. These have sharp snouts which they insert into plant tissue to suck out juices. The holes they leave are often not visible, but the plants attacked tend to wilt and grow deformed. Typical sucking insects are aphids and leaf hoppers.

The problem of pest control can be divided into two parts. First, and of major importance to the home vegetable grower, is indirect control, which can be regarded as "good-housekeeping" practices in the garden. Second is direct control, which involves using insecticides and fungicides.

Indirect Control: These simple rules represent the accumulated wisdom and experience of many gardeners:

Keep your garden clean. Neglected spots are insect-breeding places. All weeds, stalks, dead leaves, stubble, and crop wastes after harvesting should be burned promptly or placed in your compost heap. Also any hedges and borders near your vegetable garden should be kept clean and trim.

Buy good seed and plants. This is vital and more than merely money well spent. A number of bacterial and virus diseases cannot be controlled by any known chemical sprays or dusts. However, research work on selective breeding has produced many disease-resistant varieties of seeds, and also seeds yielding vigorous crops, which are not weakened by normal insect and fungus attacks. Furthermore, it has been found that, in general, insecticides are more effective on such resistant varieties. The catalogues of reputable growers will indicate whether the seeds listed are disease resistant. If you buy seedling plants of certain vegetables for setting in the garden, go to a well-established nursery where good seeds and proper cultural methods are used.

Rotate crops. Many insect pests which tend to attack specific crops or crop types live and breed in the ground from season to season. They can be starved to a considerable extent by never planting the same or similar crops twice running in the same location, either at different seasons of the year or in successive years. This merely requires a little simple planning. The problem is simplified if you can group together related types, such as the cole crops (cabbage, cauliflower, broccoli, and Brussels sprouts), cucumbers and squash, and tomatoes and potatoes.

Feed and cultivate. Controlled application of fertilizer, thorough and regular cultivation and weeding, and adequate watering during dry spells will produce healthy, vigorous and rapidly growing plants which can throw off the effects of attack by pests.

Plow in the fall. Plow up your vegetable garden thoroughly in the late fall or early winter after the majority of the remaining crops have been harvested, and before hard frosts set in. This is fatal to many pests which winter in the soil.

Destroy insects by hand. This, of course, is tedious and need not involve a regular campaign. But it is worth while to keep a few jars of kerosene handy; and, when you are walking down your rows on inspection tours, knock off and drown any particularly prominent beetles or caterpillars. Don't just tread them into the ground: they are often surprisingly tough and may survive.

Shield plants. Vegetables which have a long, thick, lower main stem, such as cabbage, broccoli, eggplant, tomato, and the like, can be protected when young from cutworms and other caterpillars by a cylindrical collar of heavy waterproofed paper or thin cardboard, about 2 inches in diameter and 3 inches long. This should be placed around the bottom of the stem and set an inch or more in the ground. Also hills of cucumber and squash vines can be protected from beetles by covering the young plants with strong cheesecloth supported by a light wood frame (for example, a couple of crossed barrel hoops) and buried in the ground at the edges or held down firmly by stones.

Direct Control: Direct attack on pests by spraying and/or dusting them with chemicals is also necessary, both as a deterrent before they appear and to kill them after they have arrived. For the average small vegetable garden the treatments can be made a relatively simple routine matter. The chemicals required can be purchased from garden supply houses in packages with full directions for use, or you can quite easily prepare them yourself with considerable economy from the cheap basic constituents. Recipes and formulas for the most commonly used chemicals are given at the end of this chapter, together with information on spraying and dusting methods and equipment.

The fungus diseases affecting leaf growth can be controlled by fungicides. The standard and long-used fungicide is *Bordeaux mixture* (containing copper sulphate and lime) which has the additional advantage that, for a number of insects, particularly leaf hoppers and flea beetles, it is also a good deterrent, though not necessarily a fatal one.

Chewing insects are destroyed by stomach poison insecticides. The most lethal are *lead arsenate, calcium arsenate,* and *Paris green* (copper aceto-arsenite). Since these are poisonous in quantity to human beings and animals, they are *not* generally advisable for regular use in the home garden unless it is very badly infested, in which case calcium arsenate is best. *Rotenone* is the modern and strongly recommended "safe" stomach poison to use. It is relatively slow acting but is poisonous only to insects. Rotenone comes from two tropical South American plants, derris and cube. Various rotenone extracts, as well as derris and cube products, are now on the market.

Sucking insects are destroyed by contact insecticides. *Nicotine sulphate* is the strongest and most effective, but it is a deadly poison and loses its strength if not kept in an airtight container. It is *not* generally advisable for regular use in the home garden unless the garden is badly infested. *Pyrethrum* (a plant extract) is recommended as a contact insecticide, and has the advantage of also acting as a stomach poison for certain chewing insects. Also *rotenone* acts to a considerable extent as a contact poison as well as a stomach poison. Ordinary *soap* solutions are quite effective against a number of sucking insects and are often included as spreaders for other insecticides.

The simplest minimum direct-control procedure for practically your whole vegetable garden (with the exception of the corn patch) is to spray with Bordeaux mixture and either spray or dust with rotenone or, preferably, a mixture of pyrethrum and rotenone. This should be done regularly throughout the growing season, about every ten days or two weeks. In dry, hot weather the intervals can be longer, and shorter in damp, muggy weather. Be sure you get at the undersides of the leaves, where many insects hide out. This routine procedure will keep down the general garden pests (aphids, flea beetles, and the like) which tend to attack all crops indiscriminately.

Fortunately there are a number of crops which do not suffer greatly from diseases or insects. This is particularly true of the root crops—beets, carrots, turnips and rutabagas, parsnips and radishes, parsley, eggplant, peppers, chard, New Zealand spinach, and to a considerable extent spinach and lettuce. Your regular routine control treatment can often be skipped if they appear in good shape. Even if a few leaves get eaten, this will not bother a healthy plant. However, if you find aphids getting thick on any of these crops, an extra treatment with pyrethrum or rotenone would be advisable. Poisonous nicotine sulphate should be used only as a last resort to cope with a real infestation—and then the plants should obviously be thoroughly washed before eating.

Certain crops may be attacked by insects or diseases which leave other crops alone. The earnest gardener would be wise to watch these crops carefully and if necessary give them the special treatment which is indicated for each crop.

Lengthy books have been written on vegetable pests and specific methods of control for commercial growers. But for the home gardener the brief information given above should be fairly adequate. However, if any of your crops suffer from a particularly fierce infestation, it may be due to local conditions, and it would be wise to consult your state agricultural experimental station.

These are a few minor tricks that you can practice if you have time:

Grasshoppers, earwigs, and *cutworms* can be dealt with successfully by scattering poison bran bait (containing Paris green) over the garden after sunset or very early in the morning.

Ants can be reduced by injecting a few teaspoonfuls of carbon bisulphide deeply into the nest at several places and closing up the openings with earth. (*Caution:* carbon bisulphide is inflammable.)

Trap crops consisting of a few plants at the end of each row can be left untreated with insecticides. Insects will tend to congregate on them and can then be slaughtered at one blow. Don't do this unless you have plenty of space and can afford to waste the trap plants.

Spraying and Dusting: Experts cannot agree as to which method is preferable, and there is considerable controversy as to the relative effectiveness of individual insecticides and fungicides when sprayed or dusted on specific crops. Most of them can be used either way, so for the home gardener it is largely a question of which is more convenient. Spraying is usually quicker over a large area, though obviously it is more messy. The arsenate poisons and nicotine sulphate, which should be used only sparingly, are probably better as dusts to avoid having to clean out your spray equipment after use.

Whichever method you use, do the job regularly and thoroughly so that all exposed portions of your plants are covered.

Equipment: *Spraying.* The best spray is a fine mist. An ordinary atomizer is adequate for a very small garden. However, for larger gardens a compressed-air sprayer is better. Be sure that the top is screwed on firmly against the rubber gasket before you start pumping. The nozzle should be angled so that you can get at the undersides of leaves. Clean out your equipment, particularly the nozzle, with water after each use. Bordeaux mixture particularly is quite corrosive.

Dusting. Insecticidal dusts can be shaken out from a bag of fine cheesecloth or a can with a finely perforated bottom. However, unless you are very expert, this results in uneven dusting and considerable waste. It is better to use a powder gun designed for this purpose. Various types can be bought and are quite cheap. Obviously the dust should go onto the plants, not as a cloud in the air.

Recipes and Formulas:

Bordeaux mixture.

Copper sulphate (bluestone).............	4 ounces
Quicklime	4 ounces
Water	3 gallons

These proportions can be varied a little either way. Dissolve the copper sulphate in a little hot water and add 1½ gallons of water. Shake the quicklime and add the remaining water. Mix the two solutions when ready for spraying and preferably strain through cheesecloth.

For dusting, it is better to buy a prepared mixture, which will have the requisite fineness.

Arsenic poisons. For sprays, dissolve 10 teaspoonfuls of calcium arsenate or lead arsenate, or 2 teaspoonfuls of Paris green, in each gallon of water. The addition of three or four times as much lime to the solution reduces the likelihood of plant injury. For dusts, thoroughly mix the poisons with from five to ten times their quantity of slaked lime or gypsum or any other inert powdery diluting agent you may have available, such as soybean flour.

Rotenone. This is usually purchased as a powder containing about 4 per cent rotenone. For a spray, mix 2 or 3 ounces with each 3 gallons of water. The powder should be made into a paste before mixing. For dusting, add to the powder about four times its weight of wheat flour or gypsum, and mix thoroughly. A keg with a number of pebbles in it makes a simple mixer.

Pyrethrum. Pyrethrum and pyrethrum extracts are sold as powders of varying strengths. Follow the manufacturer's directions for sprays and dusts.

Nicotine sulphate. This is sold as a 40 per cent liquid or as a powder. For a spray, add 1 or 2 tablespoonfuls of liquid to each

3 gallons of water, together with about 3 ounces of soap previously dissolved in hot water. (Laundry soap or soap flakes will do.) The soap acts as a spreader and itself is insecticidal. For a dust, thoroughly mix together the nicotine sulphate powder and slaked lime in the proportions of 1 ounce of powder to 1 pound of lime.

Poison bran mash.

Bran	5 pounds
Paris green	4 ounces
Molasses	1 pint

Mix the Paris green in the bran and add the molasses diluted with water. This should form a stiff mash.

1. Asparagus

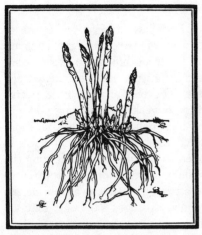

(*Asparagus officinalis. Liliaceae,* lily family.)

HISTORY: Asparagus is native to Europe—the southern parts of Russia, the steppes of Poland and Siberia. It grows wild there and is well liked by the cattle, which eat the asparagus as grass.

It has been in cultivation for over 2000 years. Cato's directions for growing asparagus almost could be used today, except that he recommends starting with seed from the wild plant. Pliny claimed that highly fertilized asparagus stalks grew as heavy as three pounds.

Asparagus has been grown in this country ever since the first colonists settled here, and today it is grown extensively both for the market and for canning. The name is derived from the Greek, meaning *to swell* or *be ripe*.

Food Value: Asparagus is a good source of vitamin A, an excellent source of vitamin C, and contains some vitamin B_1. These vitamins are contained only in green asparagus. Bleached white asparagus is almost totally lacking in vitamins.

Culture: Two factors connected with the growing of asparagus do not generally apply to the other vegetables included in this book.

In the first place, asparagus is a hardy perennial crop, which means that instead of the production of the crop being limited to a single year it will bear for many years. For that reason, precise care in establishing a permanent asparagus bed will pay long-enduring dividends.

The other factor is that asparagus is a plant that requires a dormant period each year; and, since it rests only when the growth is checked by frost, it cannot be grown in frost-free sections of the country.

I would add that asparagus is not suitable for a small vegetable garden. It also should be ignored if you do not intend to remain a gardener for a number of years.

Asparagus is propagated either from seeds or by roots bought from a reliable nursery. It takes 4 years from seed for the plants to be ready for initial harvesting, 3 years from year-old bought plants. If you are willing to wait this extra year, plant your own seeds, since sowing your own seeds is less expensive and most satisfactory. Otherwise buy one-year plants from a first-class nursery or seedsman.

An asparagus bed takes up quite a bit of space, but it will remain productive for 10 to 15 years. It is not at all difficult to grow excellent asparagus now that rust-resistant varieties have eliminated the formerly often fatal asparagus rust. The bed requires little yearly care; the rewards are ample. For 6 to 10 weeks every spring you will have a continual table supply of this most delicate vegetable, far more than you would probably feel justified in purchasing at retail prices in the market. And some may be canned for future use. Considering the price of bought canned asparagus, home canning of this crop represents a considerable saving. Since asparagus is not available in the market except during the spring, canned asparagus is the only kind we can eat during the remainder of the year.

Certain crops taste best only when eaten immediately after they are harvested. Corn, peas, and asparagus are all conspicuous in this respect. For this reason, anyone who hasn't eaten them within an hour after they are picked just never has tasted the real vegetables. After asparagus is cut, there occur certain chemical changes in the spears which reduce the amount of sugar and increase the amount of tough, fibrous material. These changes take place most rapidly during the first twenty-four hours after cutting. So if you and your family like asparagus, grow your own and taste perfection by cutting just before each meal what you need.

Habits of Growth: The perennial part of the asparagus plant is composed of a subterranean crown with very long, thick, fleshy roots. Each spring this crown produces a number of annual shoots or spears 8–10 inches long which arise erect from the crown. These spears are the edible part of the plant and are produced from early spring until an end is put to the harvesting period arbitrarily in order to give the plant time to store up food and get some rest before the next harvesting period comes around.

The plant has no true leaves; the tall green branches that grow when the cutting season is over function as leaves. The fruit is a berry which is green when young and turns red as it matures.

The life of a bed varies with conditions and treatment. The bed should last, at the minimum, 10 or 12 years; and it will sometimes produce for 15 or 20 years if the feeding has been constant and good. The general trend is toward an increase in production and weight of the spears for several years, with a gradual decline coming

Food Value: Snap beans are an excellent source of vitamins A and G, and a good source of vitamin B_1 and C. They are also a good source of calcium and iron.

Lima beans are an excellent source of vitamin B_1 and a good source of vitamin G, and they contain some vitamin C. They are also an excellent source of phosphorus and iron.

Culture: There are two types of both snap and lima beans: the bush or dwarf type and the tall or pole type. It is extremely easy to grow both types, especially the dwarf type which does not require any staking. Snap beans are tender and lima beans are very tender crops. Since snap beans can stand cold weather better than can the limas, the first planting can be made about the date that the last spring frost is due, while the limas should wait another 2 weeks until the soil has warmed up.

The seed is sown directly in the garden, and it germinates readily. The growth of the plant is quick and vigorous and presents no difficulty even to the beginning gardener. In fact, bush snap beans should be one of the indispensables in every garden because of the ease in growing and the wealth in harvesting them.

Snap beans are used in an immature state and can therefore be harvested about 50 days after the seeds are sown. The harvesting period of the dwarf plants is not long, one or two pickings is usually all you get, so successive plantings must be made every week or so to assure a continual supply. But pole beans, both snap and lima, bear continually until frost and one planting is enough.

Lima beans are used when the pod is almost fully mature, and therefore they cannot be harvested so quickly as snap beans. The small Sieva beans, although of inferior quality, are earlier than the large-seeded varieties and can be harvested in about 70 days as against 80 for the large seeded. The pole varieties take 10 days longer. This long maturing time, plus the fact that limas are a warm-season crop, limits the culture of these beans to sections of the country with a relatively long frost-free season—at least 4 months to allow time both for growing and for harvesting enough to warrant growing the crop. Snap beans can be grown anywhere, but a large part of the commercial crop is grown in the South in the spring, with sometimes a second planting in the fall.

Beans are especially nutritious and are also one of the vegetables that taste infinitely better when harvested young and eaten just after they are picked—which is an added reason for growing your own.

Habits of Growth: The general habits of growth are the same for both snap and lima beans. For the gardener in this country they are annuals (though limas are perennial in tropical countries). They produce stems about 15–20 inches tall, which, in the dwarf varieties, stand erect. The pole varieties are 8–10 feet tall. The latter have no tendrils to help the plant climb, but the stems are twining and coil from left to right up the supporting pole. In the dwarf varieties the main axis ends in a flower cluster, which prevents the stem from growing farther. In the pole varieties, on the other hand, the flowers are axillary and the stem can elongate indefinitely. The stems branch little. In the dwarf varieties there are four to eight sets of leaves on the main stem; in the pole varieties the nodes keep on growing until frost kills the plant.

The flowers are large and showy, white, rose, violet, or yellow. In the dwarf varieties all the short branches flower at about the same time, and for that reason all the pods similarly mature at about the same time. The flowering season is indeterminate in the pole varieties.

The fruit is an elongated pod, which is straight in most snap beans and curved in limas. The seeds are within the pod and may be white, red, black, or speckled when mature. Beans that are green when harvested are actually immature beans.

Snap beans are commonly eaten before they are fully grown, both the pod and the bean being used; however, when the pod is mature, the bean may be used alone in a dried state. On the other hand, with limas only the bean is ever eaten.

Types and Varieties:

SNAP BEANS: Snap beans, both bush and pole, are divided into two types, the *green podded* and the *wax* or *yellow podded*. These beans are still often called string beans, but now that the strings have been bred out of most varieties, the name no longer seems suitable. They have fleshy-walled pods and small seeds when immature and can readily be snapped into pieces in this state.

There are still a great many varieties on the market and the choice to a novice is bewildering. However, we're not so badly off. In 1921 seedsmen listed 962 varieties of bush snap beans and 604 varieties of pole beans.

Bush green: Tendergreen is one of the best bush, green-podded, snap-bean varieties. It is ready to eat in about 50 days and has an excellent quality. Burpee's *Stringless Green Pod* is another first-class variety, maturing in 49 days. *Stringless Refugee* is slower, about 70 days to maturity, but very popular for canning. *Bountiful*, a popular market variety, especially in the South, is ready in 48 days, but the quality is only fair and it is not a desirable variety for home gardens.

Bush wax: Good varieties of bush wax beans are *Brittle Wax*, *Pencil Pod Black Wax*, and *Sure Crop Wax*.

Pole green and *pole wax:* The outstanding variety of green snap pole beans is *Kentucky Wonder* (maturity, 65 days). Of the pole wax beans, *Golden Cluster Wax* is an excellent variety.

LIMA BEANS: Bush and pole lima beans likewise are divided into two types, the *small seeded*, such as the Sieva, and the *large seeded*, such as the Trua. The small-seeded type is hardier and earlier and it is useful for northern parts of the country where large-seeded limas are too late to provide much of a harvest. The small-seeded type is used also for dry beans to some extent and produces the tiny baby limas popular for canning.

Bush limas: Henderson Bush and *Wood's Prolific Bush* lima, which is an improved Henderson Bush, are among the best small-seeded varieties. The best large-seeded bush lima is probably *Fordhook Bush*, with fat, rounded seeds of potato shape. If you prefer a flatter bean, plant *Burpee's Improved*. Both are ready to harvest in 75 days.

Pole limas: Recommended pole lima varieties are *Sieva* (maturity, 78 days) for the small beans, *King of the Garden* (maturity, 88 days) and *Burpee's Best* (maturity, 92 days) for the large beans.

How Much to Buy:

Bush snap or limas:	1 package	for	20 feet
	1 pound	for	150 feet
Pole snap:	1 package	for	15 poles
	1 pound	for	100 poles
Pole limas:	1 package	for	10 poles
	1 pound	for	50 poles

For an all-summer supply you will want successive sowings of the bush beans but only one sowing of the pole beans. Remember this when you place your order. Also remember to plant enough to supply your table and to can. Good beans rarely appear in the

markets during the winter, so if your family is partial to this vegetable, a generous supply should be canned.

Planting:

Germination time: 7–10 days.

Depth for seed: 1 inch is sufficient, but if the soil is dry, plant
the seed 2 inches deep so that it will have more
moisture for germination.

Spacing of plants for *Snap beans,* 3–4 inches. *Lima beans,* 6–12
bush beans: inches. (12 inches advisable for the large-
seeded kind.)

Spacing of rows for 24–30 inches.
bush beans:

Spacing for pole beans: 3–4 feet apart each way for the poles. (If pole
beans are planted in rows, the plants should
be 1 foot apart in the rows, and the rows 3–4
feet apart.)

When to Plant:

	EARLY CROP	LATE CROP
	Earliest Safe Date for Planting Seed in Garden	*Latest Safe Date for Planting Seed in Garden*
Zone A. Lima,	March 1 – March 15	Lima, Oct. 1
Snap,	Feb. 15 – March 1	Snap, Oct. 1
" B. Lima,	March 15 – April 1	Lima, Oct. 15
Snap,	March 1 – March 15	Snap, Oct. 15
" C. Lima,	April 1 – April 15	Lima, Sept. 1
Snap,	March 15 – April 1	Snap, Sept. 1
" D. Lima,	May 1 – May 15	Lima –
Snap,	April 1 – May 1	Snap, Aug. 15
" E. Lima,	May 15 – June 1	Lima –
Snap,	May 1 – May 15	Snap, Aug. 1
" F. Lima,	May 15 – June 15	Lima –
Snap,	May 15 – June 1	Snap, Aug. 15
" G. Lima	–	Lima –
Snap,	May 15 – June 15	Snap, Aug. 15

(See maps at back of book showing locations of zones for spring and fall frosts.
Remember that the boundaries of the spring frost zones are not the same as those of
the fall frost zones, and your locality may be in different zones for the spring and
fall frosts. If you live in the West outside the zones, for an approximate guide take
the frost dates in your individual locality, find similar frost dates in one of the zones,
and use the corresponding dates for that zone.)

Bean seeds rot in cold soil and there is no point in doing any planting until about the date of the last spring frost for snap beans, two weeks later for the limas. The frost dates given in the maps are, of course, merely averages. During some seasons the last frost may be before these dates, and a chance planting of bush snap beans a week or 10 days earlier might produce results, if you are very eager for an early crop. But, as a rule, the gardener had better play safe and wait. A frost will definitely injure the crop. Successive plantings a week or two apart will provide a continual supply. The last planting should be 8 weeks before the first frost date.

Delay planting limas until the soil is thoroughly warmed up because they will not stand the cold so well as snap beans will.

If you have room, make one planting of snap and lima pole beans as soon as you can plant them with reasonable safety. The great advantage with pole beans is that, once they start to produce, under proper. conditions they will continue bearing until frost. But since they take longer to provide this harvest, a good planting scheme is to sow two or three plantings of the bush varieties to keep you supplied until the pole beans begin bearing; once the pole beans do begin, they'll take care of you from then on.

Beans do not transplant readily because they have a long tap root; but, if you want to have pole limas and if your frost-free season is short, the seeds can be started in a hotbed or in the house if you plant them in individual containers, such as pots, berry baskets, or inverted pieces of sod. The individual container is essential because in that way the plant can be set in the garden without any disturbance of the roots.

How to Plant: Bush beans are simply planted in rows, in drills about an inch apart, and thinned when the plants are up; don't delay the thinning long since the growth of the plant is vigorous. Planting lima bean seeds with the eye down is often advised, but is not necessary if the soil is in proper condition. Discard cracked seed since they germinate poorly or not at all.

Pole beans, which must be staked, require a different seeding practice. The poles are best placed before planting to avoid disturbing the roots and to give the plants something to climb up as soon as they are ready. The best poles are made of cedar and are obtainable from seed houses and lumber yards. They are rather expensive, but if they are put away carefully they will last for several years. However, any kind of sturdy pole or lath will do for a single season. The poles should be up to 12 feet tall. If the soil is hard, open it up with a crowbar or push the poles deep into the soil when it is wet. See that they are a good 18 inches deep so they'll stick, and leave 8–10 feet above ground. Four poles are frequently tied together, wigwam fashion. Plant 8–10 seeds in a circle around the pole, and thin to 4 or 5 plants. The poles should stand 3–4 feet apart each way.

Some gardeners prefer to plant the seed in rows and support the climbing beans with wire mesh or a trellis arrangement. For the trellis, heavy posts go at each end of the row, with some lighter poles in between, 15–20 feet apart. No. 10 wire is strung from post to post near the ground and at the top, and then twine is wrapped vertically between the two wires. The posts must be well dug in or the combined weight of the bean plants may produce a catastrophe.

Where to Plant: Bush beans, being temporary residents of the garden, belong with the other quick-maturing, succession crops. The first planting may have to have space reserved for it from the beginning, but further plantings can follow such cold-season, early crops as spinach, lettuce, carrots, beets, or early potatoes. The plants bear prolifically but not for long, so you don't need many of them at a time. There is probably always 10 feet or so of space available in your garden that a few bean plants can fit into.

The pole varieties, once started, use the ground for the remainder of the season. They are tall and need space, and they should be put near one end, preferably toward the north, where they won't shade low-growing plants.

Soil: Beans aren't fussy about their soil requirements, but they will grow more readily in a warm soil. Any soil that cakes or forms a hard crust isn't suitable because the cotyledons of the seed have to be thrust up through an inch of soil, which should therefore be porous.

Very rich, heavily fertilized land causes a tendency for the plant to run to vine rather than fruit, so don't apply fertilizer with a lavish hand. If the garden was fertilized before any planting at all was done in the spring, it is probably rich enough for beans without any further applications. If the soil has not had any feeding, use 1 or 2 pounds of 4–12–4 or 4–16–4 fertilizer per 100 feet.

Cultivation and Care: If a hard rim has caused the ground to crust before the seedlings show above ground, break it up gently with a rake. For weed control, go over the ground a few times, just scraping the weeds away. But don't go in for heavy hoeing; the roots are close enough to the surface so that any deep or extensive cultivation will result in unnecessary and undesirable root pruning.

Never cultivate when the foliage is wet from either dew or rain, or you may spread the spores of the anthracnose fungus, which will cause damage if it takes hold of your plants.

The commonest pests are aphids and the Mexican bean beetle. If they are bad, and if routine spraying or dusting is not sufficient, extra pyrethrum or rotenone should be applied. Badly infested vines should be destroyed at once after harvesting.

Harvesting: Snap beans are picked while the pods are immature and before they have finished growing. The seeds should still be small, when the tough strings in the pod won't have had time to make an appearance; the tips should be soft and the bean should snap readily. The plant must be watched carefully to make sure that the beans are caught at the right time—when they are large enough to eat but before the flesh gets tough and the beans make lumps in the pod. The proper time of harvesting lasts only a day or two, and even a few days delay means a poor crop. If the pods are allowed to ripen fully, the plants stop producing and will die. Bush plants usually afford two or three pickings, a few days apart or every day if the weather is warm and the growth vigorous.

The pole varieties can be harvested indefinitely as long as the pods that are ready to be used are removed regularly. If the supply of snap beans is suddenly overpowering for the table, the surplus should at once be canned or salted down.

Limas are allowed to develop further since the beans are shelled. The pods should be picked when both the shell and the bean are fully grown but before the pods begin to turn yellow and the beans harden and get dry. Bush limas can be picked several times before the harvest is exhausted; pole limas will produce indefinitely until frost.

All the picking is done by hand—and carefully, to avoid tearing up the plant. Don't forget that if any pods ripen and die on the plant the production of that particular plant is finished.

Storing: Snap beans and green limas cannot be stored in any of the regular ways, but salting snap beans keeps them quite successfully. Mix tender, young snap beans with salt, a pound of salt to four pounds of beans. Put them in a stone crock with a layer of salt on top and cover with a weight. They make their own brine, and when the bubbling has stopped you can either leave them in the crock or put them in sterilized glass jars and seal them.

Canning: Snap beans are a good crop for canning. Remember to use them when they are young. For canning directions see the chapter on "Canning."

Uses: Snap beans are one of the most difficult vegetables to cook to perfection. Most people ruin them, even when they are young and stringless. But I shall always remember a meal I had in a small restaurant in Paris, where snap beans were served as a separate course. This is a favorite practice of the French; and it is a good one, putting vegetables in their proper place as a real delicacy instead of considering them as something that should be eaten, but not relished. Those Paris beans were cut the long way, they were like a heap of grass on the plate, the color was so green, and they were as tender and melting as spun sugar.

To produce snap beans that are green and tender, and not gray and tough, you should cook them in plenty of rapidly boiling water, with the slightest pinch of soda added before the beans are put in. Soda does destroy vitamins—and this is the only vegetable I ever use soda with—but it does keep them green. Take them off the fire the instant they are done, even a few minutes of overcooking turns them gray. Fifteen to twenty minutes is plenty for young beans. Put your salt on after they are cooked, don't add it to the cooking water. And preferably cut them thin, the long way.

Another way of serving very young snap beans is to cook them in butter, slowly.

Snap beans are good if cooked and served with crumbled crisp bacon, with sauté mushrooms, or on toast covered with grated cheese and left under the broiler just long enough to melt the cheese.

Lima beans take longer to cook than snap beans and do not need the soda to keep them green if they are not overcooked. A little cream added to the butter you pour over your lima beans seems to hit just the right note with this already nourishing vegetable; sautéed mushrooms are good with lima beans; and nobody needs to be reminded of the classic combination of corn and lima beans. A good variation of succotash is succotash pudding—corn pudding with cooked lima beans added.

3. Beets

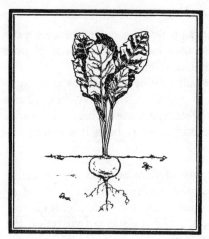

(*Beta vulgaris.Chenopodiaceae*, goose-foot family.)

HISTORY: The modern beet as such was not apparently known in ancient times. There is a story that when the Greeks paid homage to Apollo they served him beet roots on a silver platter, but the first recorded specific reference to beets is in the third century in Rome. They were mentioned in 1390 in some old English cooking recipes. Beets are natives of Europe and North Africa, and were originally found near the sea in southern Europe and around the coasts of the Mediterranean as far east as the Caspian Sea and Persia.

The name beet comes from the fact that when the seed pods swell they look like the Greek letter beta, β.

Food Value: Beet greens are one of the best vegetable sources of vitamin A; they are also an excellent source of vitamin G and of iron. The beet roots are not so rich in food value as the greens, but they are a good source of vitamins B_1 and G. Eaten with the greens they can provide an exceptionally valuable part of your diet.

Culture: Beets can be grown all over the country, and they are among the most important home-grown vegetables. They are an easy crop to grow, are very hardy, and are quite resistant to insects and diseases. They use little garden space; they grow quickly; and they can be planted where they are to mature. Successive plantings will provide a continual supply for the table most of the summer in the North, while a late planting yields beets for winter storage.

Beets are reasonably easy to store, are delicious canned, and all in all are indispensable in the home vegetable garden.

Habits of Growth: The plant is a half-hardy biennial which produces a tuft of large succulent leaves and a thickened, rounded, dark-red tap root 2–4 inches in diameter the first year. It produces flowers and seeds the second year. Both the leaves and roots can be eaten; and, since they are both part of the first year's efforts, the crop is an annual as far as the average gardener is concerned. An old gardening book describes a beet as "beautiful and much admired for its flavour."

It is a most attractive vegetable to grow. The colorful leaves vary from dark red to light green, and they can even be grown in your flower beds purely for their decorative effect.

The rounded root is made up of alternating bands known as "zoning." There are narrow light bands which are the conducting tissues and broad dark bands which are the storage tissues. This zoning varies considerably in different varieties, and in many beets it is almost imperceptible.

Types and Varieties: Four types of *Beta vulgaris* are generally recognized by botanists: the ordinary garden beet; Swiss chard or leaf beet; the sugar beet; and the mangel or stock beet. This chapter is concerned with the garden beet which falls into two types, the *early* type and the *late* or main-crop type.

Early type. Early beets are planted in the North during the spring and in the South all winter. They are usually harvested when they are small and tender. They grow best when the weather is cool, have a sweeter flavor than the late beets, and are the ones that are used for canning and pickling.

VARIETIES: *Crosby's Egyptian* is a very popular early variety which matures in about 60 days. *Early Wonder* is another good early variety.

Late type. Late or main-crop beets are sown in the North in the late spring or early summer for table use in the fall and for winter storage. They grow larger than the early crop and grow better when the weather is warm.

VARIETIES: *Detroit Dark Red* is the best main-crop variety. It matures in 60–65 days, is the most widely grown beet there is, and is well liked by commercial canners. *Winter Keeper* is one of the best varieties to use for winter storage.

How Much to Buy:

1 package for   25 feet
1 ounce   for 100 feet

The yield from beets is large, since each root requires only a little space. A 20-foot row supplies 60–80 beets, plus all the thinnings which can be eaten as greens. The return is large, but so is the demand in most families, especially if you are planning to can some of the baby beets. Also, since beets are a succession crop, careful planning will keep the table well supplied. Hence you should plant at regular intervals, the length of the row depending upon the size of your family and its liking for this delectable vegetable.

Planting:

Germination time: 8–10 days.

Depth for seed: ½–1 inch.

Spacing of plants: 3–4 inches.

Spacing of rows: 12–18 inches.

When to Plant:

	EARLY CROP	LATE CROP
	Earliest Safe Date for Planting Seed in Garden	*Latest Safe Date for Planting Seed in Garden*
Zone A.	Feb. 1 – Feb. 15	Nov. 1
" B.	Feb. 15 – March 1	Oct. 1
" C.	March 1 – March 15	Sept. 1
" D.	March 15 – April 15	Aug. 15
" E.	April 15 – May 1	Aug. 1
" F.	May 1 – May 15	July 15
" G.	May 15 – June 1	July 1

(See maps at back of book showing locations of zones for spring and fall frosts. Remember that the boundaries of the spring frost zones are not the same as those of the fall frost zones, and your locality may be in different zones for the spring and fall frosts. If you live in the West outside the zones, for an approximate guide take the frost dates in your individual locality, find similar frost dates in one of the zones, and use the corresponding dates for that zone.)

Since beets are hardy and can stand a light frost, you do not have to wait until all danger of frost is over to make your first planting. However in regions of the country where the last frost is likely to be a severe one, it is better to wait until it is over before planting. In the North, beets are planted about 2 weeks before the last frost date, and every 3 weeks or so after that until 2½ months before the first fall frost date. The last planting should be a crop that will mature just about the time frost is due and is intended primarily for storage. All the late plantings should be the late or main-crop varieties, while the first plantings should be early varieties.

Beets are easy to transplant and can be started in the hotbed for an

extra early crop. However, unless you have room to spare in the hotbed, the latter had best be saved for some crop that requires special
seeding, since beets grow so easily when sown directly in the garden.

But if you're impatient and want to prove what a smart gardener
you are, sow some seed in the hotbed 4 weeks or so before your
normal date for outdoor planting.

How to Plant: Beet seeds will remain viable for about 5 or 6 years;
but since the rate of germination is poor, they should be planted quite
thickly. You can eat the thinnings, so the seed won't be wasted. The
seeds are large enough to handle easily; they germinate quickly; and
you'll have your first pair of true leaves in 8–20 days.

Where to Plant: Early beets should be planted with the other
early short-season crops, such as carrots and onion sets, that are to be
harvested green. They can be followed by a late crop of turnips,
beans, celery, cauliflower, lettuce, and so on.

The late beet crop can follow the short-season crops, such as carrots, lettuce, and spinach.

Soil: Like all root crops, beets do best in a loose, well-drained, sandy
soil, which is easily broken down, so that they can expand and grow
properly. They also require a rich soil. Hence, if you want a superior
product, give them a little extra feeding with a quick-acting commercial fertilizer during their growing period. But never plant beets
(or any root crop) in a soil full of fresh manure; well rotted manure
is the only kind they will tolerate.

Cultivation and Care: Beets do not require intensive cultivation.
Weeds, of course, must be removed before they reach a size that will
interfere with the development and therefore the yield of the beets.
But, other than that, just an occasional shallow cultivation is sufficient.
It must be shallow since the roots are close to the surface and deep cul-
tivation would harm them.

Some care is needed in thinning the seedlings when they are 4–5
inches tall. The thinnings with the tiny beets attached can all be
eaten and are perfectly delicious. Don't delay too long on this thinning because the plants that are to remain need the room. And take
out the largest plants, leaving the smaller ones in the ground to develop. Each plant needs no more than 3–4 inches space.

Harvesting: Harvesting is simply a matter of pulling the beets out of the ground. When you remove the tops, leave an inch or two attached to the root so that it will not bleed.

The early beets should be harvested when they are small, 1½ inches in diameter or, at the most, not more than 2 inches. When they are any larger they have a woody taste and never become tender upon being cooked. For canning they can be pulled when they are even smaller than 1½ inches.

The late beets are sometimes allowed to get as large as 3 inches in diameter, and beets for storage are allowed to stay in the ground until just before heavy frosts.

Storing: Late beets can be stored successfully during the winter under proper conditions. However they keep best at temperatures around freezing, and the temperature should never exceed 40° F. Also they must be kept moist, with little air circulation. These conditions require a special storage room in the cellar or an outside storage room, or if neither is available an outside storage pit (see the chapter on "Storing").

Late beets for storage should be dug up when the soil is dry, and should be about 3–4 inches in diameter. Examine them carefully and discard any with flaws. The tops should be cut off about 1 inch or less above the crown. They can be kept in crates or moist sand, but will wilt and shrivel if kept too dry.

The maximum storage period is 4–5 months.

Canning: For the average home gardener, canning is probably a better method for preserving beets. You will then be able to have beets at a moment's notice, while beets that have been stored take a long time to cook and do not have the fine flavor of tiny canned beets which were picked when the crop was the finest. Both the tops and the roots can be canned. For canning directions see the chapter on "Canning."

Uses: The thinnings are eaten, leaves, roots and all. Try boiling them in milk instead of water for a change and a treat. Young tops by themselves make excellent greens, especially if a piece or two of bacon is cooked along with them.

Harvard beets are a variation from ordinary boiled beets. Make a sauce by mixing ½ cup of sugar and ¾ tablespoon of cornstarch;

then add ¼ cup of water and ¼ cup of vinegar. Cut up 10 beets and add them to the sauce and simmer for half an hour. Just before serving, add 2 tablespoonfuls of butter.

As another variation, add a sour sauce to boiled beets. This sauce is made by stirring 2 tablespoonfuls of flour into 2 tablespoonfuls of butter in a saucepan, mixing in either ¾ cup of the water the beets were cooked in, or ½ cup of this water and ¼ cup of cream. When this is blended, stir in ½ teaspoonful of salt, 1 tablespoonful of sugar, ½ cup of vinegar, and a dash of pepper. Cut up the previously boiled beets and heat them in this sauce.

Also, boiled beets cut up fine, heated with salt, pepper, butter, and ½ cup of sour cream, are easy to prepare and something the family will clamor for.

To prepare pickled beets, take beets about the size of a walnut which can be pickled whole. Clean and wash the beets, leaving the tail and more than an inch of the tops on. Boil until tender. While the beets are cooking, put on the stove to heat: 3 pints of vinegar, 1 pint of water, 1 cup of sugar, and 1 teaspoonful of salt. Peel the beets while hot, sort according to size, and pack in glass jars. Pour boiling liquid to fill the jars and seal.

4. Broccoli

(*Brassica oleracea var. botyris; Brassica oleracea var. italica. Cruciferae*, mustard family.)

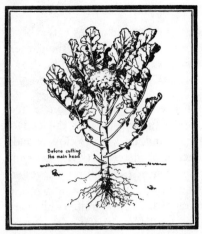

Before cutting the main head

HISTORY: It is believed that broccoli was known to the Romans at the time of Pliny, but references to this vegetable group it with cauliflower. The first notice of broccoli as such was made in 1724 by an English writer who called it "sprout colliflower or Italian asparagus." In 1729 another English gardener reported that there were several kinds that he had been growing in London for two years; "that with small, whitish-yellow flowers like the cauliflower; others like the common sprouts and flowers of a colewart; a third with purple flowers; all of which come mixed together." The seeds of the plants that he described came from Italy, and all the types now grown originated there since it has been extensively cultivated in that country for many years. It has been grown also in America for a number of years. Thomas Jefferson mentions that it was available in Washington markets, but it has become popular only within recent years. In fact, it probably holds a record for the short time required to gain wide acceptance by the public and importance as a commercial crop.

The type of broccoli now generally grown is often called sprouting broccoli, branching broccoli, asparagus broccoli, or calabrese (which was the original Italian name for it).

———•———

Food Value: Sprouting broccoli is an especially valuable nutritive crop, so valuable, in fact, that it should be a staple part of the family diet whenever it is available either in the garden or in the market. It is an excellent source of vitamins A, C, and G and a fair source of vitamin B_1. It is also an excellent source of calcium and a good source of phosphorus and iron.

Culture: Sprouting broccoli is a hardy, fairly quick-maturing crop of the cabbage family, which can be grown practically anywhere in the country. It is delicious and not difficult to grow, but certain basic demands must be satisfied to assure success. It is a crop that requires *coolness and moisture* and will not head satisfactorily when the weather is hot and dry. The planting, therefore, must be timed carefully. Most varieties take 80–90 days to mature; and, once matured, the harvesting lasts several weeks. Since cool weather is necessary for heading, 3 to 4 months of reasonably cool weather are needed. In the north and central states this means planting the seeds in a hotbed or in the house; and, in those regions where summer comes early, broccoli does best as a fall crop, which can be seeded right in the garden. In the far North where the summers are cool, broccoli can be grown all summer.

Habits of Growth: Sprouting broccoli is a plant about 2 feet tall, which produces a main, thickened flower stalk, at the end of which first develops a central cluster of tiny, dark-green flower buds. This head of flower buds is 3–6 inches in diameter. Both the stem and the head are edible. The head is compact at first; but, if not harvested, it gradually separates and the individual buds open, showing whitish-yellow petals. The leaves are large, ragged, bluish green. While they can be eaten, they are not nearly so tender or palatable as the remainder of the plant.

After the central head has been cut, a number of small lateral shoots develop in the axils of the leaves remaining on the stalks. These shoots in turn form flower-bud heads 1–4 inches in diameter. Four or six cuttings are possible from each stalk, and these lateral shoots provide a continuous harvest for several weeks.

Types and Varieties: There are actually two types of broccoli—heading and sprouting. We shall discuss only sprouting broccoli in this book, but it is of interest to note them both.

Sprouting broccoli. Inasmuch as there are few varieties of sprouting broccoli on the market, the choice is not difficult. But it is of vital importance to get a good strain of seed from a first-class seedsman to ensure getting a pure strain. Buy the best seed procurable of *Italian Green Sprouting* or *Calabrese.*

Heading broccoli. This vegetable is very much like cauliflower, although many people consider the taste inferior. This is the type that is grown very commonly in England and France, being much more prominent in those two countries than cauliflower is. It has the same kind of white head surrounded by large leaves. It takes 3 to 4 months to mature and must have cool, uniform weather with abundant moisture to mature properly. Even a few days of heat or dryness will ruin the crop. For that reason its culture is very limited in America, and it is grown to any extent only in parts of Washington and Oregon. Elsewhere it is better for the ambitious gardener to grow cauliflower. Only one variety of heading broccoli is listed in catalogues, and some do not list any.

How Much to Buy:

1 package for 250 plants

One package is ample for a home garden. A 100-foot row consisting of 50 plants (2 feet apart) divided into a spring and a fall crop will give a family of 5 people all the broccoli it needs. A 100-foot row will produce about 100 pounds.

Planting:

Germination time: 6–10 days.

Depth for seed: ½ inch.

Spacing of plants: 18–24 inches.

Spacing of rows: 36 inches.

When to Plant:

	EARLY CROP	LATE CROP
	Earliest Safe Date for Planting Seed in Garden	*Latest Safe Date for Planting Seed in Garden*
Zone A. Jan. 1 – Feb. 1		Nov. 1
" B. Jan. 15 – Feb. 15		Oct. 1
" C. Feb. 15 – March 1		Sept. 1
" D. March 1 – March 15		Aug. 15
" E. March 15 – April 15		Aug. 1
" F. April 15 – May 1		July 15
" G. May 1 – May 15		July 1

(See maps at back of book showing locations of zones for spring and fall frosts. Remember that the boundaries of the spring frost zones are not the same as those of the fall frost zones, and your locality may be in different zones for the spring and fall frosts. If you live in the West outside the zones, for an approximate guide take the frost dates in your individual locality, find similar frost dates in one of the zones, and use the corresponding dates for that zone.)

Broccoli is best treated as a two-season crop for spring and fall, except in the South where it is grown during the winter.

The early crop can be grown by seed sown in the garden about the time of the last frost date. This planting will give you a crop to harvest in about three months, and the harvesting itself lasts several weeks.

The late crop can be sown either directly in the garden 3–3½ months before the first fall frost date or in a special seedbed and transplanted to the garden proper about 4 weeks later.

In parts of the country where summer comes quickly, it is better to start the early broccoli in the hotbed or in the house 4–6 weeks before the earliest outdoor planting date and transplant it in the garden at the dates given above for outdoor seed planting. Broccoli plants can be purchased for the early crop for about 25 cents per dozen plants.

Broccoli will not fail to produce shoots even when the weather is hot, but it will not head well and the flowers will open up very quickly, necessitating immediate harvesting. It is definitely better tasting when grown in cool weather.

How to Plant: The seeds for indoor or hotbed seeding are easy to manage. They should be planted ½ inch deep and either transplanted once to stand 2½ inches apart when they have shown their first pair of true leaves or put right into the garden without any transplanting. One transplanting will give you sturdier plants though.

If the seed is sown directly in the garden, thin or transplant the young seedlings when they are 3–4 inches high so that they stand 18–24 inches apart in the row.

Where to Plant: One spring and one fall crop of broccoli are sufficient because the harvesting lasts quite a time. This means that a late crop of corn, beans, lettuce, beets, or spinach can follow the early crop of broccoli, while the late crop can be preceded by peas, lettuce, carrots, or onion sets. Keep the early and late cole crops together to facilitate pest control, but do not follow one cole crop by another in the same place since insects that feed on such crops live over in the ground.

Soil: Broccoli, like the other cole crops, needs a moderately rich soil and one that is easily worked and well drained. Either manure or commercial fertilizers should be applied. Either the manure should be well rotted or, if fresh manure is to be used, it should be applied in the fall and turned under in the spring. If you are using a commercial fertilizer, 5–8–6 is a good one. Mix about 1 pound per 50 feet of row in the soil at planting time and an equal amount as a side dressing when the plants have been in the garden for 3–4 weeks. If the plants seem to need a little urging, you can top-dress with nitrate of soda, about ¼ ounce per plant.

Cultivation and Care: The plants require no special attention except that they do thrive on ample moisture. Hence, keep them well watered if the weather turns dry.

Soon after the plants have been put in the ground, start giving them fairly deep cultivation. Later, as the plants grow, make the cultivation shallower and push the ground in toward the row in order to smother the small weeds. When the plants are large enough to touch each other you can stop your cultivation altogether.

Broccoli may be attacked by the same pests as cabbage and cauliflower—worms and aphids. If routine spraying or dusting is not effective, give them extra dusting with pyrethrum or rotenone.

Harvesting: The first and probably the most essential thing to remember about harvesting broccoli is that if you want to eat it in its prime it must be cut before the flower buds open while it is still green and tender and delicious. The large central head is cut with the stem and attached leaves, making a total length of about 8–10 inches. The smaller heads that subsequently sprout are cut when they are in the same stage as the original central bud—that is, compact and green. The length of stems of the smaller heads depends upon the vigor of the plant; usually they are about 4–6 inches long. Since these small shoots keep on growing in the axils of the leaves, the harvesting continues for a few weeks.

Uses: Broccoli is usually boiled and drenched in butter. To boil it, stand the broccoli up, tied in bunches, and cook the stems for 10 minutes, then push it over and cook both the stems and flowers for another 10 minutes. Don't overcook it. A little lemon juice or mustard seems to accentuate the flavor. For a change, try cooking it the Italian way. After boiling it until almost tender, drain and fry gently in hot olive oil until it is light brown. Sprinkle it with Parmesan cheese before serving. The heads of raw broccoli, chopped fine, make a palatable salad combined with tomatoes and French dressing or sour cream.

Another good way to use broccoli is the way it is served as the speciality of the house in a New York restaurant. Boiled broccoli is placed on the bottom of a casserole and covered with diced cooked chicken, a rich cream sauce flavored with sherry, and grated Parmesan cheese. The whole thing is then put into a moderate oven to brown. This is a meal in itself and fit for the most special company.

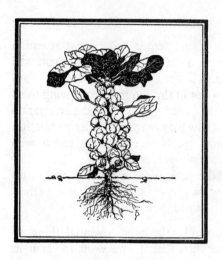

5. Brussels Sprouts

(*Brassica oleracea var. gemmifera.
Cruciferae,* mustard family.)

HISTORY: Brussels sprouts are named for Brussels, the capital of Belgium. They have been grown in that vicinity for hundreds of years, records noting their appearance as early as the thirteenth century. They were grown in America in 1806, which presupposes their culture in England, at any rate, at that time. They are not very well known in other countries.

Food Value: Brussels sprouts are a valuable addition to the diet since they are an excellent source of vitamin C, a good source of vitamins A and B_1, and a good source of phosphorus and iron.

Culture: Brussels sprouts can be grown anywhere except in those sections of the country in which no frost at all occurs; there they will not be at their best and the gardener had better strike this crop off his list.

Brussels sprouts are considered by many people to be a difficult crop. This is mostly because of planting at the wrong time or using inferior seed. Get first-class seed from the best seed house you know; plant it at the right time; and you should harvest a good crop of these delicious buds. They are so very good that they deserve wider cultivation, and all gardeners who live in areas where this crop flourishes should try them. The flavor is the most delicate of a tribe not particularly noted for delicacy, and the way they grow is so interesting that it is worth while having a few plants just to watch them grow. Also, since Brussels sprouts are so hardy that the plants will stand considerable frost, they are a welcome addition to the garden because they will supply the table with fresh vegetables late in the fall when most crops have been ruined by frost.

Brussels sprouts are a hardy, slow-growing, cole crop that takes about 4 months to mature from the date of seed sowing. This crop requires cool weather but needs it only at the end of the growing period, when low temperatures are needed to make the buds hard and firm. And the buds really taste best when they have actually been touched by frost. But part of the growing period can take place in the heat of summer as long as the plant is kept moist. It's important to grow sturdy, disease-free plants. As a rule the seeds are started in a special outdoor seedbed. Bought plants can be used if you are dubious about growing your own. But it isn't difficult; just don't plant too early, give the plants a good soil and plenty of water, and you will be all right.

Although Brussels sprouts can be grown anywhere except in frost-free parts of the country, they do best in the North where they grow more or less slowly while summer heats the plants and finish off their growing vigorously and with a rush when the weather turns cool. Where the summers are long in the central states and the South, quick maturing types, which are set out in the fall, are the best to use.

Habits of Growth: The "thousand-headed cabbage" is a plant that grows about 20–30 inches tall. It has an erect, unbranched, leafy stem; and in the axils of the leaves along this stem little sprouts or buds like miniature cabbages are formed. These sprouts are 1–2 inches in diameter, grow all the way up the stem from the base to the large canopy of leaves at the top, and are the edible portion of the plant. The sprouts do not appear until toward the end of the growing period; and, if the weather is warm, the sprouts will grow open and loose instead of tight and hard. They taste nearly the same but they do not look so well.

Types of Varieties: Most of the Brussels sprouts offered for sale by seedsmen today are the semi-dwarf type which grows 20–24 inches tall. There are very few available varieties, and *Long Island Improved* is the best of the lot. If you live in a section of the country where the spring turns hot very quickly or where there is a short frost-free period, look around until you have found a variety which matures relatively quickly; some houses can supply seed that will mature in about seventy days from the time the plants are set.

How Much to Buy:

1 package for 300 plants

A plant will produce about 1 quart, or 50 to 100 sprouts. Plants can be bought for about 25 cents per dozen, 85 to 90 cents for 100. Don't forget when you are planning the number of plants you want that this crop can be harvested from early fall frost until well into the winter.

Planting:

Germination time: 6–10 days.

Depth for seed: ½ inch.

Spacing of plants: 18 inches.

Spacing of rows: 24–30 inches.

When to Plant:

	EARLY CROP	LATE CROP
	Earliest Safe Date for Planting Seed in Garden	*Latest Safe Date for Planting Seed in Garden*
Zone A.	Jan. 1 – Feb. 1	Nov. 1
" B.	Jan. 15 – Feb. 15	Oct. 1
" C.	Feb. 15 – March 1	Sept. 1
" D.	March 1 – March 15	Aug. 15
" E.	March 15 – April 15	Aug. 1
" F.	April 15 – May 1	July 15
" G.	May 1 – May 15	July 1

(See maps at back of book showing locations of zones for spring and fall frosts. Remember that the boundaries of the spring frost zones are not the same as those of the fall frost zones, and your locality may be in different zones for the spring and fall frosts. If you live in the West outside the zones, for an approximate guide take the frost dates in your individual locality, find similar frost dates in one of the zones, and use the corresponding dates for that zone.)

In general, although the earliest planting dates given above for the early crop are safe ones, they are a bit too early if you want the frost to sweeten your sprouts. These earliest dates should be used for only the tall-growing, slow-maturing Brussels sprouts, which take 120–130 days to mature. I would advise pushing the dates on a few weeks and planting your crop in the open ground about 4½ months before the first fall frost date. In zone E, for instance, May 15 would be about right. Then your crop would mature in the fall and be ready to harvest after frost.

Commercial growers on Long Island, where a large part of the market crop for the whole country is grown, set specially grown plants in the field in late June or early July for an early crop, and from July 20 to August 15 for a late crop. However, Brussels sprouts are generally just a one-crop vegetable for the home gardener since the crop takes a long time to mature and the harvesting is spread out over a considerable period. And for this one crop the late planting dates are best if you use varieties that mature reasonably quickly, except in the South where Brussels sprouts can be grown all winter if there are light frosts.

How to Plant: The seed will get off to a better start if it is planted outdoors in a special seedbed. It should be started in a special seedbed for two reasons: because certain insects that have a fondness for cole crops and are likely to attack the seedlings can be controlled more easily in a special seedbed, and because you will be more likely to remember them than if they are lost somewhere in the garden proper. Weak, spindly plants do not stand much of a chance.

When the seeds have put forth their first true leaves, thin or transplant them to stand 3 inches apart each way. When they are 3–5 inches tall, a month to six weeks after seeding, they are ready to be planted in the garden proper.

Where to Plant: Keep the cole crops together to facilitate pest and disease control. Brussels sprouts use a lot of space and they occupy this space from late spring until frost. However if you start the seed in a special bed you can have an early crop of spinach or lettuce out of the way before the Brussels sprouts will need the room.

Soil: Like all members of the cabbage family, Brussels sprouts are gross feeders and thrive on a rich and fertile soil. If the ground has not been well manured, use a commercial fertilizer. Don't expect a crop to be worth anything if it has not been fed. And keep it moist.

Cultivation and Care: Regular garden cultivation is sufficient for this crop. The one special attention that is beneficial is removing the side leaves once the sprouts begin to form. This will throw all the strength into the sprouts rather than into the leaves. Leave the large ones at the top alone, however; they are essential to the proper growth of the plant.

If the plants are attacked by worms or aphids and routine treatment is not effective, give them an extra dusting with pyrethrum or rotenone.

Harvesting: Remember that Brussels sprouts taste much better when they have been nipped by frost. Hence, leave the harvesting until then if you can. But when the lower leaves begin to turn yellow, the sprouts must be picked or they will get tough and lose their delicate taste. Start harvesting when the sprouts are an inch or so in diameter and quite hard, and when the leaves first start turning yellow. Begin at the bottom of the plant, since these lower sprouts mature first, and work upward. The sprouts can either be cut or broken from the stem; and, if the adjacent leaves have not been removed before, take them off now. Usually several pickings can be made from one plant since, as the lower leaves and sprouts are removed, the stem elongates and throws out new leaves, each having a sprout in the axil.

Storing: One of the chief virtues of Brussels sprouts is their ability to withstand freezing, which makes them available for the table until late in the fall when practically every other crop has succumbed. Where the climate is mild they can be left in the garden all winter. In the cold parts of the country, just before severe frost, dig up the plants, roots and all. Then they can be either replanted in a cold frame or just stacked upright, close together in a sheltered place (such as an unheated garage), covered with some straw. The sprouts will keep several months and can be picked off as they are needed.

Freezing itself does not harm them if they are allowed to thaw out gradually, but alternate freezing and thawing ruins them.

Uses: Brussels sprouts boiled quickly for 10 to 15 minutes and soaked in butter are one of the best vegetables to serve with steak or lamb chops. Fry left-over sprouts quickly in butter for a variation. Sprinkling them with grated cheese is a good touch for a cheese-loving family. A favorite way of cooking Brussels sprouts for a party dish is with chestnuts. Use 1 quart of cooked Brussels sprouts and about 1 cup of cooked chestnuts; slowly brown the chestnuts in 3 tablespoonfuls of butter; then add about a cup of good meat stock, ½ teaspoonful of salt, a little sugar (if your taste runs to sugar in vegetables), and the sprouts, and cook all very slowly for 5 to 10 minutes until it is thoroughly hot. Chopped chicken livers added to this dish make it a meal in itself.

6. Cabbage

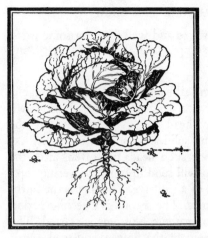

(*Brassica oleracea var. capitata. Cruciferae*, mustard family.)

HISTORY: Cabbage has been grown for so long that its culture goes back farther than the earliest historical records, probably at least 4000-5000 years. Its origin has been ascribed to Jupiter, who, struggling to explain two contradictory oracles, began in ungodlike fashion to perspire and from this divine perspiration the cabbage sprang. The Egyptians were supposed to have worshiped the cabbage, the Greeks and Romans claimed it had the fortunate quality of preserving from drunkenness whoever eats it. It is found growing wild on the seacoast of England, Denmark, and northwest France, and its growth is distributed practically over the entire world. It is one of the most generally grown of all vegetables.

Food Value: Cabbage is a good source of vitamins A, B₁, and G and an excellent source of vitamin C. It is a fair source of calcium and it is worth noting that the outside leaves have seven or eight times as much iron as the inside heart.

Culture: Cabbage is a hardy, cool-weather crop, which can stand frost but will not tolerate heat. It is not particularly easy to grow with success, but it is perfectly possible to produce cabbages if you satisfy the basic demands of the crop. It is, of course, the major cole crop grown and is used extensively all over the country. As with the other cole crops, a cool season, rich soil and plenty of moisture are essential. Since it takes 95-140 days for the crop to mature, and since it must complete its growth during the cool parts of the year, planting the seed in special seedbeds is necessary.

The plant is a hardy biennial. It forms heads the first year and seed the second year; and, since the head is the edible part, the plant is grown as an annual for the home garden. It is a plant that needs a long, steady period of uninterrupted growth. With any check—careless transplanting, lack of sufficient space, caking of the soil, a few hot days, lack of plant food, and above all else lack of water—it will tend to stop forming the desired solid head of leaves and start producing the undesirable seed stalk. *Plenty of moisture, especially during hot weather,* is the prime requisite.

The plant is subject to some diseases and well liked by some pests. But if it is grown properly and the crop is rotated, much trouble along these lines can be eliminated.

Habits of Growth: Well-grown cabbage is a handsome vegetable, with its bold lines and its robust, vital way of growing. It is grown for the large, compact rosette or "head" of leaves surrounding the terminal bud. This head is hard and solid and forms without any external aid. Each plant has only one such head; but often, after the head has been removed, the stump will send up small flowering tops. There are three periods in the life of a cabbage. The first is the fairly quick growth of the leaves and roots. The second is a resting period during which the formation of embryonic blossoms is started. The third is the growth and development of the flowers and seed, when the stalk emerges from the head and bears the flowers.

The head is formed between the first and the second periods, and sometimes if conditions are unfavorable the plant doesn't stop to form the head but throws up the seed stalk directly. Young plants exposed to low temperatures for a long time often will shoot to seed that way. That's why they should be started in heat to give them a good start. When they are well along they will head properly in weather too cold for their early growth. Too close planting also causes bolting to seed.

Types and Varieties: There are a number of types of cabbage on the market. The two general types are *early* and *late*, or main crop. If the season is a long one with cool summers, there are some intermediate varieties that can be grown. Then there are short- and long-stemmed cabbage (12–20 inches), with leaves that may be long, round or broad, smooth or savoyed, in colors ranging from light yellowish to dark green. There are also some dark red varieties to lend color to the garden and the tables. The heads themselves may be large or small, flat, elongated, or round.

The types are classified as follows:

Wakefield and *Winningstadt*. Pointed or cone-shaped small heads. Early. In the North this type has been superseded largely by Copenhagen Market, but it is very good in the South for fall planting. It will stand long exposure to cool weather and still head.

VARIETY: *Charleston Wakefield*.

Copenhagen Market. Short stemmed, slightly flat globe-shaped heads, solid, quick growing, early. This is a very popular type.

VARIETIES: *Golden Acre* and *Copenhagen Market* are by far the most important varieties. In fact, if you are going to grow only one variety of cabbage, Golden Acre is probably the best all-around choice. *Glory of Enkhuizen* is good for sauerkraut.

Flat Dutch or *Drumhead.* Large head, flattened, light green, mid-season and late. An important type.

VARIETIES: *All Head Early* and *Succession.*

Danish Ballhead. Medium size, solid, deep round head. Late. This type is most widely used for sauerkraut, fall growing, and storage.

VARIETY: *Danish Ball Head.* Best cabbage of all for storing.

Savoy. Dark green, much wrinkled leaves, nearly round heads. Late. It has a more delicate taste than the smooth leaved; considered by many the best eating cabbage. Since it is grown very little commercially, the home gardener should grow a few heads for his own use and enjoyment.

VARIETY: *Savoy Perfection Drumhead.*

Red Cabbage. Round hard heads. Late. An attractive addition to the table.

VARIETY: *Red Rock.*

Planting:

Germination time: 6–10 days.

Depth for seed: ½ inch.

Spacing of plants: *Early,* 12–15 inches.

Late, 18–24 inches, depending upon the variety. Danish Ballhead, 18 inches. Flat Dutch, 24 inches.

Spacing of rows: *Early,* 24–30 inches.

Late, at least 30 inches.

Remember, overcrowding limits the size of the head and produces a tendency to shoot to seed.

When to Plant:

	EARLY CROP	LATE CROP
	Earliest Safe Date for Setting Plants in Garden	*Latest Safe Date for Setting Plants in Garden*
Zone A.	Jan. 1 – Feb. 1	Nov. 1
" B.	Jan. 15 – Feb. 15	Oct. 1
" C.	Feb. 15 – March 1	Sept. 1
" D.	March 1 – March 15	Aug. 15
" E.	March 15 – April 15	Aug. 1
" F.	April 15 – May 1	July 15
" G.	May 1 – May 15	July 1

(See maps at back of book showing locations of zones for spring and fall frosts. Remember that the boundaries of the spring frost zones are not the same as those of the fall frost zones, and your locality may be in different zones for the spring and fall frosts. If you live in the West outside the zones, for an approximate guide take the frost dates in your individual locality, find similar frost dates in one of the zones, and use the corresponding dates for that zone.)

Cabbage should be planted to start growing in warm weather and to mature in cool weather. In the South that means starting the seed in open beds in the late summer, usually in October; 6 to 10 weeks later the plants are set in the garden where they can stay all winter. In the North, the *early crop* should be sown in heat in the hotbed or in the house, 4-6 weeks before the plants can be planted outdoors. They are hardy, and properly hardened young plants can stand a temperature of 10° or 15° F. below freezing if it doesn't last too long. Hence, they can be put outdoors almost as soon as the ground can be worked. They should be ready to harvest in another 70 days. Since they should be harvested before it gets too warm, the *planting must be early* for good heads.

The *late crop* can be started outdoors directly in a seedbed or in the garden. A seedbed is best because the young seedlings will need care to keep them healthy and sturdy, and this is easier in a special place away from the garden proper. Also, since they don't require much room at this stage, some other crop can be utilizing the regular garden space. Most late cabbages take 100-110 days to mature from the time the plants are set out, and they should be mature before frost. Also, the late cabbages will keep a long time once they have matured; therefore you can plant in time to leave plenty of leeway for harvesting.

How to Plant: The early seeds started in heat should be sown about ½ inch deep. They germinate fairly quickly and make sturdy little plants which should be either transplanted or thinned, when they have shown their first true leaves, to stand 3 inches apart each way. If you haven't the facilities for this special sowing, buy your early plants from a reliable dealer. But a simple flat in a sunny window of your house will do, and it's more fun and satisfaction if you grow your own.

Always keep the strongest seedlings, discarding the ones that look feeble; and don't use rich soil for your special seeding or the plants will be spindly and weak.

Where to Plant: It is a good practice to grow all the cole crops adjacent to one another—cabbage, cauliflower, Brussels sprouts, and broccoli—to facilitate pest control. Also, since the insects that attack these crops sometimes live through the winter in the soil, don't grow them in the same spot in your garden two years in succession. The early cabbage crop should be harvested and out of the way 2½ months after garden operations begin. It can be followed in the same place by a late planting of beets or carrots, or by corn or beans, or any crop that goes into ground in the late spring or early summer. The late cabbage crop can be preceded in the same place by any of the early harvested crops, such as peas, spinach, head lettuce, or green onions.

Soil: Cabbage produces a big plant, with the head, leaves, stump, and root all bulky and heavy. And it takes a rich soil to feed this massive crop. Indeed, cabbage is one of the coarest feeders in the vegetable world. Also, since the major part of the plant consists of water, it needs a constant and unfailing supply of moisture. The feeding should be liberal, the preparation of the soil deep so that it will hold moisture. Try to avoid planting in soil that cakes after rain.

Although cabbage wants plenty of food, it isn't fussy about the quality. Green manure, fresh manure, well-rotted manure, commercial fertilizers—any of these can be used. Well-rotted manure is best, 2 or 3 inches of this dug into the soil a couple of weeks before planting is ideal. If the soil has enough humus to make it retentive of water, commercial fertilizers can be substituted, 10 pounds per 100-foot row. The early crops need more fertilizing than the late ones because they grow and mature more quickly. The early crops respond readily to a little stimulation with nitrate of soda: 1 ounce to a square yard, worked into the soil and kept away from the foliage.

Cultivation and Care: Cultivation is important with this crop to conserve the soil moisture. Cultivate both between the rows and around the plants, deeply at first but, as the plants grow and the roots fill the earth, the cultivation had better be shallow to prevent breaking the roots. The root system of this crop is extensive and many of the roots are only an odd inch or two below the ground and almost horizontal. Therefore, merely scrape the surface to break the crust and keep down the weeds. If you find that the heads are bursting, push the plants over so that the roots on one side will be broken; and, since the plant will get less feeding, the trouble will be controlled.

If routine treatment does not seem adequate for eliminating cabbage worms and aphids, try extra dusting with pyrethrum or rotenone at frequent intervals.

Harvesting: Bend the head over and cut the stalk at the base with a large sharp knife. Early cabbages will be ready to harvest about 70 days after the plants are set out, that is they will be hard and solid— and since they have a tendency to burst if the weather turns warm they may have to be harvested quickly. The late crop, which matures during cool weather, will stay in good condition for a long time and therefore can be harvested when needed and wanted any time before freezing weather.

Storing: Late cabbage can be successfully stored during the winter under proper conditions, which are practically the same as for storing root crops. They keep best at temperatures around freezing, and the temperature should never exceed 40° F. Slight freezing does not injure them. Also they must be kept moderately moist, with little air circulation. These conditions require special storage facilities (see the chapter on "Storing"). While a cellar storage room will provide these conditions, it is not advisable to store cabbage inside the house owing to the odor given off. An outside storage pit is preferable.

A good storing variety must be used, such as *Danish Ballhead*, and the heads should be firm and mature. Any ragged outside leaves should be removed. For the usual storage pit, either the roots may be cut off, or the roots can be left on and the cabbage placed head down in the pit.

A special form of pit or trench, which can be quite shallow, is sometimes used for cabbage. The cabbages are placed in it side by side, roots down, and covered with earth. A wooden frame is made around the trench and banked over with straw and earth. Cabbages can then be removed as required from one end without disturbing the others. However, in hard freezing weather it may be difficult to get the cabbages out; therefore, storing should be tackled only by the ardent cabbage lover.

The maximum storage period is 4–5 months.

I would remind you that cabbage can easily be made into pickled relishes and sauerkraut, and you may decide that for simplicity this is the best way of preserving cabbage for the winter.

Uses: In boiling cabbage the most important thing to keep in mind is that the well-known cabbage odor is caused by overcooking; 5–15 minutes is enough cooking time for any self-respecting cabbage. There are a number of ways of cooking cabbage, but we have space for only a few. Boiled chopped cabbage placed in a baking dish covered with a cream sauce and grated cheese and baked is delectable. Another good dish is chopped cabbage placed in layers in a baking dish, each layer smothered in buttered bread crumbs and grated Parmesan cheese. Put a cup or so of a good meat stock in and bake. Or fry cabbage lightly in bacon fat and serve the dish garnished with deviled eggs. This is a hearty dish that can be used as a main course for lunch. Try cole slaw made with shredded cabbage, cut-up marshmallows, and pineapple niblets all mixed with mayonnaise that has been blended with some whipped cream. It is really delicious, and is guaranteed to make stuffing yourself with vitamins a pleasure, even for the people who ordinarily spurn raw cabbage.

To prepare Dixie Relish, take 1 quart of chopped cabbage, 2 tablespoonfuls of crushed celery seed, 3 tablespoonfuls of mustard seed, ¾ cupful of sugar, 5 tablespoonfuls of salt, 1 quart of cider vinegar, 1 pint of chopped onions, 1 pint of chopped sweet green peppers, and 1 pint of chopped sweet red peppers. Mix the chopped cabbage, onions, and peppers. Add the spice seeds, sugar, salt, and vinegar. Let stand over night. Then drain the vinegar off, pack the relish in sterilized jars, and pour back over it the vinegar that was drained off. Paddle the jar thoroughly to get every bubble out and allow the vinegar to displace all the air spaces. (Garnish each jar with two slender strips of red pepper packed vertically on opposite sides.) Cook in a pressure cooker for 10 minutes at 15 pounds pressure, and seal tightly.

Cabbage is converted into sauerkraut by a lactic acid fermentation which takes place in the brine made from the juice of the cabbage drawn out by salt.

To prepare sauerkraut, 2 cupfuls of salt are used for 40 pounds of cabbage or, in small amounts, 3½ tablespoonfuls of salt for 5 pounds of cabbage. A 2-gallon crock will hold about 10 pounds of sauerkraut. Remove the core and shred the cabbage. Either mix the salt through the cabbage or salt it down in layers right in your container. Pack the container firmly; cover with large cabbage leaves, then with a cloth; and cover over the whole top with a board or plate, weighed down. Keep at room temperature, remove scum as it forms, and leave until fermentation ceases. This will probably take from 2-4 weeks. Sauerkraut will keep almost indefinitely in a *cool* place.

7. Carrots

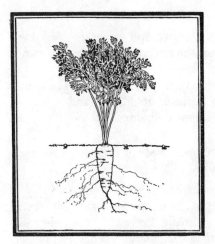

(*Daucus carota. Umbelliferae*, parsley family.)

HISTORY: Carrots are native to Europe and the adjoining portions of Asia; they were introduced from there into North and South America and China; and today they are grown throughout a large portion of the world.

It is believed that they were cultivated in early times but probably were not used generally as a food. Pliny says, "They cultivate a plant in Syria like the wild carrot, and of the same properties, which is eaten cooked or raw and is of great service as a stomachic." References to carrots are frequent in records: in China from the thirteenth century on, in Japan in 1712, in India in 1826, in Arabia in 1775, in Europe by nearly all the writers and herbalists since 1536, in Virginia in 1609, in Brazil in 1647.

In recent years carrots have become a deservedly popular vegetable primarily because their value as a food, especially as a source of vitamin A, has become recognized. The commercial acreage in America devoted to carrots has increased from 9,770 acres in 1923 to 43,500 acres in 1939.

———•———

Food Value: Carrots are not only an excellent source of vitamin A, but also a good source of vitamins B_1 and G, and a good source of calcium.

Culture: Carrots can be grown anywhere in the country, but they grow best (longer root, sweeter flavor) when the season is not too hot. They are one of the easier crops to grow and should be grown in every garden, no matter how small it is. They are produced from seed sown in the open ground; they take up little space; they do not have to be harvested at a precise time; they can be canned and they can be stored. They have an excellent taste both raw and cooked.

Carrots are a half-hardy, quick-maturing crop; the early ones can be harvested in about 10 weeks from planting, while the main crop takes 10 or 15 days longer to mature. Because carrots taste best when they are small, young, and tender, the best way to assure a supply for the table for a long period of time is to make successive plantings.

Habits of Growth: Carrots are a biennial root crop. The first year they produce feathery leaves and a thickened tap root; the second year a flower stalk arises from the crown and grows 2–3 feet high. Since the edible part of the plant is the tap root, this crop is grown as an annual by the gardener.

Different varieties vary in length from 5 to 12 inches. The root is usually from 1 to 3½ inches in diameter at the top, and it may be conical or fingerlike in shape or almost cylindrical.

Types and Varieties: The two main types of carrots are the *early* type and the *late* or main-crop type.

Early carrots, in the north and central states, are planted only in the spring, while in the South they can be used satisfactorily for all crops. These carrots, which are usually harvested when they are small, are much more succulent than the late type. They can be harvested 2 months after they are planted, before they are fully grown. This is the type to grow for canning.

VARIETIES: *Nantes* and *Chantenay*.

Late carrots are sown in midsummer in the north and central states for harvesting in the fall and for storage, although storage is more precarious and difficult than canning. This type will germinate more readily when the weather is warm and will produce good-size roots when the early type would be adversely affected. The carrots of the late crop are longer than the early ones, thicker at the top, take longer to mature (11 to 13 weeks as a rule), and are also tougher. While they are not so good as the early type, they are useful since they supply the table in the fall.

VARIETIES are *Tendersweet* (the best tasting), *Imperator* (a comparatively new variety which is proving to be very popular), and *Oxheart* (a suitable variety for heavy soils).

How Much to Buy:

1 package for   30 feet
1 ounce   for 200 feet

Sow as many early carrots as you can spare the room for. A surplus supply should be canned for the winter. Sow just enough of the late crop to supply the table in the fall, unless you have perfect storage facilities.

Planting:

Germination time: 10–15 days.

Depth for seed: ½ inch.

Spacing of plants: *Early,* 2 inches.
                       Late, 4 inches.

Spacing of rows: 12–16 inches.

When to Plant:

	EARLY CROP	LATE CROP
	Earliest Safe Date for Planting Seed in Garden	*Latest Safe Date for Planting Seed in Garden*
Zone A.	Feb. 1 – Feb. 15	Nov. 1
" B.	Feb. 15 – March 1	Oct. 1
" C.	March 1 – March 15	Sept. 1
" D.	March 15 – April 1	Aug. 15
" E.	April 15 – May 1	Aug. 1
" F.	May 1 – May 15	July 15
" G.	May 1 – June 1	July 1

(See maps at back of book showing locations of zones for spring and fall frosts. Remember that the boundaries of the spring frost zones are not the same as those of the fall frost zones, and your locality may be in different zones for the spring and fall frosts. If you live in the West outside the zones, for an approximate guide take the frost dates in your individual locality, find similar frost dates in one of the zones, and use the corresponding dates for that zone.)

Carrots are half hardy, which means that they can stand light frosts but not heavy ones. Therefore they should be first planted in the north and central states around the date of the last spring frost. Successive plantings can be made every two weeks until the latest safe planting dates given above. The late crop varieties should supplant the early varieties as the season advances; and the last planting should be made in time to harvest some for the table and possibly allow some for storage, keeping in mind that they take 75–80 days to mature. Carrots are not a fussy crop; they will grow well when the temperature is quite low and they will also stand considerable heat if they are well established. Thus, in many parts of the country carrots can be had all summer. Incidentally, a late summer planting of one of the early varieties will give you tiny carrots as big as your finger which are marvelous cooked whole or eaten raw.

In the South, in sections where there are no hard frosts, carrots are grown as a crop for harvesting in the winter and early spring.

How to Plant: Carrot seeds germinate slowly and the small plants are delicate. For that reason it is essential that the soil be kept loose so that the seeds can break through. Planting radish seeds along with your carrots is a good plan; the radishes break the soil and mark the rows so that you can cultivate before the carrots germinate. Since the carrots grow fairly slowly at first, the radishes will be out of the way before the carrots need the space.

Because the percentage of carrot seeds likely to germinate is rather low, sow quite thickly, 20–30 seeds to the foot. When the plants are an inch or two high, thin them out. Since you don't particularly want thick roots, give each plant no more than the allotted space, 2 inches for the early varieties and 4 inches for the late. And when you thin, take care not to break off the tops and leave the roots in the ground. If you thin when the ground is moist, it will be easier. And because carrots are difficult to transplant, throw the thinnings away unless they are large enough to eat.

Where to Plant: Since carrots mature quickly, they are useful as a succession crop. The first planting can go into the ground the first thing in the spring and will be out of the way in time for late plantings of turnips, rutabagas, lettuce, cabbage, beans, and so on. Late plantings of carrots can be preceded by early turnips, beets, lettuce, radishes, or spinach.

Soil: All root crops need a light soil so that the roots can penetrate easily and are not impeded in their growth. A heavy soil is likely to stunt the growth and cause forked roots. Carrots are no exception to the general rule. They prosper best in a quick, light soil which is well drained and will not bake. They do not require a particularly rich soil, so no extra feeding is necessary, but do give them a sandy enough soil so that they can grow smooth and symmetrical.

Cultivation and Care: Since the little plants are delicate at first and grow very slowly, they cannot put up an even fight with weeds. Hand-weed carefully if you want to give your carrots a fair break. Once the plants are established, they do not require any further attention except frequent cultivation, which should be shallow since many of the feeding roots grow close to the surface.

Harvesting: Early carrots are harvested when the tops are about 1–1½ inches in diameter and the carrots are sweet and tender. You can tell about the size by pushing a little soil away and looking at the top of the root. When you harvest, carefully pull the ones that are the right size so that you won't disturb the others, which must continue their growth. They can be pulled out by hand if the ground is not too hard.

Late carrots are larger, 2–3 inches in diameter, and they are best harvested by digging with a spading fork so that you won't break the roots. Either they can be harvested whenever they are large enough to eat, or they can be left in the ground until freezing weather is likely to occur and then be dug up and stored. Remember, though, that the longer a carrot stays in the ground once it is ready to be harvested, the larger and older it will get, and that means it will be tough and strong and less palatable. If you are planning to store some carrots, plant them at the latest date you can to allow them time to mature but not time enough to get old.

Storing: Late carrots can be successfully stored during the winter under proper conditions. However they keep best at temperatures around freezing, and the temperature should never exceed 40° F. Also, they must be kept moist, with little air circulation. These conditions require a special storage room in the cellar; an outside storage room; or, if neither is available, an outside storage pit (see the chapter on "Storing").

Late carrots for storage should be dug up when the soil is dry and should be of medium size. Examine them carefully and discard any with flaws. The tops should be cut off 1 inch or less above the crowns. They can be kept in crates or moist sand, but they will wilt and shrivel if kept too dry.

The maximum storage period is 4 to 5 months.

Canning: Early carrots, particularly when very young and small, are ideal canning vegetables. For canning directions see the chapter on "Canning."

Uses: Raw carrots are such an excellent source of vitamin A that they should be included in your diet at least once a week.

Grated, they make a delicious salad or sandwich filling, used either alone or with raw cabbage, or they can be cut lengthwise into strips and eaten as an appetizer.

Try cooked carrots and celery creamed together as a change from the usual carrots and peas. A tablespoonful or two of peanut butter added to the cream sauce is good.

Glazed carrots are easy to prepare and easy to eat. Cook small carrots whole, then place them in a baking pan and cover with a syrup made by cooking together for a few minutes ½ cupful of brown sugar and ½ cupful of butter. Bake in a moderate oven, basting occasionally, until the carrots are brown and glazed.

A simple but elaborate-looking vegetable combination to serve with cold roast beef or pot roast is made by baking together whole carrots, peeled good-size onions, and peeled potatoes. Cover them with melted butter, season well, and let them bake for about an hour in a moderate oven or until they are brown and the potatoes are crisp. Baking whole carrots gives them almost a caramel taste, much more pronounced than the flavor that carrots usually have when they are cut up or mashed and boiled in so much water that most of the taste is washed away. Even boiled whole carrots taste better than when they are cut up. Always cook carrots whole when they are not too monstrous. The very large ones should be cut in quarters.

8.
Cauliflower

(*Brassica oleracea var. botrytis. Cruciferae*, mustard family.)

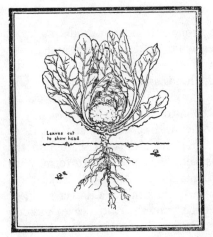

Leaves cut to show head

HISTORY: Early historians placed cauliflower and broccoli in one botanical variety, and it was not until 1724 that broccoli was mentioned separately. It is believed that the Romans knew them both, in which case they have been in cultivation for a considerable period of time, but little is known of their history. Cauliflower is a difficult crop to grow except under ideal conditions, and this has probably limited its production.

Food Value: Cauliflower is an excellent source of vitamin C, a good source of vitamins B_1 and G.

Culture: "A first rate vegetable; to obtain which, a great pains must be taken in every stage of its growth," wrote a gardener seventy-five years ago. And truthfully. If you want to be sure of success, all the necessary requirements must be followed with care. You can succeed, but don't even make the attempt if you are not willing to give all the attention it demands. Cauliflower is often called "rich-man's cabbage" because its finicky, fussy ways make it hard and time consuming to grow.

Cauliflower is a half-hardy, cool-season, slow-maturing, cole crop. It should have a more or less even and cool temperature for all its period of growth. It must have a *constant and ample supply of moisture*. It does not like heat and will not tolerate dryness. The total maturing time is about 95–140 days, depending upon the variety and the climate.

Like all cool-season crops, it does best in most parts of the country as a spring and fall crop. The seed should be started either in a hotbed, in a greenhouse, or in the house for the spring crop. The fall crop can be started outdoors in a special seedbed. It takes 30–40 days for the seedlings to grow large enough for garden planting, and another 60–90 days for the plants to reach maturity.

Getting a cauliflower to head properly is the real problem in growing this crop. The plant must be strong and lusty to produce a large, good-tasting head. And the tender, white heads do not grow that way unassisted. To keep them white they must be protected from the sun which otherwise will burn the heads and turn them brown. Unprotected heads also have a poor flavor and a tendency to throw up leaves between the segments of the curd.

If the temperature is too low (below freezing for any length of time) or very hot immediately after the plants are set out in the garden, they become weak and small. They may fail to form heads entirely; the heads may form prematurely which will make them small and useless; the head may break and send up a flower stalk; or the heads may split up into irregular growths, with leaves pushing through all over, making it useless. During the final stages of development a light frost will injure the head, while too high a temperature causes it to become yellow and leafy. Much can be done to overcome otherwise adverse conditions if the plants are given plenty of water.

"Of all the flowers in the garden," said Dr. Johnson, "I like the cauliflower best." So try your luck and see if you agree with him. The inexperienced gardener had best begin by buying six or a dozen plants of a named variety from a good grower and plan to grow them as either a spring or a fall crop, depending upon when he is most likely to have about 3 months of reasonably cool weather. Cauliflower is a crop for a gambler. If you are successful, your sense of accomplishment will compensate you for the time and trouble. If your luck is poor, you won't be the first to fail and you can try again next year.

Habits of Growth: The name "cauliflower" means "stem-flower," which accurately describes the plant growth. Cauliflower produces a plant 2–3 feet tall, consisting of a stem, a group of large leaves, and a thickened and shortened, much enlarged, crowded flower portion, which is the edible "curd" or head. Present-day cauliflower heads are usually about 6 inches in diameter. However, in 1865 a proud gardener in Massachusetts reported raising a single plant bearing a head over 12 inches in diameter and 38 inches in circumference and weighing 6 pounds, 5 ounces.

The button or tiny initial head doesn't appear until the end of the growing period. When it first emerges it is usually encircled by incurving leaves. When it is about 2 inches in diameter it begins to push through the leaves, and must then be covered from the sun by tying the large outer leaves over the head. The lack of light blanches the head. It grows quickly after tying, and will be ready to harvest 2 or 3 days later in warm weather, or 2 weeks or so later if the weather is cool.

Types and Varieties: Besides the popular and usually grown white-headed cauliflower, there is a type producing a purple head which turns green and looks like broccoli when it is cooked. It is a quick grower and disease resistant, and many people consider its flavor better than that of the white cauliflower. Not all seed houses offer it, but it is not difficult to procure if you look around a bit.

It is of the utmost importance to get the very best strain of seed available. Nothing is more disappointing than failure after months of diligence, and poor, cheap cauliflower seed dooms your crop from the outset.

VARIETIES: *Snowball* is the most widely used and best variety. Although it is usually called Early Snowball, it can be used for both early and late plantings. The purple-top type is never represented by more than one variety.

How Much to Buy:

1 package for 150–250 plants

This is more than any one family will probably want. The seed remains viable about 4 years, germinates about 75 per cent. Since cauliflower must be harvested when mature and doesn't lend itself to storage, a dozen or so plants in the spring and the fall is probably enough except for the most rabid fanciers.

Planting:

Germination time: 7–9 days.

Depth for seed: ¼ inch.

Spacing of plants: 18–24 inches.

Spacing of rows: 30–36 inches

When to Plant:

	EARLY CROP	LATE CROP
	Earliest Safe Date for Setting Plants in Garden	*Latest Safe Date for Setting Plants in Garden*
Zone A.	Aug.–Oct. (for winter crop)	Aug. 1 – Nov. 1
" B.	Jan. 15 – Feb. 15	Sept. 15 – Oct. 1
" C.	Feb. 15 – March 1	Aug. 15 – Sept. 1
" D.	March 1 – March 15	Aug. 1 – Aug. 15
" E.	March 15 – April 15	July 15 – Aug. 1
" F.	April 15 – May 1	July 1 – July 15
" G.	May 1 – May 15	June 15 – July 1

NOTE: These planting dates are the very earliest ones; a week or two later would be playing safe.

NOTE: The earlier planting date is probably the ideal one, the later date the deadline.

(See maps at back of book showing locations of zones for spring and fall frosts. Remember that the boundaries of the spring frost zones are not the same as those of the fall frost zones, and your locality may be in different zones for the spring and fall frosts. If you live in the West outside the zones, for an approximate guide take the frost dates in your individual locality, find similar frost dates in one of the zones, and use the corresponding dates for that zone.)

The early crop should not be set outdoors until all danger of a severe frost is past. This may mean delaying the planting if the season is late. But don't wait too long or the weather will get too warm for the plant to head well.

The late crop will not head until the weather gets cool, so don't plant it too early.

How to Plant: The plants can be either bought as seedlings or started from seed 30–40 days before the date for planting in the garden.

Buying plants is a recommended procedure for the inexperienced gardener. Sowing seed indoors is fun but is always a precarious undertaking because house conditions are not usually ideal and damping-off often kills the little plants. If you buy plants from a *good* grower, you can get named varieties for 24 to 30 cents per dozen, just about the same price as a package of seeds. And they will be strong plants that will get you off to a good start.

However, your own seed sowing can be done successfully, if you are careful. If you want plants for an early crop, the seed must be sown in heat either in a hotbed or in the house. Plant the seed fairly thickly ¼ inch deep, and when the little plants have produced their first pair of true leaves, transplant them so that they are 2 inches apart each way. Harden them gradually for 10 days before they are set out to prevent any severe check in their growth. And don't start them too early or they will get leggy.

For a fall crop, the seed is started in a special outdoor, shaded seedbed 5 or 6 weeks before the fall planting date given above. A special seedbed away from the regular garden will bring them better attention, and the garden space can be used for some other crop until the cauliflower plants have reached some size.

Where to Plant: Cauliflower should be planted near other cole crops, such as cabbage, for ease in insect and disease control. It takes up considerable space because the roots need room to spread out for moisture, but it occupies the ground for only 2 or 3 months either in the spring or in the fall. Other crops can thus either precede or follow it. One planting in spring and fall is generally sufficient.

Soil: Cauliflower grows best in a soil that is fertile, well drained, and with enough humus to retain moisture well. A rich soil is essential. If it has not been manured the previous fall, or if you have no well-rotted manure to use, see that it gets some commercial fertilizer, about ½ pound for every 50 feet of row before planting and another dose as a side dressing when the plants are well along. Or you can use it all before planting. Both 4–8–4 and 6–12–8 fertilizers are good.

Cauliflower also responds very well to nitrate of soda. Three applications at two-week intervals of ¼ ounce per plant are highly recommended, starting when the plants have been in the garden for 2 weeks. Scatter it in a small circle around the plant and don't let any actually touch the foliage or stem.

Cultivation and Care: Cauliflower needs plenty of cultivation. The plant must make a vigorous growth and develop large leaves early in the season. To do this you must keep the weeds under control and not allow any crust to form on the surface of the soil. Begin shallow cultivation with a hoe or wheel cultivator a few days after the plants are set and keep it up at weekly intervals until the heads are formed. Often and shallow. Deep cultivation breaks off too many of the roots. And don't forget, plenty of water!

Special care is required to blanch the heads. When the head first appears, tie the large outer leaves over it with straw, raffia, or twine.

Tie them loosely enough to allow for plenty of ventilation and to prevent the collection of moisture, which might cause the head to decay.

The usual cabbage pests will also attack cauliflower. If routine spraying or dusting is not sufficient, use an extra dusting of pyrethrum or rotenone.

Harvesting: Cauliflower is a crop that must be harvested as soon as it has matured. If it is left too long, the head may get discolored from the leaves rotting, or break, or begin to push up flower stalks. The average curd is about 6 inches in diameter. Don't expect that if you leave it for a few days longer it will grow larger. Unless the initial growth of the plant has been good, the curd will never grow large no matter how long it is left to grow.

After the leaves have been tied up to blanch the head, look inside every day to determine whether the heads are ready to harvest. They do not all mature at the same time; hence, they must be watched carefully. Harvest while the curd is firm and white. Cut well below the head with a long, sharp knife. For the market the leaves are usually cut squarely across the plant, leaving an inch to form a ruff collar around the curd. All the leaves can be trimmed off at home since they are not generally used in cooking.

Canning: It is well worth while to can a small amount of cauliflower. For canning directions see the chapter on "Canning."

Uses: Although cauliflower is usually eaten plain, boiled and served with butter sauce, this is not the only way to use it. It is delicious broken up into flowerets and eaten raw, either in a salad or dipped into Russian dressing and served as an appetizer. Left-over cauliflower becomes a main luncheon dish when it is put in a casserole, covered with a cream sauce and plenty of fresh grated cheese, and baked until brown and bubbling. Sometime try French-fried cauliflower— just break the head into flowerets, dip them in a standard batter, and fry an odd minute or two in deep fat. And don't forget, a little lemon or mustard perks up plain butter sauce; and browned bread crumbs, chopped hard-boiled eggs, or chopped nuts make an attractive garnish —and paprika is almost a must to add color.

To pickle cauliflower, break the head into flowerets to keep them from falling apart when they are done, leave a bit of the hard part of the stem on each piece. Cook them in boiling salted water for about 5 minutes; put them in jars; and cover with the following mixture, scalding hot and strained: 1 gallon of vinegar, 1 cupful of water, 1 ounce of mace, 1 ounce of peppercorns, 1 ounce of cloves, ¼ cupful of white mustard seed. Fill the jars to the top and seal immediately.

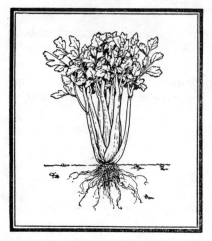

9. Celery

(Apium graveolens. Umbelliferae,
parsley family.)

HISTORY: Celery has grown wild and been used as a medicine for hundreds of years. The wild plant is a native of marshy places in European regions extending from Sweden to Algeria, Egypt, and Ethiopia, and eastward to the Caucasus. It was not until 1623 in France that any mention was made of a cultivated variety. The wild variety was called "smallage," and it was a herb eaten to purify the blood. In 1686 it was claimed "smallage transferred to culture becomes milder and less ungrateful, whence in Italy and France the leaves and stalks are esteemed as delicacies, eaten with oil and pepper." In 1776 in England celery seed was listed by a seedsman, and it has been cultivated to some extent in European countries for the past 200 years or so. It was formerly used green and as an ingredient in soups and stews. Only in England and America are the stalks blanched and eaten raw.

The first commercial production of celery in America was started by some Holland-American gardeners in Kalamazoo, Michigan, in 1874. They offered it for sale to passengers who went through Kalamazoo on the train, and later the train boys and express messengers on the Michigan Central Railroad sold celery to the passengers and to people along their routes. It was from this small beginning that celery production has now brought the crop to be the second most important salad crop in America. It is now grown in almost every state.

———•———

Food Value: Celery contains some vitamin B$_1$ and is a good source of calcium.

Culture: Celery is neither an easy nor an inexpensive crop to grow. Commercially it is considered the most expensive of all vegetables to cultivate because of the fertilizer needed, the amount of labor necessary, the cost of the seed, and the special equipment used for blanching the stalks. On a small scale these expenses are not excessive, but you must be prepared to give this crop the utmost attention or you might as well not even tackle it.

It is a slow-growing, half-hardy crop, which grows best in a rich soil, with an abundance of water, plenty of bright sun, and cool weather when it matures, particularly at night, for successful blanching. It must be propagated either from seeds sown under glass or in special seedbeds, or from bought plants. Great care is needed to get the seeds started. About 2 months is necessary for the seedlings to reach sufficient size for planting in the garden; another 4 months is required to produce mature plants.

The temperature requirements of celery are finicky. Haphazard culture may cause it to go to seed prematurely or give an inferior product; too cool weather when the plants are first set out will check their growth; and hard frosts will damage the mature crop. The plants can stand quite hot weather when they are once established; they can stand in the garden until hard frosts are due; and if necessary they can be stored in the cellar to finish blanching.

Celery stalks must be blanched if you want them to be tender and crisp and well flavored. The blanching consists of closing the light out from the inner leaves, which prevents the development of chlorophyll. (The methods used in blanching are discussed in the section on Cultivation and Care.)

Habits of Growth: Celery is a biennial which normally produces leaf stalks and leaves the first year and seed the second year. However, occasionally it behaves like an annual and shoots to seed the first year, a happening that should be prevented if possible. The first year the plant should consist of a short stem and leafy stalks 6–15 inches tall. The stalks, or elongated petioles, are ribbed and form the part commonly eaten either raw or cooked. The leaves, however, are also edible and are especially useful dried for seasoning. Each plant usually has two or three pairs of leaf stalks and a terminal leaflet. It is worth noting here that commercially one whole plant is called a "stalk" and that the bunches of celery we buy in the markets consist of three to twelve such "stalks."

The word *graveolens* means "strong-smelling" and is applied to celery because of its characteristic odor and flavor, which are due to the presence in the stalks and leaves of certain volatile oils. The color of the foliage varies from yellowish green to dark green.

Types and Varieties: There are two distinct types of celery. One is light yellowish green, and the other dark green. Before we consider the types in detail, it should be emphasized that buying the best seed available is one way of making sure that your celery will be of first-class quality and as disease free as possible. The characteristic flavor of celery is affected more by the variety of seed bought than by the growing conditions; and planting cheap, carelessly grown seed is a rank waste of time. The best seed is expensive but the average gardener doesn't require much, and it is foolish to sacrifice your whole crop for a few cents. There is also the important matter of diseases. Celery is subject to serious diseases, particularly various forms of blight. As these are often carried in the seed, it is vital to buy seed that comes from disease-free plants.

Yellow type. This is the so-called self-blanching type. The plants are light in color; but, unless they are grown in a special way, they are not actually self-blanching. In general it is used for an early crop.

VARIETIES: *Golden Self-Blanching.* This is the standard variety for market gardeners, representing well over half of the total crop. It blanches golden yellow. (The seed is normally grown in France and may now be hard to obtain.)

Golden Plume. This is earlier and more vigorous. It blanches to creamy white, is a good keeper, and is an excellent variety for home gardeners.

Green or winter type. In general the plants of this type are larger than the yellow type and mature somewhat more quickly. It is grown for winter use and for storage. The plants are harder to blanch but they are of excellent quality. Indeed, the fine nutty flavor is better than the flavor of the yellow type. An enterprising gardener should grow some of each type and decide for himself which he likes better.

VARIETIES: *Giant Pascal* is the standard leading variety. It is hard to blanch, however, and many gardeners for that reason grow *Utah* or *Salt Lake*, which matures a week earlier and blanches more readily and to a pure white.

How Much to Buy:

1 package for 300–400 plants

If properly handled, the seed should produce this much, which certainly is more than ample for most gardeners. The seed remains viable for at least 3 or 4 years, and a practice of commercial growers that you might well follow is to buy seeds a year before you intend to use them and grow a few seeds of different varieties to test for your preference. The following year you can make your major crop the variety you like best. A 100-foot row provides space for about 200 plants.

Planting:

Germination time: 5 days to 2 weeks.

Depth for seed: ⅛ inch. The seed is fine and merely needs to be pressed into the soil.

Spacing of plants: 6 inches.

Spacing of rows: 2–6 feet, depending upon the method of blanching (see Cultivation and Care).

When to Plant:

	EARLY CROP	LATE CROP
	Earliest Safe Date for Setting Plants in Garden	*Latest Safe Date for Setting Plants in Garden*
Zone A.	Jan. 1 – Feb. 1	Nov. 1
" B.	Jan. 15 – Feb. 15	Oct. 1
" C.	Feb. 15 – March 1	Oct. 1
" D.	March 1 – March 15	Sept. 1
" E.	March 15 – April 15	July 15
" F.	April 15 – May 1	July 1
" G.	May 1 – May 15	June 15

(See maps at back of book showing locations of zones for spring and fall frosts. Remember that the boundaries of the spring frost zones are not the same as those of the fall frost zones, and your locality may be in different zones for the spring and fall frosts. If you live in the West outside the zones, for an approximate guide take the frost dates in your individual locality, find similar frost dates in one of the zones, and use the corresponding dates for that zone.)

Planting should be timed so that the plants will not reach maturity until the weather is reasonably cool. A good plan in the North is to plant both an early and a late crop. In this way the harvesting will merge and provide you with a continual supply.

The *early crop* in the North must be started in heat either in a hotbed or in the house. It will be about 2 months before the plants are ready to be put in the garden.

Probably the most important fact to keep in mind is that under no circumstances should your celery bolt to seed. That can happen in the spring, but it need not if you remember that the most likely cause of this bolting to seed is subjecting the plants to a low temperature of 40°–50° F. for 2 weeks or so after they are planted out. The plants can stand a frost, but a prolonged period of cold weather does damage. If they can be set out when the temperature is around 70° F. and can keep on growing right from the start, they will be safe. Therefore, since continuous growth is important with this crop, the sowing of the seed should be timed so that the seedlings will not have to wait in the house for warm enough weather. To be sure that your plants will not be ruined by a spell of cold wet weather, the later of the two planting dates given above for the early crop is safer.

Seed for the *late crop*, while it can be sown directly in the garden, is better if it is started in a special seedbed or even in a flat in the cold frame. Do not do any outdoor sowing until you are sure that there is no danger of a long, cold wet spell. It is vital that the seedlings have heat until they are at least an inch high. If you want to start your late crop before the weather has thoroughly warmed up, start it in the cold frame.

A late crop is the wisest procedure for gardeners in the central states. The seed can be started outdoors; the crop will mature during ideal weather for celery, in the fall when it is cool; and the rains provide the abundant moisture celery flourishes on.

How to Plant: Sowing your own seeds can be done satisfactorily, but you have to take care. Celery seed is very fine and will make a good stand only in soil that is well pulverized and kept perfectly moist.

The early crop is sown in flats indoors or in a hotbed, quite thickly because there will be some loss in seeds. Do not cover the seed at all, just press it into the soil. Put a pane of glass or a piece of paper over the flat to conserve moisture. The young seedlings are delicate, and the temperature during these early stages should be 70°–75° F. When the plants show their first true leaves, transplant them to stand 2 inches apart each way. When the plants are 4–5 inches tall they are ready for planting in the garden. Plant only the sturdiest ones.

The seedlings for the late crop can be handled exactly the same way, in flats left in the cold frame. Your control over plants in a flat is excellent: they can be moved at will—indoors during heavy storms, in the sun on good days—and they can be watered from the bottom, which eliminates the possibility of washing out fine seeds. With a difficult crop such as celery, seeding in flats gives you maximum control.

However, outdoor seeding is possible in a special seedbed whose surface cultivation is perfect. Scatter the seed or sow in rows, when the weather is thoroughly warm and the ground is moist. Cover with burlap, and keep the burlap on until the seeds have germinated. Watering through the burlap breaks the force and prevents washing away the seed. Transplant once, 2 inches apart each way.

If these directions make you doubtful about your ability to grow good plants, don't give up the idea of a celery crop. Good plants can be bought from reliable dealers for about 25 cents a dozen or 100 plants for $1.25, which is a modest price when you consider the harvest.

Where to Plant: The early crop may be out of the way in time for a late planting of spinach or radishes, although it is likely to occupy the land the whole season. The late crop can be preceded by peas or potatoes or other early crops, but those two are good because they require about the same amount of row space.

Soil: Celery can be grown in any kind of soil except heavy clays, but it is a rank feeder and must be supplied with considerable fertilizer. Either well-rotted manure or a complete fertilizer can be used. If commercial fertilizer is used, it should be applied at least a week or 10 days before the plants are set. The soil should be well dug 10–12 inches deep and the fertilizer should be worked into the full depth. Five pounds of fertilizer to a 100-foot row is the right amount. If you want to have a bumper crop, make additional feedings three or four times after the plants start growing, every 3 weeks, 2 pounds for a 100-foot row.

Cultivation and Care: Cultivation should be shallow and constant until the celery has grown profusely enough to cover up most of the space between the rows. Then cultivation is no longer necessary. The top 2–3 inches of soil should be kept loosened up. The root system of a celery plant is a dense mass of roots, most of which are within a radius of 6 inches of the plant, and close to the surface. Do not hoe deeply or you will break off some of the roots. Do not cultivate when the leaves are wet.

Water copiously during a dry spell. Celery probably suffers more from a deficiency of water than does any other crop. The watering should be done by pouring water along the soil close to a row of plants. Be sure that no water gets into the hearts of the plants.

Blanching is one of the most important steps in celery culture. If it is not done, the plants have not only a dark color but also a strong and bitter flavor. The principle of blanching is simply to cover up the stalks so that all light is excluded; without light the formation of chlorophyll is stopped and the covered parts turn white. The blanching is begun when the crop is nearly mature, 2 or 3 weeks before you intend to harvest it. When the crop is growing quickly in the summer it will blanch in 10 days or 2 weeks. In the fall, when the growth has slowed up, it may take 3 weeks. Let the crop, especially the late crop, make all the growth it can before you start to blanch. But remember, since it should be harvested before heavy frosts, do not delay too long.

There are several methods of doing this job: with boards, with paper, with soil. From some varieties, planted very closely, you can get almost self-blanched stalks.

For the home gardener with comparatively few plants to worry about, individual celery blanchers are simplest. They can be bought or you can make your own. Blanchers that are sold are cylinders of heavy, specially prepared paper. Manila paper wrapped around the plant and tied is perfectly satisfactory. This is the only method that allows you to blanch just a few plants at a time, and thus extend your harvest period over several weeks.

Blanching with boards is done with 1-inch boards 12 inches wide and up to 12 or 14 feet long. The boards are laid on their edges on the ground as close to the plants as possible, held upright by cleats nailed across the top. Hill up a little soil around the base of the board to exclude all light. The boards can be put up as soon as the celery is tall enough for some of the leaves to show over the top. It will take 10 to 20 days in the summer, which is the best time to blanch this way. Do not leave the boards up too long or the celery may rot, especially if the weather gets moist.

Another method is to use specially prepared paper 10 or 12 inches wide. This comes in a long roll and it is unwound and placed around the rows of celery plants and held in place by inverted U-shaped pieces of wire imbedded in the ground.

Late celery is most successfully blanched with soil. The plants must be set about 5–6 inches apart if they are blanched this way. Just hold each plant and draw up enough earth around it to hold it firmly in place. Then finish the job with your hoe along the row, piling the dirt up until only the celery tops are exposed. Start doing this when the plants are a foot tall, and raise the soil gradually as the plants grow until they are 12–15 inches high.

So-called "self-blanching" celery is sometimes planted so densely, with the plants 6–10 inches apart each way, that when they are full grown the dense foliage hides the stalks from the light. The soil has to be excessively rich to feed celery grown in this manner; 50 pounds of well-rotted manure to each square yard of earth is not too much.

For the average gardener, the recommended procedure is the individual blanching of each stalk, unless you are growing such large quantities that the labor would be excessive.

If your celery suffers from blight treat it with an extra spraying of Bordeaux mixture, in addition to regular routine pest-control treatment.

Harvesting: Celery is harvested by cutting the root an inch or two below the crown with a sharp knife. The early crop should be harvested whenever it is fully blanched because it has a tendency to become overripe and pithy if it is held too long. This is another reason why concentrating on a fall crop is a wise course. If you blanch only a few stalks at a time, and save part of your fall crop for storage, you can harvest for months. The fall crop must be harvested before hard frosts, however. And don't fully blanch the stalks that you intend to store.

Storing: Celery can be stored in the same cellar or outside storage room used for root crops (see the chapter on "Storing") since it requires about the same conditions—temperature around freezing, high humidity, and little air circulation. The plants are dug up, roots and all, and placed in the storage room either right on the floor in a bed of soil or in boxes of earth. They should be planted with the crowns even with the surface and the roots should be kept well watered, but do not allow water to get on the stalks or foliage.

If there is some light in the storage room, the plants should be covered with a board. They will keep 3 to 5 months and should give you good celery plants all winter.

Uses: A good way to use up a sudden oversupply of celery is to put up spiced celery. Chop up 6 bunches of celery with the roots and leaves removed, 12 tomatoes, and a pepper. To 1½ cupfuls of vinegar, add 2 cupfuls of sugar, 1 teaspoonful each of mustard, clove, allspice, cinnamon, and celery seed, and 2 tablespoonfuls of salt. Put all the ingredients together in a kettle and simmer for 1½ hours. Pack into jars and cover.

Creamed celery and onions, which is made from about 2 cupfuls of celery to 1 of onions covered with melted cheese and baked in a casserole, is very good. So is the same dish made with crab meat instead of onions. Try it for Sunday night supper. Or try boiling celery in consommé instead of water, and when it is done make a sauce with the consommé, seasoning it with lemon juice and chopped parsley. Another dish is to boil some celery, sauté mushrooms in butter, add flour to the mushrooms, then cream the mushrooms enough to make a medium cream sauce, add the celery and serve. Or fry celery slowly in butter. When it is brown, remove the celery, add some bread crumbs to the butter, and serve this as a sauce over the celery.

To prepare celery relish, mix together 1½ cupfuls of chopped celery, 4 teaspoonfuls of powdered sugar, a teaspoonful of salt, ½ teaspoonful of mustard, and ¼ cupful of vinegar. Put a cover over this and place in the ice box for 2 hours. Before you serve, drain off the liquid.

10. Chard

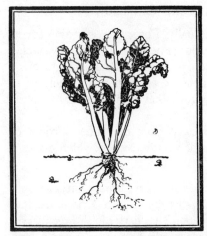

(*Beta vulgaris var. cicla. Chenopodiaceae*, goosefoot family.)

HISTORY: Chard, or Swiss chard, apparently was the so-called beet of the ancients and of the Middle Ages. Aristotle mentioned a red chard in 350 B.C.; Roman writers made frequent references to this vegetable; it is found in Chinese writings as early as the seventh century; and in Europe all the old herbalists noted it. Red, yellow, and white forms were all found in ancient times.

The wild form is found in the Canary Islands, along the coast of the Mediterranean as far as the Caspian Sea and Persia, and also along the seacoasts of England. It is a close relative of the beet, and the variety in color and leaf formation of this crop explains why it has numerous popular names, such as silver beet, leaf beet, kale beet, Swiss beet, spinach beet, asparagus beet.

Chard is not an important commercial crop because the stalks do not withstand the rigors of transportation and handling well. Since it is rather scarce in the markets, it is all the more important for the home gardener to include this little-grown but well worth while vegetable in his garden.

Food Value: Chard is an excellent source of vitamin A (and, in fact, one of the best vegetables for this important vitamin) and is also an excellent source of calcium and iron.

Culture: Chard is an accommodating half-hardy crop that can be sown when the weather is cool and will grow well when it is either cool or quite hot. It is also an easy crop to grow. The seed can be planted right in the garden when the soil has warmed up a bit; in 60 days you can start harvesting; and, since leaves can be picked from one plant until frost, the harvesting continues all summer. It is one of the very few vegetables to provide a continuous harvest without successive plantings, which is another reason why it should be an indispensable addition to every garden. It is the only kind of green, except New Zealand spinach, that is a certain midsummer potherb; it is suitable for canning; and, for ease of culture, handsome appearance, and very good taste, it deserves much wider appreciation than it at present enjoys.

Another, and by no means inconsequential, good point is that chard is not seriously affected by diseases or pests.

Habits of Growth: Chard is actually a beet that is grown for its green leaves rather than for its tap root. The plant grows 2–2½ inches tall. It consists of broad, fleshy, red or whitish leaf stalks; large, crisp, savoyed, yellow-green leaves which are sometimes as much as 10 inches wide; and a small whitish root that is not eaten. Both the stalks and the leaves are edible.

While the older leaves are harvested from the outer portions of the plant, new leaves are being formed at the center, which makes it possible to harvest it continually.

Types and Varieties: All chard is the same type plant; the only difference is in the color of the stalks and leaves. There are few varieties from which to choose. *Fordhook* has dark bluish-green leaves and an almost white stalk. This is considered a first-rate variety. *Lucullus* has light yellowish-green leaves and is the old standard variety. In 1940 Burpee's introduced a new variety called *Rhubarb Chard*, which has ribs the same color of red as rhubarb and is highly recommended as an excellent variety.

How Much to Buy:

1 package for 25 feet
1 ounce   for 100 feet

Twenty-five feet of original sowing will yield 25 plants after thinning, which is ample for the average family.

Planting:

Germination time: 8–10 days.

Depth for seed: ½ inch.

Spacing of plants: 12 inches.

Spacing of rows: 18 inches. (The tops grow so large that the plant needs this much space.)

When to Plant:

		EARLY CROP	LATE CROP
		Earliest Safe Date for Planting Seed in Garden	*Latest Safe Date for Planting Seed in Garden*
Zone	A. Jan.	1 – Feb. 1	Nov. 1
"	B. Jan.	15 – Feb. 15	Oct. 1
"	C. Feb.	15 – March 1	Oct. 1
"	D. March	1 – March 15	Sept. 1
"	E. March	15 – April 15	July 15
"	F. April	15 – May 1	July 1
"	G. May	1 – May 15	June 15

(See maps at back of book showing locations of zones for spring and fall frosts. Remember that the boundaries of the spring frost zones are not the same as those of the fall frost zones, and your locality may be in different zones for the spring and fall frosts. If you live in the West outside the zones, for an approximate guide take the frost dates in your individual locality, find similar frost dates in one of the zones, and use the corresponding dates for that zone.)

The later of the early safe planting dates is probably the best one to use since chard will get off to a fine start when the weather has warmed up. If you are impatient for an extra early crop, sow the seed in your hotbed a month before the first outdoor planting date. There is no necessity for this special planting, though, as chard grows very satisfactorily when it is seeded directly in the garden.

How to Plant: Planting chard is simply a case of sowing the seed ½ inch deep, watering it if the soil is dry, and letting nature take its course.

Where to Plant: Chard should be planted near the other crops that stay in the ground the whole season, such as parsnips, New Zealand spinach, and celery. As a matter of fact, chard grows so luxuriantly and with such great beauty that it can advantageously be grown in the flower garden. Many vegetables are lovely things to see growing. Edna Ferber's heroine in *So Big* amused and astounded the local farmers when she said she thought that cabbages were beautiful; but she was right, of course. Cabbages are beautiful, and so are chard and many other vegetables beautiful in themselves, as well as being evidences of nature's bounty and providence.

Soil: Any good garden soil will do for this crop. If you want the speedy, succulent growth that makes chard particularly good, give it two or three small feedings during the summer with a complete commercial fertilizer.

Cultivation and Care: Routine garden cultivation to keep down weeds and keep the soil porous is all that this crop needs. Later in the season when the tops are fully grown and expansive, little cultivation of any sort will be necessary.

The seedlings will need to be thinned, but thinning is a pleasure because the small greens can be eaten. Eventually the plants should stand a foot apart, but do not give them that much room all at once. Make your first thinning when the plants are 5–6 inches tall and thin to 2–3 inches. When the ones that remain in the ground begin to get crowded, thin again to 6 inches. The final thinning is made when the plants start crowding each other. Because chard transplants easily, the thinnings can be put in any spot in the garden where summer foliage is desired.

Harvesting: In about 60 days from planting the first leaves can be pulled. The outer leaves are removed an inch or so from the ground, a few at a time. Have enough plants so that no one plant need be ransacked too severely. New leaves develop in the center which keeps new foliage coming on. If you harvest with a knife, take care that you do not injure the center bud.

You will have a continual supply until late fall. With light protection the plant will probably live over the winter to give you early spring greens. However, it will go to seed quickly the second year.

Canning: Chard cannot be stored because it is too perishable. But it is very suitable for canning. For canning directions see the chapter on "Canning."

Uses: The stalks and the leaves of chard can be served separately or as a single dish. The broad, crisp stalks are cooked in the same manner as asparagus and served with either butter or a cream sauce. The leaves are treated the same as spinach or any other greens, washed free of dirt (since they are higher from the ground than spinach, getting rid of the dirt and grit is not quite such a chore), boiled in very little water, and chopped very fine and well buttered. The young thinnings can be boiled as a whole, leaves and stalks together. An elaborate dish consists of serving a platter with the stalks in the center, surrounded by a ring of the chopped greens. Rhubarb chard served in this manner with its red stalks provides a festive and unusual as well as a delicious vegetable to put before guests.

11. Corn

(Sweet Corn)

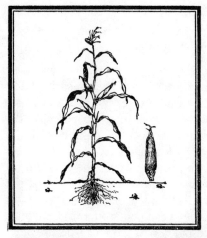

(Zea Mays var. rugosa. Gramineae, grass family.)

HISTORY: Corn is a native American plant. Inasmuch as it has always been widely grown in many parts of both North and South America, there are numerous references to it, dating back to the eighth century. The corn in these early references is grain corn or maize and not the sweet corn we eat today, which is a comparatively recent addition to the list of edible plants.

The first record of maize in the eighth century was in Mexico, where yellow and white maize played an important part in many early Indian legends and religious observances. Sturtevant [1] decribes one of their ceremonies, which is typical of many: "At harvest time in Quegolani, the priests of the maize god ceremonially visited the corn fields, sought the fairest and best-filled ear, which, after worshipping, they wrapped in cloth and at next seedtime, with processions and solemn rices, buried, wrapped in a deer skin, in a hole lined with stems in the midst of the fields. When another harvest came, if it were a fruitful one, the earth was dug up and the decayed remains distributed in small parcels to the happy populace as talismans against all kinds of evil." In a letter from Cuba in November, 1492, Columbus mentioned "a kind of grain called maiz, of which was made a very well-tasted flour."

A great variety of corn was cultivated during that period: blue, yellow, white, red, and even black. All the early explorers and settlers found corn growing wherever they went. In 1696 a Rev. John Campanius in his reading of the Lord's Prayer altered "give us this day our daily bread" to "give us a plentiful supply of venison and corn." Not only was the grain itself used; the stalks furnished sugar to the Peruvians, honey to the Mexicans, and a kind of beer to the natives everywhere.

The sweet type of corn first made its appearance when a member of General Sullivan's expedition took back to Plymouth some ears he had found among the Indians along the Susquehanna. This was in 1779. In a catalogue published in 1828, only one variety was listed, but by 1881 sixteen varieties had appeared. Incidentally, it would be a much simpler matter for the gardener if that were all he had to choose from today.

The culture of sweet corn is practically limited to North America and is almost unknown in other parts of the world.

***

Food Value: Sweet corn is a good source of vitamin B_1 and a good source of phosphorus; it also has a high carbohydrate content, which makes it a more nourishing food than many other vegetables. And

[1] *Sturtevant's Notes on Edible Plants* (U. P. Hedrick), New York State Department of Agriculture, Annual Report, 1919.

the amount of butter most people usually eat with an ear of corn supplies an excellent supplement of vitamin A.

Culture: Sweet corn is a fairly easy crop to grow. It is a tender, warm-weather crop that is sown about the date of the last spring frost, germinates readily, grows lustily with little care, and provides a harvest that is one of the treats of the whole summer. It thrives when the weather is warm both day and night, in plenty of sunshine, and in a good garden soil. But it is sensitive both to light frosts and to severe heat or drought. Sweet corn can be grown all over the country, although it usually produces a better crop in the North because the ravages of the corn ear worm are likely to be severe in the South. Different types of corn mature at times ranging from 9 to 14 weeks, and a continual harvest from midsummer to frost can be provided either by successive plantings of one type or by planting early, mid-season, and late varieties.

Sweet corn is eaten when it is immature, and it must be picked at exactly the right stage of development. One planting provides ears at this perfect stage for only a week or 10 days. But although it is something of a nuisance to make repeated plantings, the work is more than compensated for by the pleasure you will get from eating your own corn. This is a vegetable which is never tasted at its best unless it is eaten within a few hours, preferably a few minutes, after harvesting. The moment corn is picked, the sugar in the kernels starts changing into starch. This change takes place most rapidly during the first twenty-four hours. At the end of that time half the sugar has become starch. Obviously sweet corn bought in the market, which is usually more than a day old, is inferior to your own. Every gardener can find room for a row of one of the small varieties; he owes himself and his family that much sheer enjoyment and delight. Furthermore, sweet corn is suitable for canning for the winter larder.

Habits of Growth: Sweet corn is a tender annual plant, which produces one or more erect stems 4–10 feet tall, terminating in tassels. Large leaves, 2–3 feet long and about 2–4 inches wide, are produced in the joints of the stem. The male or pollen-bearing flowers are numerous. These are followed by the production of the long ears, encased in a sheath or husk, or what is more commonly called the silk. The ears are composed of a thick axis, or the cob, covered with the kernels, or seed, of which there are 8 to 24 rows. When the plant is fully mature, the seeds are hard, wrinkled, and dry. Sweet corn, however, is harvested while the grains are immature and still smooth and soft. The customary suckers are secondary stems formed from nodes either near or at the surface of the ground.

Types and Varieties: A word of warning is necessary before we discuss and recommend varieties. In the past few years plant hybridizers at various agricultural experiment stations have been doing a vast amount of work on sweet corn to produce hybrids that will be earlier, yield more heavily, and be resistant to certain prevalent diseases and pests. Corn hybrids are first-generation crosses between two different strains and are selected for advantageous properties derived from each parent strain. They are not completely sterile, like mules, but they degenerate rapidly. Therefore they are produced afresh each year for the crop they yield and not for reproduction. Modern methods make the cost of producing hybrid seed each year quite low.

The results of this research have been far reaching; and since the work is being carried on at stations in various parts of the country, and since new hybrids are constantly on the market, the best way to choose corn varieties for your particular vicinity is to obtain the latest information from your own county agricultural agent. All the varieties recommended below are good ones, but they may not be the ones best adapted to your local conditions.

There are three types of corn: the early, the midseason, and the late. These terms apply to the length of time needed for maturity rather than to the time of the season that the types should be planted. You can plant any of them all season.

There are two kinds of varieties: the standard or open-pollinated varieties, which are still popular and satisfactory, and the new hybrids, which are superior and highly recommended. So great has the demand for these new hybrids become that in 1941 more than half the corn sold was of this type. In general the hybrids have a higher yield, and are more uniform in quality, size, and time of maturity.

The old open-pollinated varieties include *Stowell's Evergreen*, which is the oldest variety in use today and was first introduced in 1845; *Country Gentleman*, another old variety; and *Golden Bantam*, which made its first appearance about forty years ago and had to overcome enormous opposition because nobody considered yellow corn fit for anything but horses. Luther Burbank increased the number of rows on the cob from eight to twelve, and W. Atlee Burpee popularized it.

Early type. This type matures in 65–75 days, grows about 4–6 feet tall. The plants and ears are relatively small. It requires less space than the other types and grows faster. The ears are of excellent quality even though they are small, and many people prefer to plant this type successively all season.

VARIETIES: *Golden Sunshine* (74 days) and *Golden Early Market* (72 days) are standard varieties; among the hybrids, *Spancross* (71 days), earliest of the hybrids, and *Marcross* (69–75 days), one of the largest of the early type.

Midseason type. This type matures in about 80-90 days, is 6–8 feet tall, and includes some of the most popular varieties.

VARIETIES: *Golden Bantam* (82 days), one of the sweetest varieties that grows, and *Whipple's Early Yellow* (84 days) are both popular standard varieties; *Golden Cross Bantam* (88–89 days), wilt resistant, and *Whipcross 39* (81 days), which is of the same type as Whipple's Early Yellow but practically immune to bacterial wilt, are hybrids.

Black Mexican is a variety that many people shy away from because of its appearance, but it has a delicious flavor and some people think it is by far the best of all. It matures in about 86 days, and the kernels have a purplish or bluish-black tinge. This does not improve the appearance of the ears, but it certainly does not impair the flavor, and most of the color cooks out.

Late type. This type is 7–10 feet tall, matures in 90–100 days, has the largest ears, and is the heaviest yielding of all the types. It is the one most generally used for canning because of the size of the yield and the sweet flavor.

VARIETIES: *Country Gentleman* (94 days), having very sweet white "shoe-peg" kernels, is the widely known standard variety. Another good standard variety is *White Evergreen* (90 days), which is an improved *Stowell's Evergreen*. A new introduction is the hybrid, *Stowell's Evergreen Hybrid,* an improvement over both of the older varieties. For the South, two varieties which are highly resistant to the ear worm are *Honey June* and *Surecropper Sugar.*

The days to maturity are only approximate because the growth is not the same under all climatic conditions. Very hot weather hastens maturity; a spell of long, cold weather will slow it up.

How Much to Buy:

1 package for 100 feet or 25 hills
1 pound for 300 feet or 75 hills

If you have the space, plant enough to allow for canning. Do not try to save your own seed from the hybrids; the crosses must be made every year and home grown seed will not produce true to type.

Planting:

Germination time: 5–8 days.

Depth for seed: 1 inch early in the season, 1½–2 inches later.

Spacing of plants: In rows, the plants should stand 10–18 inches apart, depending upon the size of the variety.

Spacing of rows: *Early,* 30 inches.
Midseason, 36 inches.
Late, 42 inches.

Spacing of hills: *Early,* 2 by 2½ feet to 2 by 3 feet.
Midseason and *late,* 3 by 3 feet to 3½ by 3½ feet.

When to Plant:

	EARLY CROP	LATE CROP
	Earliest Safe Date for Planting Seed in Garden	*Latest Safe Date for Planting Seed in Garden*
Zone A.	Feb. 15 – March 1	Oct. 1
" B.	March 1 – March 15	Sept. 1
" C.	March 15 – April 1	Aug. 15
" D.	April 1 – May 1	Aug. 1
" E.	April 15 – May 15	July 15
" F.	May 1 – June 1	July 1
" G.	May 15 – June 15	June 15

(See maps at back of book showing locations of zones for spring and fall frosts. Remember that the boundaries of the spring frost zones are not the same as those of the fall frost zones, and your locality may be in different zones for the spring and fall frosts. If you live in the West outside the zones, for an approximate guide take the frost dates in your individual locality, find similar frost dates in one of the zones, and use the corresponding dates for that zone.)

The first planting is made at about the date of the last killing spring frost. Corn seed can stand a light frost, and a small planting can be made a week or two before this date as a gamble if an especially early crop is wanted. But the seed rots in the ground if it is cold and damp, and planting any earlier than the last frost date is risky. It is a warmth-loving plant, and seed planted when the soil has warmed up makes up for lost time quickly.

There are two ways of managing a successive corn harvest. One is to plant the early, midseason, and late varieties all at the same time. Since the early varieties are ready to harvest a month before the late varieties are, in theory you should have a month's harvesting. Actually you may have some overlapping or gaps, but it is a good plan if you have the room and do not relish frequent plantings. It also works best in the South where the weather later is so hot that the corn may have trouble getting started. A continual harvest is more surely attained, though, by successive plantings, made every week or two. The first and last plantings can be of the early, quick-maturing type. Between these you can plant some of the midseason and late varieties if you favor certain of these. The last planting, of an early variety, should be sown at least 10 weeks before the first fall frost date.

How to Plant: There is not much choice between planting in rows and planting in hills. If you plant in hills, you can cultivate crosswise and that saves some hand weeding. On the other hand, rows are easier for the small home gardener and probably are to be preferred there.

If you plant in rows, the most important thing to remember is that the pollen necessary for fertilization is carried by the wind, and you should plant several short rows in a square rather than string your planting out in one long row.

The first planting should be heavy because some of the seed will probably rot. You can thin either by pulling up the excess plants or by cutting them off with a hoe. The hoe method is good because you do not disturb the plants that are to remain in the ground.

In a hill, 6 to 8 seeds are planted and later thinned to 4 plants for the small varieties and 3 plants for the large.

If your enthusiasm for corn is unbounded and you cannot wait for the first corn planted outdoors, seed can be started 3 weeks early in a cold frame or in the house. The roots do not take to transplanting readily; therefore the seed must be sown in individual containers—pots, berry baskets, or cardboard containers.

Where to Plant: Even the early varieties of corn are fairly tall; so plant corn at one end of the garden with other tall-growing plants so that you will not shade the short ones. Early corn can be followed by any of the cool-season crops, such as spinach, beets, lettuce, or turnips; while late plantings of corn are a good follow-up crop for peas or early cabbage.

Soil: The question of just how to fertilize a corn patch is one that should be determined by each gardener according to the type of soil in his garden. Corn needs a good soil but not an overly rich one. If your soil has been manured before planting, that is all the fertilizer you will need. If not, use a commercial fertilizer at the time of planting your seed. Since the fertilizer should not come into direct contact with the seed, the best plan is to apply it in bands an inch wide about 2 or 3 inches from the seeds. A good type is 4–8–4, and the application should be moderate, about 2 pounds per 100 feet of row or 25 hills.

Cultivation and Care: The main purpose of cultivation is to keep down weeds. The root system of corn is large and the roots are close to the surface. Hence, deep tilling harms the roots and should be avoided. Cultivate often and shallow. When the plants start to form ears, cultivation can cease except for a little hand weeding when necessary.

Although corn is a warm-weather plant, it reacts badly to drought. Without water the yield is seriously affected. If possible, irrigate when the weather turns dry. A casual sprinkling with a hose is no good; the plant needs an adequate supply. A good way to provide it is to hollow out a trench alongside the plants, and flood the trench with water two or three times a week.

Much time used to be spent removing the suckers from the plant, but recent investigations have proved that this sucker removal does the plant more harm than good, and it is no longer an advisable procedure.

Sweet corn is a problem if attacked by corn ear worms and borers. Clean gardening is the best preventative. However, if you find worms, dust the silk every few days with calcium arsenate or squirt a little mineral oil from an oil can into the silk. Corn-ear worms also attack tomatoes, which should then be sprayed or dusted with calcium arsenate.

Harvesting: Harvesting of this crop is no haphazard business to be undertaken when you think of it. Corn ears should be harvested at a precise stage of their growth. A delay is disastrous. The ears are harvested while immature. The young kernels pass through three stages. During the first, called the pre-milk stage, the kernels are tender and sweet but small and the juice is clear like water. Then the kernels swell and get plumper and the juice turns milky. This is the milk stage, when they should be harvested. The last stage is the dough stage. The juice thickens; the sugar turns to starch; the kernel becomes hard, and the peak of perfection is past.

The milk stage never lasts long—a week or 10 days normally, longer if the weather is cool, only a day or two in a hot spell. Unless you are experienced and can tell by feeling the ears whether they have reached the exact moment of perfection, you should pull down a bit of the husk and use the thumbnail test. Puncture a kernel; if a milky fluid comes out, the corn is right, if what comes out is thick and doughy, the corn is too ripe. Start testing when the silk turns brown. If a planting all reaches harvesting stage at about the same time and you have more than you can eat, don't let the ears grow old on the plant; pick them and either can the surplus or give it away. It's nothing short of a crime to let corn spoil.

The actual picking is simply a matter of jerking the ear off the stalk with a slight twist.

Canning: Canned corn is an excellent product. Do your canning immediately after the corn is picked, because of the rapidity with which the sugar starts turning to starch. For canning directions see the chapter on "Canning."

Uses: There is only one proper use for fresh, home-grown sweet corn, apart from canning, and that is to eat it on the cob. Half an hour before dinner put your water on to boil, go out to the corn patch and pick your corn. By the time the water is boiling the corn will be husked, and 10 or 15 minutes later you should be eating it. Steamed corn is still better, but it takes longer to cook unless you use a pressure cooker.

There are many recipes for corn dishes, such as corn pudding. Only left-over or canned corn should be used in them.

12.
Cucumbers

(Cucumis sativus. Cucurbitaceae, gourd or melon family.)

HISTORY: Cucumbers date back probably 3000 years. They are mentioned in the Old Testament as an article of food the lack of which the Israelites lamented in the wilderness. The Roman Emperor Tiberius grew cucumbers in heat and had a supply for his table every day of the year. They are definitely identified in Chinese writings by the fifth century. Charlemagne had cucumbers planted on his estates. Columbus found cucumbers growing in Haiti in 1494, and the early French explorers in the United States found cucumbers grown by the Indians both in the North around what is now Montreal and also in Florida. The English colonists started planting them in 1609. Botanical books from the sixteenth century on mention their culture.

Today they are an important commercial crop, being produced for the market in twenty-nine states; and they are grown extensively by home gardeners.

Food Value: Cucumbers are a good source of vitamin C, but that is about the extent of their value from a nutritive standpoint. They are a supplementary rather than a main food item. They are usually eaten either in salads or as pickles and relishes with other foods that make up for the dietary deficiencies of the cucumber.

Culture: Cucumbers need warm weather to grow and produce fruit, and they are killed by even a light frost. However, they mature quickly, and hence can be grown anywhere if planted at the right time.

Cucumbers are not a particularly difficult crop to grow, but they are a very tender, hot-weather crop and it is perfectly useless to attempt growing them except when the weather is thoroughly warm. But they also do not thrive in extreme heat. Thus, the growing season must be chosen with some care.

Cucumbers are not demanding in other respects, however. They can be planted in either hills or rows, but adequate room must be left for the vines to spread out. The seeds can usually be planted in the garden, and they start producing fruit in 60–70 days. The harvest continues for several weeks if the immature fruits are picked regularly. They can be eaten immediately or can be made into pickles.

They do not require special seeding in heat, although they can be started in a hotbed or in the house if an especially early crop is desired. In sections of the country where the season of warm weather is sufficiently long, several successive plantings can be made to ensure a prolonged harvesting period.

Habits of Growth: The cucumber plant is a trailing vine producing fruits which are the edible part of the plant. At first the plant grows erect; then it falls over and starts to run or vine. The stems are hairy and angular and the leaves are quite large. The stems produce many tendrils, enabling the vines to climb over bushes or obstacles in their path.

On the first node of each fruiting branch the cucumbers are borne. The fruit is usually oval or elongated, although sometimes it is nearly globular, and varies in size from an inch or two to 2 feet in some of the English varieties (which are grown in greenhouses). The fruit is always harvested when it is immature. As soon as one fruit is allowed to ripen fully on a vine, it prevents the setting of any more fruit and the productivity of the vine is over. The rind of the immature fruit is green; when it reaches maturity it turns yellowish white in some varieties and brown in others. Also the seeds start to harden and the fruit is no longer worth eating.

The green fruits are usually covered with white or black spines or prickles.

Types and Varieties: There are three types of cucumbers: the English type and two American types, the slicing and the pickling.

English type. This can be grown only in greenhouses. It produces mammoth fruits usually from vines that have climbed up and covered the ceiling of the greenhouse, allowing the fruits to hang down. Since they cannot be grown outdoors, we shall not consider them for the home gardener.

Slicing type. These cucumbers grow quite large and are harvested when they are about 10 inches long and 2–3 inches in diameter if they are to be used for the table. If harvested when 3–5 inches long, they can be used for dill pickles.

VARIETIES: *White Spine* is a good standard kind, and *Davis Perfect* is excellent; *Kirby* is a popular variety in the South.

Pickling type. Pickling cucumbers are usually smaller fruited than the slicing type, and they have a larger number of spines. The very small pickling cucumbers, called "gherkins," are little, bur-like fruits

2–3 inches long and 1–1½ inches thick, which make excellent pickles. Gherkins are actually quite different from the regular cucumber and are often classed in an entirely different botanical group, but they are included here for simplicity.

VARIETIES: Pickling cucumbers: *Chicago Pickling* and *National Pickling*. Gherkins: *West India Gherkin*.

How Much to Buy:

1 package for 15 hills or 15 feet
1 ounce for 50 hills or 50 feet

A few cucumber plants are sufficient for most families since each plant produces numerous fruits. It is a good idea, however, to grow a few plants of both the slicing and the pickling types because each type is best for its own purpose. And one plant of gherkins will produce many fruits for pickling because they are especially prolific.

Planting:

Germination time:	8–10 days.
Depth for seed:	1 inch.
Spacing of plants:	18 inches (if planted in rows).
Spacing of rows:	4–5 feet.
Spacing of hills:	It is probably better for the home gardener, who does not need a very large crop, to grow cucumbers in hills; each hill should be about 4 or 5 feet square.

When to Plant:

	EARLY CROP *Earliest Safe Date for Planting Seed in Garden*	LATE CROP *Latest Safe Date for Planting Seed in Garden*
Zone A.	March 1 – March 15	—
" B.	March 15 – April 1	—
" C.	April 1 – April 15	Aug. 15
" D.	April 15 – May 1	Aug. 1
" E.	May 1 – June 1	July 15
" F.	May 15 – June 15	July 1
" G.	June 1 – June 15	June 1

(See maps at back of book showing locations of zones for spring and fall frosts. Remember that the boundaries of the spring frost zones are not the same as those of the fall frost zones, and your locality may be in different zones for the spring and fall frosts. If you live in the West outside the zones, for an approximate guide take the frost dates in your individual locality, find similar frost dates in one of the zones, and use the corresponding dates for that zone.)

The point has already been made that cucumbers are a tender, warm-season crop, but it can stand repeating because it is the most important point to remember if you want to be sure of success. The seed will not germinate in cold soil, and a frost will kill the plants. Be sure that all danger of frost is over.

The cucumbers for pickles can be planted later than the slicing ones—and it is wise to postpone planting as long as possible because this late planting may permit the plants to escape the severest attacks of the striped cucumber beetle, a pernicious pest.

How to Plant: The hill system was formerly the accepted way of handling cucumber plants. The hills are just large 4- or 5-foot squares, which can be raked up a foot or so high in the center where the seeds are planted. This allows the vines plenty of room to roam in all directions. However, when they are grown on a reasonably large scale, it is now quite usual to sow in rows 4 or 5 feet apart, with the plants 18 inches apart in the rows so that the vines can only spread sideways. A few hills should be enough for most families, but cucumber addicts can plant in rows if they can spare the space.

Whichever method you use, sow plenty of seeds. There's an old saying that goes:

> "Two for the cutworm, one for the crow,
> One for the beetle, and four to grow."

And it is true that the devastations are likely to be severe. Therefore, plant about 12 seeds in the center of a hill in an area 6–12 inches in diameter, and if your thinning is not already taken care of by the striped beetle, thin to 2 or 3 plants when they are well established, discarding the weaker and smaller plants. In a row sow a seed every inch or two and thin finally to stand 18 inches apart. Don't be too hasty about thinning, though, and be sure that you will have enough plants left before you throw any away.

If seeds are started in heat or in the house, since the roots are set back by being disturbed, the plants must be grown in special containers so that the entire plant can be set in the garden without disturbing the roots. Berry boxes, pots, special cardboard containers are all good —and a common way of sowing is to stick the seeds in a piece of inverted sod. Sow 2 or 3 seeds in each container and thin to one plant. This operation should start about a month before the outdoor planting date. Such special sowing is by no means necessary, but it does allow for earlier harvesting.

Where to Plant: If you have some odd space available outside the garden proper, it is not a bad idea to put the cucumbers there because they do take up a lot of space in the garden. A few vines could be planted along a wall or fence, or in a sunny spot by the garage. In the vegetable garden they can be preceded by a very early crop of radishes, lettuce, or spinach; they grow too late in the fall in most regions to have any crop follow them. You can, however, do some intercropping if you plan carefully. Small early crops, such as lettuce or carrots, could be planted between the hills or rows as long as they are out of the way when the cucumbers begin to vine and need all the room they can get.

Soil: Cucumbers will grow in almost any kind of soil, but it does need an abundance of fertilizer. Well-rotted manure is good, and the best way to apply it is to put a forkful or two right where you are going to plant the seeds, and cover the manure with 3–4 inches of soil. Then you'll have the manure where the roots can use it. If you broadcast it all over the space intended for the crop, most of it will be wasted. Commercial fertilizers can be used in a soil that already has plenty of humus; 5–7–5 is good, dug into the soil a week before planting time.

Cultivation and Care: Cultivation is important in the early stages of the plant growth because when the vine starts to run and cover the ground the only possible cultivation is weeding by hand. Therefore, cultivate frequently at first and keep it up until you run the risk of injuring the vine. Don't let the weeds get a head start or you will never be able to get them under control.

The worst enemy of cucumbers, particularly young plants, is the striped cucumber beetle. It is tiny but most energetic. A method of control suggested in *Cornell Extension Bulletin*, No. 344, is helpful:

If the cucumbers are planted in hills, they can be protected easily against the striped cucumber beetle by covering the hills with a cheese-cloth screen when the plants are young. This is usually done by removing both the top and the bottom of a box 12 to 18 inches square and 6 to 8 inches deep. A piece of cheesecloth, single thickness, is tacked over the top of the box, and the box is set over the hill as soon as the cucumbers are planted. Such a protector not only keeps the beetles away from the plants, but also hastens germination and increases the rate of growth early in the season. The boxes are left in place until the plants become crowded. As soon as the boxes are removed, the plants should be dusted thoroly with 0.5 or 0.75 per cent rotenone dust.

Another treatment is to apply a calcium arsenate spray, preferably just after a rain.

Harvesting: Cucumbers are always harvested when the fruit is immature. Mature fruit is not palatable; the seed coats are hard; and the flavor is poor. But another reason for picking the fruit when it is immature is that the maturing of the seed causes such a heavy drain on the plant that it is afterward unable to set any more fruits. Any imperfect fruits should be removed also.

The fruits are picked by size rather than by age. They are ready to be picked when the furrows are well filled out and the cucumber is almost cylindrical, while the fruit is still green and plump and crisp, before the skin begins to turn yellow. Slicing cucumbers for the table are picked when they are 6–10 inches long; the ones for pickling, anywhere from ½ to 6 inches long, depending upon your own preference.

The fruit is picked by hand. A short piece of the stem an inch or so long should remain attached. It takes only a day or two for the tiny cucumbers to reach harvesting size and it may take a month for the large ones to grow big enough. Since the fruit grows rapidly and prolifically when it is set, you should go over the vines every day to remove any fruit that shows signs of maturing. This is an easy task in a small home garden, but this constant hand picking jumps the labor cost tremendously in commercial growing.

Uses: Cucumbers are delicious raw either in salads, sliced and served with French dressing, or in sandwiches. They have a crisp coolness which is particularly satisfying on hot summer days. The phrase "cool as a cucumber" is an apt one, and it is interesting to note that the expression was prevalent in writings at least a hundred years ago. Fried cucumbers are a pleasant change and easy to prepare; just dip ¼-inch slices in egg and bread crumbs and fry. Or you can stuff cucumbers. Cut them in half lengthwise, take out the inside and boil gently for five minutes; then fill the centers with any chopped leftover meat mixed with a little minced onion and some bread crumbs and bake until brown. Stewed cucumbers are another good dish. The slices are boiled until tender (about 20 minutes), drained, and seasoned. Vinegar and butter are added, and the whole is thoroughly heated.

Cucumbers can be preserved as pickles or relishes. There are innumerable recipes. The following are some good standard ones:

Sweet cucumber pickles. Soak small, fresh cucumbers overnight in brine (in the proportion of ½ cupful of salt to 1 quart of water). Boil a vinegar-sugar mixture (in the proportion of 1 pound of granulated sugar to 1 quart of vinegar), sufficient to cover the cucumbers when placed in a jar. A small amount of whole mixed spices, tied in a cloth, can be boiled in the vinegar mixture for about 15 minutes and then removed. The mixture should be poured over the cucumbers and left overnight. Then pour off the liquid; add a small amount of sugar to the liquid; reheat and again pour over the cucumbers. This process should be repeated until the desired sweetness is obtained.

Sour cucumber pickles. Soak small, fresh cucumbers in brine (in the proportion of ½ cupful of salt to 1 quart of water). Rinse and drain. Cover them with plain vinegar or with vinegar to which about a tablespoonful of brown sugar and a tablespoonful of mixed spices have been added for each quart of vinegar. Bring slowly to boiling and then pack the pickles in a jar with the hot vinegar poured over them.

Dill Pickles. Soak medium-size cucumbers in water for about 24 hours. Pack the cucumbers tightly in layers in a jar with dill leaves between the layers. Prepare a salt-vinegar mixture in the proportion of ½ cupful of salt, 1 cupful of vinegar, and 1 gallon of water (which is sufficient for a two-gallon jar of pickles). Pour this liquid over the cucumbers and hold them down solidly in the jar by a weight on top. When pickles are removed, the weight should be replaced.

Crisp pickle chips. Scald and peel a quart of sliced cucumbers. Cut them into pieces and cook for an hour in two quarts of water. Chop up a green pepper, a red pepper, and a large onion and add them to the cucumbers and cook another half hour. Add 1 pint of vinegar, 1 cupful of brown sugar, ¼ cupful of salt, ½ teaspoonful of mustard seed, and ¼ teaspoonful of tumeric, and boil for ten minutes. Put into jars and seal.

Mustard pickle. Cut up about 6 cucumbers into thick slices and soak for 24 hours in brine (in the proportion of ½ cupful of salt to 1 quart of water). Add a cupful of small pickling onions. Scald the cucumbers and onions in a vinegar mixture consisting of 2 cupfuls of vinegar, 1 tablespoonful of salt, 4 tablespoonfuls of brown sugar, 1 tablespoonful of mustard seed, 1 teaspoonful of pepper, ½ teaspoonful of celery seed, ½ tablespoonful of turmeric. After scalding, pack in jars and seal.

Cucumber relish. Sprinkle ½ cupful of salt over 1 gallon of pared and diced cucumbers and 2 finely chopped onions. Let stand overnight. In the morning drain well, add 1 quart of vinegar and 1 pint of water, boil for 15 minutes and drain again. Add 1 pound of brown sugar, ¼ cupful of mustard seed, ¼ cupful of celery seed, 2 teaspoonfuls of allspice, and 1½ cupfuls of fresh vinegar. Boil slowly for fifteen minutes.

13. Eggplant

*(Solanum melongena var. esculentum.
Solanaceae,* nightshade family.)

HISTORY: Eggplant is called by a variety of names, such as guinea squash, mad apple, and the French word *aubergine.* It is a close relative of the potato, and its name undoubtedly comes from the fact that there is a small white kind that looks very much like a chicken's egg.

Its exact history is unknown, but its growth in India and China has been recorded for at least 1500 years. Probably India is the original habitat, and it still grows wild there. It was not known in Europe in ancient times but was first introduced when trade routes with the Orient were opened up. The kind of eggplant originally grown there was small, egg-shaped, white, yellow, and brown ones which are grown today only for decoration or as curiosities.

Food Value: Eggplant in itself has little value as a food, containing only a fair amount of vitamin B_1. But since it is commonly cooked together with other vegetables, this lack of vitamins and minerals can be made up.

Culture: Eggplant is a very tender, hot-weather crop which can grow properly only when the season is very warm. Care is needed if good fruits are to be obtained. The plant is long growing and heat loving, and it must not be checked in any stage of its growth. *Eggplant is always a seedbed crop;* it is never started directly in the garden. In the South it is started in cold frames, in the north and central states the seed must be started in a hotbed or in the house. The seed is sown indoors 8 to 10 weeks before the date for outdoor planting, and it will be another 60 to 70 days after the plants have been set in the garden before the fruit will be ready to harvest. The instructions for growing the young seedlings (see How to Plant) must be followed with extreme care so that you will have strong plants to put in the garden. And above all, do not even attempt to transplant this crop outdoors until the weather is very warm. Eggplant grows rapidly during hot weather and very slowly when it is cool. If it grows slowly, it may never produce any fruit.

Habits of Growth: Eggplant is an annual, bushy, branched herb or sub-shrub 2–3 feet tall, with woody stems, large grayish-green leaves, big violet-colored flowers, and finally the fruit, which is the edible part of the plant. This fruit is a large, pendent, heavy-fleshed berry which is held to the plant by a greatly enlarged hard stalk and an enormous calyx. The fruit varies in length from 2–3 inches to 1 foot. The color may be black and purple, yellow, white, or striped, although the black and purple is the type generally grown today. The fruit may be oval, round, long, or pear shaped; the skin is smooth and shiny. The stem and leaves are often covered with spines.

A good-size fruit is about 6–9 inches in diameter, and a plant will bear 3–8 fruits.

Types and Varieties: There are two types of eggplant, the *black and purple* and the *white*.

Black and purple. Only the black and purple type is grown to any extent for eating. This is available both as a tall, large-fruited plant and as a dwarf plant with small fruit 4–5 inches long, which matures more quickly than the large fruit and should be used where the season is very short.

VARIETIES: Large-fruited: *Black Beauty* is the most generally grown large-fruited variety. A new variety, *New Hampshire Hybrid*, matures about 2 weeks earlier than Black Beauty. The fruit is a little smaller but very prolific and it is a variety well worth growing, especially where the summer season is short.

Dwarf: these are listed merely as dwarf or early.

White. It may take some scratching around to find a house that has the white-fruited type. Burpee's lists one, *Burpee White Beauty*, which produces large, oval-shaped, ivory-white fruit. This is interesting to grow as a novelty.

How Much to Buy:

1 package for 50–100 plants

This is more than the average family would want or at least have room for. Eggplant produces more fruit per plant in the South where the climate is more to its liking than in the North. Two or three fruits of a large variety, such as *Black Beauty*, are probably all you will get in the North, while a smaller-fruited variety, such as *New Hampshire Hybrid*, will give you a larger yield.

A dozen plants are usually adequate for the family garden, but since the fruits can be stored and it is such an adaptable vegetable, if you have the room you may want to grow more. Plants can be bought for setting in the garden for about $1.00 a dozen.

Planting:

Germination time: 10–12 days.

Depth for seed: ¼ inch.

Spacing of plants: *Large-fruited*, 3 feet. *Dwarf*, 2 feet.

Spacing of rows: 3–4 feet (depending upon the size of the variety).

When to Plant:

		EARLY CROP	LATE CROP
		Earliest Safe Date for Setting Plants in Garden	*Latest Safe Date for Setting Plants in Garden*
Zone	A.	March 1 – March 15	Sept. 1
"	B.	March 15 – April 1	Aug. 1
"	C.	April 1 – April 15	July 15
"	D.	April 15 – May 1	July 1
"	E.	May 1 – June 1	June 15
"	F.	May 15 – June 15	June 1
"	G.	June 1 – June 15	—

(See maps at back of book showing locations of zones for spring and fall frosts. Remember that the boundaries of the spring frost zones are not the same as those of the fall frost zones, and your locality may be in different zones for the spring and fall frosts. If you live in the West outside the zones, for an approximate guide take the frost dates in your individual locality, find similar frost dates in one of the zones, and use the corresponding dates for that zone.)

In the South there can be two crops of eggplant, one in the spring and one in the fall. In the North eggplant is a one-crop plant. It should be sown in a cold frame in the South, in a hotbed or in the house in the North, and it should never be planted outdoors until the weather has thoroughly warmed up and will stay warm for the next 2–2½ months while the plants are maturing. Eggplant takes a long time to produce edible fruits, and during all that time it must have very warm climate.

For that reason, the later date given above for the early crop should be used as a general rule. If the weather has not thoroughly warmed up then, delay outdoor planting still longer until it has.

How to Plant: The seed should be started 8 to 10 weeks before the date for outdoor planting. This seed requires rather special care since it must be kept in a stage of continuous development. One serious check in growth may be enough to keep the plant from ever producing any fruit, and it will surely result in a yield of smaller fruits.

For the home gardener, a flat in a warm, sunny spot in the house is the easiest method of handling this crop. Make a furrow 1 inch wide in rows 4 inches apart, and sow the seed thinly in the furrow. The soil should be rich and the temperature around 80°–85° F. during the day and not lower than 65° F. at night.

When the seedlings are 3–4 weeks old, they are ready to be transplanted. Since the root system should be disturbed as little as possible when the plants are finally set in the garden, the best way of handling them is to put them into individual containers. These can be either clay flower pots or cardboard containers, 2 inches in size. If the plant grows to such a size that the roots fill these containers, they should be moved again into 4-inch pots to avoid checking the growth. However, the roots should be kept in a solid, compact mass that can be moved into the garden with little or no disturbance. When the plants are 6–8 inches high and the weather is warm, set them in the garden.

Where to Plant: Eggplant should be put in a spot that is warm and sunny. It will occupy the space several months, but a short-season crop, such as spinach or lettuce, can precede it. It takes up considerable space, and is best planted near the other long-season summer crops, such as tomatoes and peppers.

Soil: The soil for this crop should be very fertile and thoroughly prepared. A commercial fertilizer, since it supplies quickly available plant nutrients, is a good source of soil enrichment. A 5–8–7 mixture is good, about 1 ounce per plant applied when setting out the plants and another dose used as a side dressing 3 weeks later.

Cultivation and Care: Cultivation should begin as soon as the plants have been set in the garden and continue at 10-day intervals during the whole growing season. It can be deep at first and close to the plant; but, as the root system extends, the cultivation should become more sallow. Do not cultivate when the foliage is wet. Other than this routine care, eggplant makes no special demands.

Harvesting: The harvesting of eggplant can begin in midsummer when the plant is one-third grown and can continue until the fruit is fully mature. Even after the fruits are fully grown they can stay on the plant for some time, but they should be picked while the skin is still bright and glossy. When the skin becomes dull, the fruit is over-mature and the flesh dry and tough and not much good for eating.

Because the fruit is heavy, cut it from the plant with a large knife or sharp pruning shears rather than try to pull it and risk damaging the plant. The large calyx is left attached to the fruit.

Storing: Mature eggplants can be kept for a month or two in the house. Put them on a shelf in a light room where the temperature is well above freezing, for example, in a cool cellar closet or a heated attic with windows. Each fruit must be handled very carefully; one bruise will make it rot. Do not allow the fruits to touch each other on the shelf.

Uses: There are many delicious ways of using eggplant.

Peel the eggplant; cut it in cubes; and stew it gently in boiling water for about 10 minutes. Remove from the fire; drain well and put it in a baking dish; season with salt and pepper; cover with buttered bread crumbs, and bake until the crumbs are brown. Or remove from the fire; season with salt and pepper; add some butter and thoroughly mix the eggplant with sour cream; and heat it over a low fire but do not boil it.

Cook cubed eggplant with a little sliced onion, 2 to 3 tomatoes, and 10 or 12 sliced okras, for 25–30 minutes. Or, after the cubed eggplant has been stewed, mix it with tomato sauce and put it in a casserole; cover the top with sausages; and bake until the sausages are cooked, turning them once.

Fried eggplant is a meal in itself. Peel the eggplant and cut it up into ½-inch thick slices. Salt the slices and lay on a plate for half an hour to drain. Then dip each slice in slightly beaten egg and then in bread crumbs, and fry in deep fat. Serve with tomato sauce. This should be eaten immediately or the eggplant loses its crispness.

A particularly good way to cook eggplant consists of first boiling the eggplant whole for 20 minutes in salt water. Rinse it in cold water, peel, and cut into small cubes. Brown a chopped onion slowly in olive oil and add it to the eggplant along with a cubed tomato, a green pepper cut into very small cubes, and some grated Parmesan cheese. Mix all the ingredients; place in a baking dish; cover with buttered bread crumbs; and bake until the top is brown, about half an hour.

Almost any filling can go into a stuffed eggplant, but the procedure is always the same. Cut the eggplant in half; parboil for 10 minutes; then scoop out the inside, leaving a good half inch of the shell. The filling is put in, covered with buttered bread crumbs, and baked until brown. The filling can be just the mashed-up center mixed with some bread crumbs and a little cream; or the center can be mixed with cut-up tomatoes, crumbled crisp bacon and mushrooms, with cooked shrimps, with ground ham, or with almost anything that is sitting in the refrigerator. It's an easy and economical way of using up the tag end of a roast and still give your family a real treat.

14. Lettuce

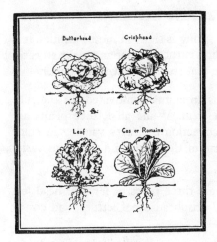

(Lactuca sativa. Compositae, composite or sunflower family.)

HISTORY: Lettuce has been cultivated for so many hundreds of years that no one knows when and where its beginnings were. It was served at the royal tables of the Persian kings about 550 B.C.; it was used as a salad by the Greeks and Romans; and Chaucer makes an allusion to it in 1340. Numerous varieties have been grown in Europe and in this country for many years.

Today it is the standard salad crop, and as such it should have a place in every garden. As a result of the growing interest in diets containing adequate vitamins and minerals, lettuce has assumed a special importance. The total acreage devoted to lettuce by commercial growers in this country has increased seven times in the past ten years and in 1937 the commercial value of the lettuce crop was greater than that of any other vegetables except potatoes and tomatoes.

Food Value: It is well to remember when you are preparing salads for the table that the richest part of lettuce, as far as the vitamins and minerals are concerned, is not the tender hearts but the big, green outside leaves. Use them all. Lettuce is an excellent health food. It is low in calories and rich in health-building properties. Green lettuce is an excellent source of vitamin A, a good source of vitamins B_1 and G, and a good source of calcium and iron.

Culture: Lettuce is a hardy, cool-season, moisture-loving, annual crop. It is easy to grow if its requirements are understood and catered to. It is useful in the garden because it matures fairly quickly and can be used as a succession or companion crop. In hot weather it becomes tough and bitter, gets sunburned, and very probably will prematurely push a flower stalk up through what you had expected to be the head. Certain varieties will grow better than others in warm weather but none is good in hot weather, and the heading varieties are hopeless.

Lettuce should make a rapid, continuous growth from beginning to end. This means a rich soil, ample water, and frequent cultivation. Slow-growing lettuce does not amount to much. The time required for maturity varies considerably with different varieties, ranging from 45 to 90 days, but it is safe to count on at least 8 to 10 weeks.

Since the cool outdoor season in spring is short in most localities, it is best to start a flat or two of heading lettuce in heat and make an early outdoor planting of a leaf lettuce that stands hot weather better.

Habits of Growth: Lettuce is an annual, cultivated for the root leaves which arise from a short stem. While all lettuce plants are basically alike, and comprise a collection of leaves varying in color from light to dark green, the form of the leaves and the heads varies considerably.

Types and Varieties: There are three types of lettuce: head lettuce (comprising butterhead and crisphead), leaf lettuce, and cos or romaine.

Head lettuce. This type of lettuce is good and very popular, but it is the hardest kind to grow because of the difficulty of getting it to head unless the weather is cool and the plant has had plenty of moisture. The leaves should fold over one another and form a more or less solid, well-defined head. The outside leaves are green and few; the inside leaves blanch much lighter. Many people like the taste of head lettuce better than that of the other types because it is more delicate. But if you grow nothing else you will miss a lot of salad pleasure. Lettuce should be eaten often and in large amounts, and the same kind day in and day out is monotonous. Therefore, don't think that head lettuce is the only kind worth growing; try all three.

There are two forms of head lettuce, *butterhead* and *crisphead*. Butterhead has smooth, soft-textured, finely veined leaves, the inside leaves being light yellow. A good variety is *White Boston*, maturing in about 80 days. This resembles the old favorite *Big Boston* but is earlier and has no red tinge. Crisphead has brittle, crisp, coarsely veined leaves and a white center. It is often erroneously called *Iceberg*. *Iceberg* is a variety of this type, not the type itself, and is exceedingly good. Another good variety is *New York No. 12* which matures in 80–85 days.

Leaf lettuce. This type of lettuce has large, loose, frilled leaves which are spreading in growth. The leaves grow in a bunch and the inner ones do not overlap to form a definite head. There are a lot of green outside leaves and just a few white ones in the center. This type is easier to grow than head lettuce because it matures quickly, about a month sooner than most heading varieties, and it is more heat resistant. In sections of the country where periods of moderately cool weather are short, this loose lettuce is more reliable, and it is good. Varieties are *Grand Rapids* and *Black Seeded Simpson*, both maturing in 45 days.

Cos or romaine. This type of lettuce grows upright with large, smooth, erect, crisp, oblong leaves having broad midribs. The outside leaves are dark green, while the inside of the head may blanch somewhat. You can tie the leaves together at the top of the head if you want it blanched more, but don't forget that the green leaves have the most nutritive value. Cos lettuce withstands hot weather better than either of the other types since it will not run to seed as soon as the weather turns warm. Good varieties are *Paris White* and *Trianon*, maturing in 80 days.

(Besides the three main types, there is also another kind of lettuce which is a cross between the heading and the cos types. It forms a loose leafy head and has an excellent quality. It is available in just one variety, *Matchless*, and is highly recommended.)

How Much to Buy:

1 package for   50 feet
1 ounce   for 200–300 feet

Since lettuce must be harvested when it is mature, and since it cannot be canned and storage is extremely difficult, it is best to sow a little as often as you can at week or 10-day intervals, to give you a continual supply during the lettuce season. Five or six fully grown heads of lettuce for each member of the family are probably all that most families can consume from a single planting. If you eat the thinnings it will prolong the harvesting time considerably.

Planting:

Germination time: 6–8 days.

Depth for seed: ¼ inch.

Spacing of plants: Leaf and *cos* types, 8–12 inches. *Heading* type, 12–18 inches.

Spacing of rows: Leaf and *cos* types, 12 inches. *Heading* type, 14–18 inches.

When to Plant:

	EARLY CROP	LATE CROP
	Earliest Safe Date for Planting Seed or Setting Plants in Garden	*Latest Safe Date for Planting Seed in Garden*
Zone A.	Feb. 1 – Feb. 15	Dec. 1
" B.	Feb. 15 – March 1	Nov. 1
" C.	March 1 – March 15	Oct. 1
" D.	March 15 – April 15	Sept. 1
" E.	April 1 – May 1	Aug. 1
" F.	May 1 – May 15	July 15
" G.	May 15 – June 1	July 1

NOTE: The earlier of the two planting dates can be used with safety in all except unusually late seasons.

(See maps at back of book showing locations of zones for spring and fall frosts. Remember that the boundaries of the spring frost zones are not the same as those of the fall frost zones, and your locality may be in different zones for the spring and fall frosts. If you live in the West outside the zones, for an approximate guide take the frost dates in your individual locality, find similar frost dates in one of the zones, and use the corresponding dates for that zone.)

If you wish to have more than one early crop in the spring, some seed must be started either in a hotbed or in the house. This is especially advisable with heading lettuce since it will not head well when the weather gets warm. This seed should be started 6–8 weeks before the above outdoor planting dates. Seed can be sown in the garden at about the same time that you put your plants in, and again in two weeks, provided that your spring season is long enough to allow these plantings to come to maturity before hot weather. Choose fast-maturing varieties for the late spring plantings. And don't try sowing head-lettuce seed outdoors in the spring in parts of the country where you cannot count on 2½ months of cool weather. *Plant early—both plants and seeds.*

For the late crop, plant the seed outdoors in a shady spot, late in the summer in time for the crop to mature before frost. Well-hardened young plants can stand a light frost, but freezing weather is likely to damage a mature crop. One fall crop is all that you are likely to get in the North; but you might sow a few seeds in the cold frame 6 weeks or so before the earliest fall frost and have a supply for the table well into the fall. *Consider maturity dates before planting.*

How to Plant: Sow the seed in a flat or in the hotbed in rows 2 inches apart and ¼ inch deep. The seedlings should be transplanted at least once, when the first pair of true leaves appear, to stand 2 inches apart both ways. The transplanting is necessary to keep them from getting spindly. Harden them off well 10 days before setting in the garden and they will be able to stand temperatures below freezing.

Handle the seeds in the seedbed the same way, transplanting once before they are put in the garden proper.

Where to Plant: Lettuce is an accommodating plant. It neither uses much space nor stays around long. It is therefore useful for inter-cropping. A common practice is to sow lettuce plants between rows of early cabbage and cauliflower—the lettuce will be ready to harvest before the other plants need the room and a row will have been saved. If you are not too particular about having your garden neat and precise, sow a few feet of lettuce seed and transplant the small seedlings into any odd foot or so of ground that happens to be empty at the moment. I don't endorse this because I favor a spic and span vegetable garden, but it is a way of obtaining a large supply without much cost in precious row space. One writer says that a friend of hers put lettuce in her rose bed. This is a good use of otherwise wasted space. Lettuce is shallow rooting and will not interfere with the greedy rose roots—and the perky lettuce will dress up the bed.

Soil: Lettuce requires a rich soil that is kept well moist. Lettuce, to be crisp and well flavored, should have a rapid growth. The best way to ensure this is to see that the soil has plenty of readily available fertilizer. Soil that has been well manured is good, but satisfactory results can be obtained by the use of commercial fertilizer, 3–4 pounds per 100 feet. And a teaspoonful of nitrate of soda worked into the soil around the plant when it has done some growing is a good prod to speedy growing.

Cultivation and Care: Lettuce seed sown direct in the garden requires some thinning, but the easiest course is to wait until the plants have leaves that are big enough to eat. Then the thinnings can be used at the table. Pick the largest plants, at various times, and let the smallest plants keep on growing. Don't wait too long, however, because the remaining plants shouldn't get so crowded that their growth will be stunted.

Cultivation consists of keeping weeds out and moisture in. It should be shallow to avoid injuring the roots. But lettuce has a small root system and is close to the surface; hence, it cannot put up a fair fight against weeds. Therefore, if you want good lettuce, weed regularly.

Water lettuce well if the weather turns dry. Lettuce is an ardent moisture lover and produces crisp, first-class leaves only when it has water in abundance.

Harvesting: Lettuce should be harvested in its prime, when the leaves are young and tender. One way of stretching a planting is to eat all reasonably large thinnings. If you wait too long to pick, the plants get old, tough, and bitter; and sometimes they will develop a seed stalk.

To harvest, just cut the head off level with the ground with a sharp knife.

Uses: Most lettuce is, of course, used in salads. Many people think a crisp, fresh piece of lettuce cannot be improved by anything except a well-seasoned dressing. But if you have a sudden flood of lettuce crying to be eaten, you may want some variations. Here are two suggestions.

Boiled lettuce. Quarter the head, wash it, and cook it in the water clinging to the leaves for about 10 minutes. Chop it up fine; season it with salt, pepper, and melted butter; and mix some crumbled crisp bacon or toasted bread crumbs—or both—in it.

Wilted lettuce. Shred two or three heads of lettuce into a warmed mixing bowl. Fry several slices of bacon until they are crisp, remove the bacon and pour into the hot fat ¼ to ½ cupful of vinegar that has been seasoned with ½ teaspoonful of salt and ⅛ teaspoonful of pepper. As soon as the grease and vinegar have come together, remove the pan from the fire and pour the contents over the lettuce. Cover the bowl and let it stand for 5 minutes. The lettuce is ready to serve then, sprinkled with the bacon crumbled or with finely chopped hard-boiled egg.

15. Onions

(Allium Cepa. Liliaceae, lily family.)

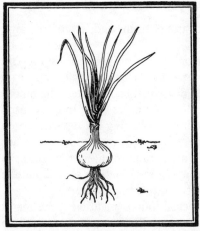

HISTORY: Onions have been grown and used as a food since the beginnings of recorded history. One story traces the origin of the onion back to the Garden of Eden, relating that when Satan stepped out of the Garden of Eden after the fall of man, onions sprang up from the spot where he placed his right foot and garlic from where his left foot touched. Onions, radishes, and garlic were consumed in quantity by the laborers who built the Great Pyramid in Egypt. Among the complaints which the Israelites made to Moses was one about food. "We remember the fish, which we did eat in Egypt freely; the cucumbers, and the melons, and the leeks, and the onions, and the garlic."

Pliny said that the Romans used onions to cure the sting of serpents and other reptiles, that they made poultices of onions and barley meal for those who had watery eyes because onions clear the sight by the tears they draw, and that onion juice was given to those who suddenly became speechless.

By A.D., 60 varieties were mentioned that were long or round, yellow or white. Chaucer makes a reference to onions, "wel loved he garleek, onyons and ek leekes." Today onions are grown throughout most of the temperate regions of the world. The onion was cultivated in this country as early as 1629. In 1935 it was the sixth largest commercial vegetable crop in the United States, exceeded only by Irish potatoes, sweet potatoes, tomatoes, lettuce, and English peas. Today, it is shipped in car lots by forty of the forty-eight states.

Food Value: Onions are a good source of vitamins B_1 and C.

Culture: Onions are a hardy bulb crop which should start growing when the weather is cool and moist and which mature best when the weather is hot and dry. They have a long period of production since they can be harvested when they are young, small, and green, or when they are older, fully ripe, and quite large. Some varieties store well; hence they can be used over a long period extending from about 6 weeks after sets are planted until the end of the winter. Onions are good by themselves: they are also an essential ingredient of many relishes; they are a standard food seasoning; and they are delicious pickled. Thus a surplus supply will never go to waste. Some onions should be grown by every gardener, no matter how small his space. They are a relatively easy crop to grow, especially if grown from sets or seedlings rather than from seed.

There are three ways of propagating: from seed, from seedlings, and from sets.

Seed. It takes 130–150 days for onion seed to produce thoroughly ripe onions. Onions for storage must ripen before the fall rains begin because the rain, coming on top of dry weather, will start the onions growing again and they will be useless for harvesting. In the central states the climate is ideal for outdoor seed planting because the season is so long. But in the North, where outdoor planting must take place too late in the spring to give the onions time to mature, planting in heat, in a hotbed, or indoors must be resorted to. The seed should be sown about 10 weeks before the outdoor planting dates.

For the average gardener any special indoor planting space might better be reserved for some other crop, such as eggplant, that has to be started from seed and cannot be grown, as onions can, from sets.

Propagation from seedlings or sets is much easier and costs so little that seed sowing is the simplest course only in the South, where the seed, sown in the fall, has the whole winter in which to mature. However, certain varieties can be obtained only from seed. If you expect to harvest these while the onions are young and do not plan to store them (they must be thoroughly ripe for storage), outdoor seed sowing is satisfactory. The seed must go in the ground as soon as the soil can be worked.

Seedlings. Seedlings, sometimes called "transplants" or "green sets," are young onions grown from seed in the South. These can be bought by the bunch and planted in the garden to finish their growing. In the North this is the only way by which gardeners can get good-size bulbs of the large Spanish and Bermuda onions since these are not obtainable in sets and are difficult to grow from seed anywhere but in a warm climate.

Sets. Onion sets are nothing but small, dry, immature, year-old onions about ½–¾ inch in diameter, which have been crowded and starved to such an extent that they have been unable to develop naturally. When they are planted again they resume their growth and can be harvested after 6 or 8 weeks if you like them tender and green, or after about 14 weeks if you want them ripe. The sets are easy to plant, usually give you larger bulbs than the ones grown from seed, can be pulled sooner, and above all are much easier to handle.

Habits of Growth: The onion forms a single bulb, without offset bulblets which most other bulbs have. The shape of the bulb is either globular or flattened, the colors, red, white, or yellow. It is an underground bulb, with cylindrical, hollow-leaf blades which arise from a very short conical stem. The bases of the leaves thicken and become the scales of the onion bulb. This bulb is the part that is usually eaten, although the leaves can be used in stews and seasonings.

Onions are usually left to grow until they are fully ripe. But you do not have to wait until the bulb is ripe. Onions can be eaten as soon as they are large enough, and they are perfectly delicious when they are young and green.

Types and Varieties: There are two general types of onions:

American type. These onions are small, have a denser texture and a sharper quality, ripen earlier, and are the best keepers. They are yellow, white, or red. Seventy-five per cent of the commercial crop is yellow.

VARIETIES: Good varieties of seed are *Yellow Globe Danvers* (an excellent keeper), and *Yellow, White,* or *Red Southport Globe.* White sets are not sold by variety. The best yellow sets are *Ebenezer.*

Foreign or European type. These onions are larger, have a milder flavor and more tender flesh, and do not usually keep very well. The flavor is good enough, however, to warrant growing them. These are the Spanish and Bermuda onions.

VARIETIES: While two varieties, *Riverside Sweet Spanish* and *Prizetaker,* can be grown from seed in the North, the easiest and most reliable course is to buy seedlings of the Riverside Sweet Spanish. Most commercial Bermuda onions are grown in Texas, make a poor growth in the North, and should be attempted only by the gardener in Texas and Southern California.

How Much to Buy:

1 package of seed for   30 feet
1 ounce of seed for 200 feet
1 quart of sets for 100 feet

A quart of sets, which costs about 35 cents, will yield 120 bunches of green onions and 2 bushels of dry bulbs. It is hard to have too many onions, when they lend themselves to a great many uses; and a bushel or two of ripe bulbs will be a grateful help all winter. I would say plant as many onions as you can find room for. None of them will go to waste.

Planting:

Germination time:	8–10 days.
Depth for seed:	½ inch.
Depth for seedlings:	2 inches.
Depth for sets:	1–2 inches. (If you want long, white necks, plant 2 inches deep.)
Spacing of seedlings and sets:	For green onions, 2–3 inches. For ripe onions, 3–4 inches (no wider or you are likely to get split bulbs.)
Spacing of rows:	12–14 inches.

When to Plant:

		EARLY CROP			LATE CROP	
		Earliest Safe Date for Planting in Garden			*Latest Safe Date for Planting in Garden*	
Zone A.	Sets	Jan.	1 – Feb.	1	Sets	Dec. 15
	Seedlings	Jan.	1 – Feb.	1	Seedlings	Dec. 15
	Seed	Feb.	1 – Feb.	15	Seed	Dec. 1
" B.	Sets	Feb.	1 – Feb.	15	Sets	Dec. 1
	Seedlings	Feb.	1 – Feb.	15	Seedlings	Dec. 1
	Seed	Feb.	15 – March	1	Seed	Nov. 1
" C.	Sets	Feb.	15 – March	1	Sets	July 15
	Seedlings	Feb.	15 – March	1	Seedlings	July 15
	Seed	March	1 – March	15	Seed	Oct. 15
" D.	Sets	March	1 – March	15	Sets	July 1
	Seedlings	March	1 – March	15	Seedlings	July 1
	Seed	March	15 – April	1	Seed	–
" E.	Sets	March	15 – April	15	Sets	June 15
	Seedlings	March	15 – April	15	Seedlings	June 15
	Seed	April	1 – May	1	Seed	–
" F.	Sets	April	1 – May	1	Sets	June 1
	Seedlings	April	1 – May	1	Seedlings	June 1
	Seed	May	1 – May	15	Seed	–
" G.	Sets	May	1 – May	15	Sets	May 15
	Seedlings	May	1 – May	15	Seedlings	May 15
	Seed	May	15 – June	1	Seed	–

(See maps at back of book showing locations of zones for spring and fall frosts. Remember that the boundaries of the spring frost zones are not the same as those of the fall frost zones, and your locality may be in different zones for the spring and fall frosts. If you live in the West outside the zones, for an approximate guide take the frost dates in your individual locality, find similar frost dates in one of the zones, and use the corresponding dates for that zone.)

Onions are hardy and can stand considerable frost; therefore both the seed and the sets can be planted outdoors at the end of the winter as soon as the ground can be worked, even before the latest spring frost date. It is vital that both seed and sets get a good start before the weather gets warm. This is particularly true for the seed. Hence I repeat, *plant at the very earliest date that the land can be worked.*

How to Plant: Seed indoors should be started about 8–10 weeks before the date for outdoor garden planting since seed growth is slower in the late winter months when the sunlight is weak and limited. Sow in flats, in rows 6 inches apart, and cover with ½ inch of soil. The seed germinates slowly. The temperature should remain relatively low, about 60° F., and there should be plenty of ventilation or the seedlings may damp-off. As soon as the seedlings have straightened up, transplant them to stand ½ inch apart. They can be put into the garden at about the same time that sets are planted. It should be emphasized that only in the North is indoor planting of onion seed necessary, unless you wish to grow Riverside Sweet Spanish from seed—and even then the safest and easiest way to grow that type of onion is from bought seedlings.

Outdoor planting of seed starts early. Sow the seed in moist, well-pulverized soil, ½ inch deep, in rows 12–14 inches apart. Since the seed germinates slowly, a few radish seeds sown along with the onion seeds will mark the rows and facilitate cultivation. Thin before the plants get so large that pulling some will mean seriously disturbing the roots of the ones you intend to leave in the ground. Thinning when the ground is moist simplifies your job. And leave the strongest plants. The thinnings probably will be big enough for table use.

Sets should obviously be planted right side up. It is easy to spot the top because it usually has a little neck, often with a tiny green sprout. Set them in the ground 1–2 inches deep. And select which sets you will plant—½–¾ inch in diameter is the best size. If they are too large, they may send up a premature seed stalk or give you a strong-flavored, tough bulb. The small ones make a weak start and are likely to be too little to amount to much.

Seedlings are set 2 inches deep, and part of the tops can be cut off to prevent wilting.

Where to Plant: Sets grown for green onions are harvested in 6–8 weeks. Another crop can then follow in the same ground. But onions grown to full maturity and for storage occupy the ground until late in the summer. Hence, the only follow-up crop, in parts of the country where frost does not come too soon, would be a late planting of a quickly maturing crop, such as spinach or radishes. Onions should be grown adjacent to other crops that occupy the ground the whole summer season, such as chard and parsnips, and in a row by themselves.

Soil: Since the roots of the onion have a limited feeding range, there must be plenty of available plant food to keep the roots well supplied. Well-rotted manure dug into the soil the previous fall is good, or a complete fertilizer worked into the soil 10 days or so before planting. The New Jersey Agricultural Experiment Station recommends 5–8–7, about 5 pounds for 100 feet of row.

And if you are planting seed, have the soil in the bed very well pulverized. Onion seedlings aren't the huskiest things in the world; they have difficulty with a lumpy soil or one that is caked.

Cultivation and Care: Cultivation should be frequent with this crop. The roots need all the food available, and weeds deprive them of essential nourishment. Hand weeding will be necessary between plants; you cannot grow both weeds and onions together. Don't put your hoe or wheel hoe too deep or too close to the bulbs, or you may cut off many of the lateral feeding roots. Without these feeding roots the bulb will be considerably smaller. Give onions plenty of water.

Your onions may need special spraying or dusting with nicotine sulphate if infested with onion thrips during a hot spell.

Harvesting: Onions can be harvested for weeks, since they are equally good pulled when young or left to ripen thoroughly. They are harvested by simply pulling them out of the ground, and the early spring onions have a delicate, sweet taste that will surprise anyone who has eaten only store onions.

A ripe onion can be spotted by its leaves, which fall over. If it has ripened properly, the neck shrivels first and the leaves fall over while they are still green. If the leaves start drying from the tips downward while the neck remains erect, the plant has not ripened properly and should not be stored. If you wish to hasten the ripening process, the tops should be broken down by pushing the leaves over.

Storing: Onions for storage should be harvested only when fully mature—that is, when the tops have fallen over. (Onions with thick necks do not store well.) The bulbs must then be cured by leaving them in the garden on top of the soil, after pulling, until withered.

This takes from 5 to 10 days. If it has rained, dry them thoroughly in well-aired boxes or seed flats, under cover (for example, in the garage). After they are cured, cut off the withered tops about an inch above the bulb—no shorter or they will shrivel or rot. The onions should be so dry that they rattle. They are then ready for storing in a cool, dry place—but not so cold that they will be frozen hard. An unheated attic is a good place, since light freezing does not harm them. Put them in seed flats or porous bags or hampers—anything that will allow them the ventilation they require. They will keep at least 5 months—long enough for the whole winter. Do not attempt to store them in a storage room with root crops—root crops need a moist atmosphere, which will ruin onions very quickly.

Uses:

> "This is every cook's opinion,
> No savory dish without an onion,
> But lest your kissing should be spoil'd,
> Your onions must be thoroughly boil'd."

This was Dean Swift's advice, but perhaps you will be willing occasionally to place an onion sandwich, made with fresh white bread, plenty of butter and salt, and a thick slice of sweet Spanish onion, even above kissing.

There are so many ways to use onions that no cook should feel at a loss to deal with a supply of any size. Onion soup is a heartening dish at any time and very easy to prepare. Cook a cupful of onions thinly sliced in 2 or 3 tablespoonfuls of butter until they are nicely browned. Then add 6 or 7 cupfuls of consommé and bring to a boil. Put a piece of buttered toast in each soup bowl, sprinkle with grated cheese, preferably Parmesan, and fill with the soup. Serve more grated cheese in a separate dish for the real cheese lovers.

French-fried onions are easy to prepare and yet taste like a gourmet's dream. All you have to do is slice large onions a little less than ¼ inch thick, separate into rings, dip them into milk and then flour, and fry in deep hot fat. The milk is the trick that makes them crisp. An exceptionally good luncheon dish is a casserole of creamed, young, boiled onions and sliced hard-boiled eggs. Make your cream sauce with half chicken consommé and half rich milk, which takes the insipidness out of cream sauce, and top the dish with crumbled salted crackers browned in butter. Bake until the dish is bubbling, and you'll have a treat.

To prepare sweet onion pickle, use the small silver-skinned onions. Remove the skins until the smooth surface is reached. Place them in a large jar or crock and let stand for 24 hours in a strong brine in the proportion of 1 cupful of salt to 4 quarts of onions. The next day make fresh strong brine, bring to a boil, and boil the onions in it for 5 minutes. Remove the onions and put in cold water for one hour. Drain, place in large jars and pour over them boiled spiced vinegar made from the following ingredients: 1 gallon of vinegar, 1 tablespoonful of allspice, 1 tablespoonful of cloves, 1 stick of cinnamon, 1 piece of mace, 2 pounds of sugar. The spices should be put in a muslin bag and boiled in the vinegar for 15 minutes. Remove spices, put in onions, and bring to a boil. Pack while hot in hot jars and seal immediately.

To prepare mustard onion pickle, take 4 quarts of small white onions, 4 sweet red peppers, and ½ cupful of salt. Peel onions and cut peppers into strips. Place in brine (½ cupful of salt to 1 gallon of water), bring to scald, and drain. In a separate saucepan make a sauce of the following: 5 tablespoonfuls of dry mustard, 5 tablespoonfuls of flour, 2 tablespoonfuls of turmeric, 2 cupfuls of sugar, 2 quarts of vinegar, 1 pint of water. Mix the dry ingredients; add the water and the vinegar; bring to a boil; then add onions and peppers. Let boil gently for 10 minutes. Cool and seal.

16. Parsley

*(Petroselinum hortense. Umbelliferae,
parsley family.)*

HISTORY: Parsley has been in cultivation for over 2000 years. The Greeks made wreaths and decorative garlands of it, dedicating it to the gods. During the time of Pliny there was not a sauce or a salad served without parsley. Its smell was supposed to absorb the intoxicating fumes of wine and thus prevent any of the usual effects of overindulgence. Another use of parsley was as a planting over graves to keep them green with the decorative foliage. Horace includes parsley in one of his odes:

> "I have a cask of Alban wine,
> Phyllis, that counts its years at nine,
> And parsley in my garden grounds
> For garlands, ivy too abounds
> To deck thy shining tresses."

Parsley was one of the few seasonings grown in England before the Norman Conquest, the others being garlic, onions, leeks, sage, and thyme. Mothers during the Middle Ages used to answer children's inquisitive questions by stating that babies were found in parsley beds; and John Gay in instructions for stewing veal recommends including,

> "Some sprigs of that bed,
> Where children are bred."

It was well liked in Cornwall in England, where it was used mostly in parsley pies, for which unfortunately we have no recipe. Today it is far and away the favorite garnish, and is the most popular garden herb grown in this country.

* * *

Food Value: Recent investigations have shown that parsley is one of the best of all sources of vitamin A, one ounce supplying 30,000 international units. When fresh and raw it is also an excellent source of vitamin C and a good source of vitamin B_1. So parsley should be eaten as well as looked at.

Culture: Parsley is an accommodating crop and has simple climate requirements. Thus it can be grown anywhere in the country. It is hardy and will stand hot weather, a combination not often found. However, although it can stand heat well when it is established, it should not actually be started when the weather is hot. And it is so resistant to frost that it will live over the winter, even in the North if put in a cold frame. Or it can be potted and brought into the house to supply the table and gladden the eye.

Parsley is an easy crop to grow. The plant is propagated from seed sown in the garden where the plants are to mature. The seed is slow to germinate, but once the seedlings are off to a good start the crop requires no more attention. The leaves can be picked from the plant all summer long. Although it is an all-season crop the space is well occupied.

Habits of Growth: Parsley is quite a beautiful decorative biennial plant. The first year the plant grows 12–20 inches tall, is much branched and covered with the dark green leaves. A few of these leaves are harvested at one time, and the plant keeps on yielding new leaves until it throws up a seed stalk after it is about a year old. It produces seed in abundance; but, by keeping the seed stalks closely cut, you can prolong the season of leaf yield.

Types and Varieties: There are five different types of parsley.

Common or plain-leafed. This type has been largely superseded by the curled-leaf type, but the leaves are full of flavor and it is grown for seasoning soups and stews. It is listed as *Plain* or *Single* and takes about 70 days to mature.

Celery-leafed. This type is scarcely known outside Italy and is difficult to obtain here. Its leaves can be blanched the same as celery.

Curled-leaf. This is by far the most common and popular type. *Paramount* is the best variety and takes 70–80 days to mature.

Fern-leafed. This is an attractive variant but not easily available since most growers now prefer the curled-leaf type.

Hamburg or *turnip-rooted.* This type is plain leaved. It produces also a thickened tap root 8 inches long which resembles and can be eaten as parsnips. There is only the one variety, *Hamburg*, which takes 90 days to mature.

How Much to Buy:

1 package for 50 feet

Since a few plants are sufficient for most gardens, one package is ample. If you want to use parsley as an edging (the plants can be dug up and transplanted at any time), 1 ounce will sow 200 feet.

Planting:

Germination time: 2–4 weeks.

Depth for seed: ⅛ inch.

Spacing of plants: 6–8 inches.

Spacing of rows: 12–18 inches.

When to Plant:

	EARLY CROP	LATE CROP
	Earliest Safe Date for Planting Seed in Garden	*Latest Safe Date for Planting Seed in Garden*
Zone A.	Feb. 1 – Feb. 15	Dec. 1
" B.	Feb. 15 – March 1	Nov. 1
" C.	March 1 – March 15	Nov. 1
" D.	March 15 – April 1	Sept. 1
" E.	April 1 – May 1	Aug. 1
" F.	May 1 – May 15	July 15
" G.	May 15 – June 1	July 1

(See maps at back of book showing locations of zones for spring and fall frosts. Remember that the boundaries of the spring frost zones are not the same as those of the fall frost zones, and your locality may be in different zones for the spring and fall frosts. If you live in the West outside the zones, for an approximate guide take the frost dates in your individual locality, find similar frost dates in one of the zones, and use the corresponding dates for that zone.)

Parsley is quite hardy and can be planted either in the spring anywhere as soon as the ground can be worked, or during the summer in the North and during the fall in the South. The spring planting is usually the main crop and will provide harvesting for the entire summer. The fall planting in the South affords plants for winter harvesting. In the North the plants are carried through the winter in the garden with a little protection or in the cold frame, and they are ready for use in the spring.

How to Plant: The one difficulty likely to be encountered with the growing of parsley is that the seed requires such a long time to germinate, and there's an old saying that the reason the seed is so slow is that it goes to the devil and back seven times. But the devil can be cheated and the process hastened considerably by soaking the seed in warm water overnight just before you plant it. The seeds should be planted quite thickly and barely covered with soil.

Once you have parsley in your garden, you never need to buy or plant seed again. You can follow an old-fashioned procedure and tie a ripe seed head on a string and attach it to a tree where it can swing about in the wind. You will have to wait 3–4 weeks for the wind-blown seed to germinate though.

Where to Plant: Parsley is so decorative and attractive that the plants can be grown anywhere, even in flower beds or as an edging for the vegetable garden. Since they stay in the ground all season they should be given a spot where they will not interfere with the succession crops that are coming and going. As good a place in the vegetable garden proper as any is at one end, preferably a conspicuous one. Or if the garden is any distance from the house, try to have a few plants somewhere near the kitchen so that the sprigs can be picked at a moment's notice. Parsley is one of the few vegetables that can be grown in partial shade.

Soil: Any good garden soil will do for parsley. However, since the seed is slow to germinate, see that the soil is well worked and in fine loose condition, so that the seed encounters no opposition. Keeping the soil moist will speed up the germination.

Cultivation and Care: Thin the small plants to stand 6–8 inches apart, and your work for the summer is over. The plants soon make a full growth that covers the ground, and they are practically free from diseases and insects. All they require is routine weeding and hoeing.

Harvesting: Harvesting is merely a matter of picking leaves as you need them. The plant will bear better if you pick just a few of the outer leaves at a time. It takes about 80–90 days from planting before you will have leaves large enough to use.

Storing: To store for use in the winter, either dry some leaves and keep them in an air-tight container or put some plants in a box in the cellar window or in pots in the kitchen or even the living room.

If you experiment with the Hamburg type, the roots can be harvested and stored the same as parsnips.

Uses: Parsley is used, of course, largely as a garnish and for flavoring stews and sauces. It is such a valuable source of vitamin A that chopped parsley should be used in cooking as frequently as possible, even if you merely add it to the melted butter that you pour over

other vegetables. Parsley can also be served boiled, seasoned with salt
and pepper, and drenched in melted butter. And fried parsley is easy
to prepare and an unusual accompaniment to meats. Just drop some
parsley into hot deep fat for a minute or two until it is crisp.

17. Parsnips

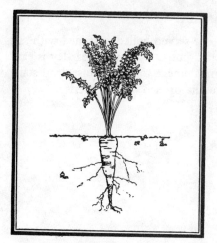

(*Pastinaca sativa. Umbelliferae,* parsley family.)

HISTORY: All evidence seems to indicate that the cultivated parsnip was known to the ancient Greeks and Romans. The Romans were supposed to have served parsnips boiled with a sauce made with mead or honey wine; and the Emperor Tiberius liked parsnips so much that every year he had them brought from Germany, where the climate enabled them to be grown to perfection. The plant grows wild in parts of Europe and the United States and in South America around Buenos Aires. The cultivated varieties were brought here from England by the early colonists and were generally grown by 1630.

It is not an important commercial crop, mainly because it occupies the land for a long period of time during which two or three other quickly maturing crops could be grown and sold.

Food Value: Parsnips are a good source of vitamins B_1 and C, and a good source of calcium and phosphorus.

Culture: Parsnips grow best if they are planted when the weather is warm and allowed to mature when it has turned cool. However, they cannot stand extreme summer heat.

Parsnips are quite an easy crop to grow, can be seeded out in the garden, do not require great care, and have a fine flavor. Since they take 3–4 months to mature, they occupy the ground the entire season. But they have one advantage which is unique to parsnips—they are not harmed by frosts and can stay right in the garden the entire winter and be harvested during open spells in the winter or as soon as they can be dug out of the ground the following spring. They therefore provide a table vegetable at a time when nothing else is available.

Parsnips are not subject to any serious diseases or pests, and they do not require much space.

Habits of Growth: Parsnips are a half-hardy biennial root crop. The first year the plant produces a rosette of leaves and a long, tapering, fleshy root which is the edible portion of the plant, 12–15 inches long and 2½–3½ inches wide at the shoulder and creamy yellow in color. The second year the plant sends up a branched stem 3–5 feet tall which produces flowers and seeds. Since the gardener is interested in only the root, the crop can be treated as an annual.

Types and Varieties: There is only one general type of parsnips and few varieties. *Hollow Crown* is the most generally grown, although many people prefer the flavor of *Guernsey*. Both of these varieties require about 4 months to mature. Some seed houses also supply a variety 6–8 inches long and about 3 inches thick at the shoulder which will mature in about 12 weeks. It is called *Short Thick*.

How Much to Buy:

> 1 package for   20 feet
> 1 ounce   for 200 feet

A 20-foot row will supply 40 roots. A good-size root is almost a meal in itself. Hence, even a short row will provide an ample supply for the average family.

Planting:

Germination time: 12–18 days.

Depth for seed: ½ inch.

Spacing of plants: 6 inches.

Spacing of rows: 12–18 inches (just enough to allow for easy cultivation).

When to Plant:

	EARLY CROP	LATE CROP
	Earliest Safe Date for Planting Seed in Garden	*Latest Safe Date for Planting Seed in Garden*
Zone A.	Feb. 1 – Feb. 15	Dec. 1
" B.	Feb. 15 – March 1	Nov. 1
" C.	March 1 – March 15	June 15
" D.	March 15 – April 1	June 1
" E.	April 1 – May 1	—
" F.	May 1 – May 15	—
" G.	May 15 – June 1	—

(See maps at back of book showing locations of zones for spring and fall frosts. Remember that the boundaries of the spring frost zones are not the same as those of the fall frost zones, and your locality may be in different zones for the spring and fall frosts. If you live in the West outside the zones, for an approximate guide take the frost dates in your individual locality, find similar frost dates in one of the zones, and use the corresponding dates for that zone.)

Parsnips are a one-crop vegetable except in the South, where one planting can be made in the fall and another in the winter. In the North, parsnips should be planted while the soil is still moist and cool. However, there is no great need to hurry about it because if they are planted too early the seeds may rot in the ground. Also, the roots continue growing until frost comes, and if they are allowed to grow for too long a period of time they get a woody, tasteless flavor. Hence, the later of the earliest safe planting dates given for the early crop is the better. Then your crop will have time to mature before frost but not get too ripe.

How to Plant: In planting, you need to take some precautions. Be sure that you have fresh seed because parsnip seed has a longevity of only a year or two. And plant thickly to allow for some failure in germination. These seeds are very slow to germinate and the young seedlings are delicate. That means that no hard crust should be allowed to form or the sprouts may not be able to push through. The easiest way both to break up the soil and to mark the rows so that you can cultivate before the parsnip seed has germinated is to sow radish seed along with your parsnip. The radishes will have been pulled and eaten before the parsnip plants need the space.

Where to Plant: Parsnips should be planted in a section of the garden with other crops, such as chard and New Zealand spinach, that require their space all season.

Soil: Parsnips do not have particular soil requirements. Good garden earth will produce adequate parsnips. They do respond to well-rotted manure that has been dug into the soil the previous fall or to an application of a complete commercial fertilizer like 4–10–6, used before planting at the rate 3 to 5 pounds per 100 feet. No additional feeding is necessary throughout the growing period. The soil should be well dug, though, and thoroughly pulverized. It takes a deep, light soil for the roots to grow properly, long, smooth and unbranched. In a heavy or shallow soil they are likely to become crooked or forked.

Cultivation and Care: The young plants are delicate in the beginning and cannot compete with robust weeds. Therefore, cultivate between the rows to keep the weeds' down, and hand-weed in the row. Do not disturb the small seedlings any more than you have to. When they once get started, they are strong, need no further care, and make a thick leaf growth which covers the ground and makes weeding unnecessary. Indeed, you can really forget about them because they do not require even watering; the roots make such a deep growth that they are very resistant to drought.

Since parsnips germinate and grow slowly, your thinning will not take place for several weeks. When the plants are 2–3 inches tall, thin them to stand 4–6 inches apart. Do not delay thinning too long; the plants are hard to pull easily when they have reached much size. And the ones that are to remain should be given sufficient space at the outset. Because parsnips do not transplant easily, you will have to discard your thinnings.

One word of advice—do not worry if the plants seem to stand still during the summer. When it gets cool and the fall rains begin, the plants will grow quickly and make up for lost time.

Harvesting: Parsnips "are not sweet 'til bit by frosts," according to an old gardening book. Frost changes the starch in the parsnip root to sugar and greatly improves the taste. Hence, you should preferably delay your harvesting until after frost. However, this transformation from starch to sugar is effected by cold temperatures of around 32° F., whether the root is in the ground or in storage. Although it is claimed that the taste is not quite the same if the parsnip has been dug from the ground, it is perfectly possible to dig them four months after they have been sown, eat them as they are, or put them in storage to be nipped by the cold there.

In any event, if you intend to harvest in the fall, do not put it off until the ground is frozen solid. It will not hurt the parsnips, but the roots are difficult to dig out.

The roots can be dug with a garden fork, but you run the risk of injuring them because they are so long. The best method of harvesting is to dig a trench or run your wheel plow along the side of the row and then remove the roots by hand. Since winter does not harm the roots, they can be harvested in the spring when the ground is again soft enough to work. Do not wait long enough to let them start the second-year growth or the flavor will be very poor.

Your harvest for the table can extend continually from fall until late spring if you dig part of your crop in the fall and store it, and dig the remainder in the spring.

Storing: As previously pointed out, parsnips have the great advantage that they are not injured by freezing, and therefore storage is successfully and automatically taken care of by leaving them out in the garden during the winter. However, it may be difficult to dig them without injury when the ground is frozen solid. If you wish to store some separately to tide you over such occasions, they can be handled exactly the same as beets and carrots, except that they will keep better if the temperature of the storage room does not go much above freezing. They also should not be allowed to become too dry. (See the chapter on "Storing.")

The maximum storage period (out of the ground) is 4–5 months.

Uses: An old English gardening book warns that "parsnips eaten too old, and in great quantities, cause delirium and insanity, on which account they have been called fools' parsnips." However, you probably won't suffer if you take a chance.

Parsnips taste well sliced, boiled, and then fried in butter. Or they can be French-fried in deep fat and served either plain or with tomato sauce. Mashed parsnips are good, and any that are left over can be made into cakes, floured, and sautéed in butter. Try boiled parsnips placed in a casserole with tomato sauce, bread crumbs, and grated Parmesan cheese. The whole thing should be baked until hot and brown. Or place boiled parsnips in a baking pan, cover with brown sugar, melted butter, and a little dry mustard, and bake until brown. Another method is to combine boiled parsnips and boiled sweet potatoes and serve them either creamed or candied.

18. Peas

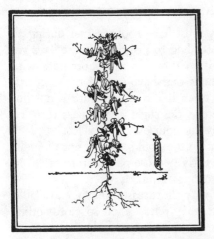

(Pisum sativum. Leguminoseae, pulse or pea family.)

HISTORY: The pea is native to Europe and northern Asia. The fact that pea seeds were found in a tomb at Thebes points to a possible Egyptian origin. Peas of some sort have been cultivated since long before the Christian era. Lentils, which are in the pea family, are mentioned in the Old Testament: "Then Jacob gave Esau bread and pottage of lentils." Pliny says writers before his time held that the eating of lentils caused men to be mild and patient. However, references to peas in early writings are not common, and it is believed that cultivated peas were not well known until the end of the seventeenth century, when apparently they became extremely popular in French court circles, as a letter written by Madame de Maintenon in 1696 shows: "This subject of peas continues to absorb all others, the anxiety to eat them, the pleasure of having eaten them and the desire to eat them again, are the three great matters which have been discussed by our princes for four days past. Some ladies, even after having supped at the Royal table and well supped too, returning to their own homes, at the risk of suffering from indigestion, will again eat peas before going to bed. It is both a fashion and a madness."

Peas were grown in England after the Norman Conquest. In America they were grown by the Indians, in as varied spots as what are now Montreal and Mexico, before the colonists came over.

Today peas are the second largest canning crop, topped only by tomatoes. The acreage used for the canning crop during the period 1933–1937 was 282,034, more than twice the acreage for the market crop, which itself has increased ten times in the past fifteen years.

***

Food Value: Peas are a highly important food. Their vitamin content is tremendous. They are an excellent source of vitamins A and C and a good source of vitamin G; and they are one of the two vegetables (lima beans being the other) which are excellent sources of vitamin B_1. They are also a good source of phosphorus and iron, and their percentage of carbohydrates is high.

Culture: Peas are a hardy, cool-season, quick maturing crop. They are so hardy that they are about the first seeds, along with onions and spinach, to be planted in the garden after winter is over. They are an easy crop to grow since they are sown directly in the garden where they are to stand, requiring no special seeding. On the other hand, you will never have any luck with peas if you try to grow them when the weather is warm. They must have cool weather during all the stages of their growth, from seeding to maturity. If the days get very warm, either the plants may yield only a few short pods with a poor production of seeds, or pods that have started their growth may just dry up and be useless. Even if the temperature is not hot enough to ruin the crop completely, the sugar in the peas turns to starch and the whole point of growing your own crop is lost.

Keeping the growth period within the cool season is not difficult, however, if you are sure to plant early because peas mature in 60–80 days and the harvesting of each sowing is quickly over.

One disadvantage of peas is the very short season they are available in the garden—although, of course, they release their space for other crops. They are worth growing even if you get only one or two messes because you have never tasted peas until you've had them straight from the vine. You can somewhat extend the possible period of harvesting by carefully choosing the varieties you plant. Both the quick-maturing and the slow-maturing varieties should be grown if you have the space. This will give a continual supply for about six weeks in most climates. In the northern and central states, except in those farthest north where the summers are cool, peas are a spring crop. Fall planting is possible, but the cool season before frost is seldom long enough to make them very successful. In the South and in California, where there is a little or no frost, peas are grown in the fall and in the winter.

Habits of Growth: Peas are an annual crop, producing thin, vining stems, which will barely support themselves in the bush varieties but which need staking for the tall varieties. The stems have tendrils, and the plant will cling to any support. The bush varieties are fairly small, while the tall varieties grow up to 6 feet or more. The flowers are white and are followed by the fruit, which consists of a pod 2–4 inches long enclosing up to about ten edible pea seeds. These seeds are 1/4–1/2 inch in diameter; either green, yellow, or white; smooth and hard or soft and wrinkled. In some varieties the pods are so large that the seeds never fill them; in other varieties the seeds almost burst the pods. The differences in both the size and flavor between varieties necessitate careful selection.

Types and Varieties: There are actually four types of peas: forage or green-manure peas; dry, edible peas; green peas, used either fresh or canned; and edible-podded peas.

Green peas. We are concerned only with the last two types, and primarily with green peas. Green peas are of two kinds—smooth seeded and wrinkled seeded. Because the wrinkled seeded are much sweeter in flavor and more tender, they are preferred. Their use was formerly curtailed for the earliest plantings because there was a prevalent theory that they were not so hardy as the smooth seeds and might rot in the ground. Recent investigations have proved this theory false, and today there is no reason why the smooth-seeded kind need ever be sown in the home garden. There is one variety of smooth-seeded peas, *Alaska,* that is popular with the canners because the peas are small, but the flavor is inferior, and it is not a recommended home-garden variety.

Buy wrinkled seeds of several varieties. And before you buy, plan to fit your varieties into your garden space and your time schedule. The problem of selecting varieties is not easy. A gardener in 1820 found the same situation that confronts us today. Writing about the pea, he says discouragingly, "the varieties are now, like most other plants, so greatly increased, that it would be uninteresting to go through a description of the various kinds." At the present time, new varieties are constantly replacing old favorites. In many cases the new ones are better and worth experimenting with. In general you want a large-podded, very green, large-producing, well-flavored pea.

Green peas are dwarf (early), half-dwarf (midseason), and tall (late).

The *dwarf* varieties are up to 2 feet tall, mature in about 60 days, and usually do not need support of any sort. They bear well, considering their small size, and require less garden space and the least care.

VARIETIES: *Little Marvel* (63 days) is one of the best, as is *Laxton's Progress,* which is the earliest of the large-podded dwarf peas, 62 days.

The *half-dwarf* varieties grow 2–4 feet tall, mature in about 70 days, and can be grown either with or without a support. They need more space than the dwarf, less than the tall. They are a good choice if your space is limited, because the peas are large and abundantly produced and yet the plant does not have to be staked.

VARIETIES: *Potlatch* or *Stratagem Improved* is a relatively new variety that is excellent. It matures in about 79 days. Another new variety, *Asgrow 40,* is similar but matures 4 or 5 days sooner.

These two are probably the best half-dwarf varieties, but *Midseason Giant* and *Morse Market* are both worth recommending.

The *tall* varieties grow from 4 to 6 feet or more in height. They are the most prolific bearers and usually mature in about 80 days. They take up the most space and need support in the home vegetable garden, although commercial growers often leave them unstaked to trail over the ground.

VARIETY: *Alderman* is the standard variety and certainly one of the finest peas grown; the quality cannot be beaten.

Edible-podded peas. This type of peas has a pod without any lining membrane. The entire pea is eaten, pod and all. They are very good and economical to grow since there is no waste. The pods are usually harvested when the pea is about half grown and are cooked like string beans.

VARIETY: *Mammoth Melting Sugar*, 73 days, is the best variety.

How Much to Buy: The number of seeds in an ounce of peas varies considerably with different varieties; therefore, exact figures cannot be given. But one package will sow 10 to 20 feet, and 1–1½ pounds, 100 feet. The seeds are sown 8 or 10 to the foot. If you want to be very accurate get a catalogue from American Seed Growers, Inc., New Haven, Connecticut, which gives the number of seeds to the ounce for each variety.

If you have the space, plant 50 feet of early crop, 50 feet of midseason, and 100 feet of late. I don't suppose anyone (except Madame de Maintenon's friends) ever had too many green peas; but, if you do have more than you are able to cope with, can the surplus. Try to can some anyway, even if it does break your heart not to eat them at once. Bought canned peas are expensive. And there are many times during the winter when fresh peas are either hard to obtain or prohibitive in price. When we pay a high price for peas in the market, it is hardly consoling to read that in England in 1820 "green peas are now often cried through the streets at four-pence [8¢] and six-pence a peck."

The yield of peas differs with the variety; the tall ones are the most productive but each plant also uses more space. The Illinois Agricultural Experiment Station gives the following interesting figures on yields, which are naturally not conclusive but are useful in guiding your planning:

	BUSHELS PER 100 FEET OF ROW
Little Marvel	26
Morse Market	28½
Asgrow 40	21½
Midseason Giant	15½

Planting:

Germination time: 7–10 days.

Depth for seed: 1 inch very early in the season, 1½ inches later.

Spacing of plants: Dwarf, 2–3 inches.
Tall, 3–4 inches.

Spacing of rows: Dwarf, 18–24 inches.
Half-dwarf, 30–36 inches.
Tall, 48 inches.

When to Plant:

	EARLY CROP	LATE CROP
	Earliest Safe Date for Planting Seed in Garden	Latest Safe Date for Planting Seed in Garden
Zone A.	Jan. 1 – Feb. 1	Nov. 1
" B.	Feb. 1 – Feb. 15	Oct. 1
" C.	Feb. 15 – March 1	Sept. 1
" D.	March 1 – March 15	Aug. 15
" E.	March 15 – April 15	Aug. 15
" F.	April 15 – May 1	Aug. 15
" G.	May 1 – June 1	Aug. 15

(See maps at back of book showing locations of zones for spring and fall frosts. Remember that the boundaries of the spring frost zones are not the same as those of the fall frost zones, and your locality may be in different zones for the spring and fall frosts. If you live in the West outside the zones, for an approximate guide take the frost dates in your individual locality, find similar frost dates in one of the zones, and use the corresponding dates for that zone.)

In sections of the country where the winters are mild, in the South and in California, peas can be planted any time during the fall and winter when you are reasonably assured of 60–80 days of cool weather without hard frosts.

In most parts of the country, however, peas are essentially a spring crop. The seeds should be sown just as close to the earliest planting dates as possible. In Zone E around New York, try to get your seeds planted by St. Patrick's Day. The early, midseason, and late varieties are all planted at the same time; the differences in maturity dates provide a continuous supply. Farther north, where the summers are cool, successive plantings may be satisfactory. But, as a rule, the later the planting, the smaller the yield; and the earliest plantings are by far the most productive ones.

Don't wait for the end of frosts; peas will germinate and make a perfectly healthy growth when the temperature is low. However, a frost, which doesn't affect the plant, may kill the blossoms or young pods. Late frosts hold little danger for spring plantings, but frost damage to pods is one reason that fall plantings are unsatisfactory and not advised. Another reason is that the seed must be started while the temperature is still high if the plants are to reach maturity before frost, and planting in warm weather stunts the growth of the plant. Hence, the yield, if any, is never more than half the yield of a spring-sown crop.

How to Plant: The seed is planted an inch or so apart and 1 inch deep at the beginning of the season. If you have a later planting, the seed is put 1½ inches deep so that it will be in cooler soil. The plants should be thinned when they are up a few inches; the dwarf ones 2–3 inches apart, the tall ones about 4 inches. The seed can be planted in either a single or a double row. The double rows should be about 6 inches apart. The usefulness of this system of planting is that it enables dwarf plants to hold one another up; and, if the plants are to be staked, the wire netting or brush can be put between the two rows. The double rows do enable you to get more plants in your space; on the other hand, there is some doubt as to whether the vines all crowded on the support yield much more than a single row would. Possibly the simplest way to plant is to use the double row and space your seed 2 inches apart. Practically all thinning will be eliminated, and if some of the seeds don't germinate you will still have plenty of plants left.

Where to Plant: Peas occupy the ground for only a short time. They should therefore be planted near the other crops that are not permanent occupants, and they can be followed by late cabbage, rutabagas, carrots, lettuce, spinach, and so on.

Soil: An especially rich soil is bad for peas because it encourages a rank vine growth at the expense of pod production. Manure can be dug into the soil the previous fall, or a complete plant food can be used. The most satisfactory way of applying the plant food is in drills 2 inches or so from the row, before planting the seeds. Peas are likely to suffer from direct contact with the fertilizer. Do not fertilize with too lavish a hand, 1–2 pounds for 100 feet will be sufficient for a reasonably good garden soil.

The soil should be fertilized, well dug, and turned over the fall before planting. You should be ready to plant your seed in the spring even before the frost is out of the ground.

Cultivation and Care: Cultivation is simply a matter of killing the weeds. If the plants are not staked, they will smother the weeds themselves; but staked plants may call for some hand weeding. Do not hoe deeply into the soil; it does more harm than good.

The only special care that tall varieties of peas require is staking. There are several ways of doing this. The best is to use brush, which should stand 4 inches apart and 4–5 feet deep after it is set in the ground. Another possibility is chicken wire, attached to strong stakes at the ends of the rows. If the rows are long, poles had better be thrust into the ground every 10 feet or so and the wire attached to the poles with cord. Or poles can be driven into the ground at the ends of the rows; two wires can be strung from pole to pole, one near the ground and the other 5 feet above it, and twine strung between the wires, parallel to the poles. Some growers like old fish net strung up between poles. All these methods are satisfactory. If you cannot get brush, the chicken wire is probably easiest, and it can be rolled up when the peas are finished and used over again many times.

Special spraying or dusting with rotenone or pyrethrum may be necessary if your peas are badly infested with aphids.

Harvesting: Peas should be harvested just as soon as the pods are filled and while the peas are still young and tender. It is necessary to watch the crop carefully because if the harvest is delayed the peas will cook up hard and the flavor will be very poor. The number of pickings should be two or three since peas of most varieties do not all mature at exactly the same time but keep on maturing for possibly a week or 10 days.

Don't just jerk the pods off the vine, or you may uproot it. Hold the vine carefully with one hand while you pick off the pods with the other. And do not do any picking until just before you are ready to cook the peas; after only a few hours off the vine the sugar starts turning to starch. If for any reason you cannot avoid delay before cooking, do not shell them until the last minute.

Canning: Green peas can be stored for possibly 2 weeks if they are kept at a temperature of 32° F. However, storing is not a practicable proposition for the home gardener. By far the best way to keep peas for future use is by canning them. They can then be used at the peak of their flavor and will last indefinitely. For canning directions see the chapter on "Canning."

Uses: Peas do not last long enough in the garden to set the housewife racking her brain for new ways to serve them. They are so delicious that any camouflaging or altering of their own flavor is not only foolish but a crime. So cook them to enhance their flavor—do not drown them in floods of water but cook them in such a small amount that when they are cooked the water will be gone. Very tender peas can be cooked in butter instead of water, with some lettuce leaves placed over them and with the pan covered. In water cook them fast; in butter, very slowly. And to keep them very sweet do not use any salt until after the peas have finished cooking. English people like a sprig of mint cooked with peas. This herb does seem to be a natural flavoring. But do not go any further in adding flavors. Cream sauces, for example, are all right in their place, but fresh peas do not need them.

However, one recipe is an exception to the rule that no other flavors should be mixed with peas. Put peas and some small, sweet, green onions in a saucepan and cover with lettuce leaves. Cook in a very small amount of water. When they are done, in about 20 minutes, add butter, seasoning, and heavy cream. Two pounds of peas, about a dozen onions, and half a pint of cream are good proportions.

19. Peppers

(*Capsicum frutescens. Solanaceae,* nightshade family.)

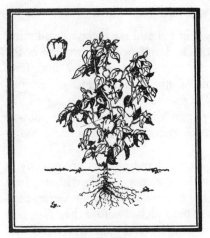

HISTORY: The pepper appears to be native to tropical America. It was cultivated in Mexico and Peru long before the arrival of Columbus and formed one of the favorite dishes of the Aztecs. It was also used as a spice by the Indians. Columbus took peppers back to Europe on his first voyage, and a record dated 1493 refers to such peppers as being more pungent than the previously known black pepper obtained from the Caucasus. A writer in 1550 mentions the pepper obtained from America as being of two kinds: "The one yellow, the other red, both, however, grow in like manner. When green, it is as large as the haws that grow on hawthorns. It is a small shrub, about half a fathom high and has small leaves; it is full of peppers which burn the mouth." In the following century peppers were used for a variety of purposes, including dyeing. Medicinally they were used both externally and internally for numerous ailments—with results which history does not reveal.

The cultivation of peppers rapidly spread throughout southern Europe, especially Spain, Greece, and Hungary. In Hungary very pungent varieties were developed for the manufacture of paprika.

At the present time the use of peppers as a vegetable is somewhat limited here, but in warm countries, particularly Mexico, the pungent hot type forms a seasoning in almost every dish.

———•◆•———

Food Value: Sweet peppers are an excellent source of vitamins A and C and contain some vitamin B_1.

Culture: Peppers are a very tender, warm-weather crop, and the seed must be started in a hotbed or indoors in most parts of the country except the South and Southwest. However, the plants will stand a considerable amount of cool weather. Cool weather is actually advantageous when the flower buds and blossoms are forming. Peppers will also stand extreme heat and dryness, though they flourish best with an ample supply of soil and moisture.

The growing season is quite long, and they take from 120 to 150 days to mature from seed. When the seed is started in heat, the plants require at least three months' growing season following setting out in the garden to produce a crop.

Habits of Growth: Peppers are perennials in tropical climates and annuals in temperate zones.

The plants are usually 1 to 2½ feet tall and are compact and stand erect. The main stem is well branched and becomes woody as the plant grows older. The leaves are smooth, glossy, and elongated. Flowers occur singly in the axils of the branches and are formed continually throughout the growing season. The fruit is a pod-like berry, carried by a short, strong stem which usually curves downward as the fruit matures. The fruit generally has prominent longitudinal ribs.

Actually what are known as green and red peppers are essentially the same. The immature fruit in all varieties is yellowish to deep green in color but turns either red or yellow on maturing. Green peppers are merely peppers which have been picked before they turn red.

Don't be alarmed if your plants tend to shed their blossoms. This is characteristic of the pepper plant, particularly the large-fruited varieties, since they produce far more flowers than can develop into mature fruit. As soon as the plants have set all the fruit they are able to carry, the subsequently formed flowers fall off. Also, many climatic conditions, such as very high temperature or insufficient moisture, cause dropping of the flowers and may render the plant unfruitful while these conditions last, though the plants are vigorous, and usually recover rapidly when more normal conditions obtain.

Types and Varieties: All peppers are of the same kind, but they are classified for convenience into two types according to the taste: the sweet or mild type and the hot or pungent type. The sweet type is usually harvested and used while still green, while the hot type is normally used after it has attained its final mature red color.

There are numerous varieties of peppers and some confusion in their nomenclature. The following are a few good, typical varieties:

Sweet type: Ruby King, a very deep green color when immature. *California Wonder,* a good, slow-maturing variety of the large-fruited sweet type. *King of the North,* a new variety which is rapidly gaining favor. *Windsor A,* another new variety, having very thick flesh. *Sweet Meat Glory,* a so-called pimento or Spanish pepper which is quite mild and thick-fleshed but takes a long time to mature.

Hot type: Long Red Cayenne, long and pointed, and fiery. *Tabasco South,* grown commercially only in the Southwest, since its growing season is too long for the North. *Red Chili,* a good average variety for the home gardener.

How Much to Buy:

1 package for 100 plants

A dozen or so plants, including a few plants of the hot type and the rest of the sweet type, should meet all the requirements of an average family of five persons.

Planting:

Germination time: 12–20 days.

Depth for seed: ½ inch.

Spacing of plants: 18 inches.

Spacing of rows: 2 feet.

When to Plant:

		EARLY CROP	LATE CROP
		Earliest Safe Date for Setting Plants in Garden	*Latest Safe Date for Setting Plants in Garden*
Zone	A.	March 1 – March 15	Sept. 15
"	B.	March 15 – April 1	Sept. 1
"	C.	April 1 – April 15	July 15
"	D.	April 15 – May 1	July 1
"	E.	May 1 – June 1	June 15
"	F.	June 1 – June 15	–
"	G.	–	–

(See maps at back of book showing locations of zones for spring and fall frosts. Remember that the boundaries of the spring frost zones are not the same as those of the fall frost zones, and your locality may be in different zones for the spring and fall frosts. If you live in the West outside the zones, for an approximate guide take the frost dates in your individual locality, find similar frost dates in one of the zones, and use the corresponding dates for that zone.)

For the more northerly zones peppers are essentially a one-season crop. The plants must be set out in the garden when all danger of frost is past and the weather is warm. However, a long growing season is required before heavy fall frosts occur.

How to Plant: The seeds must be started either in a hotbed or indoors, except in the South. Indoors they should be planted in flats and kept under glass at a relatively high temperature. A temperature as high as 75°–85° F. is necessary. It is advisable to cover the seed with sand to reduce the likelihood of damping-off. The seed takes

12 to 20 days to germinate. When the seedlings are 3 or 4 inches tall, they should be thinned out to a 3- to 4-inch spacing in the flat; or the sturdier plants can be transplanted to individual pots or boxes. The seed should be sown about 8 to 10 weeks before the first frost-free date. The plants will then be of suitable size for setting out in the garden, when they should be 6 to 8 inches tall.

Where to Plant: They should preferably be placed near other all-season crops. A very suitable place is close to eggplant, in view of the general similarity in maturity time and growing conditions. Because of the relatively late planting date in the garden, they can be preceded in the same space by crops of early lettuce, spinach, onions, or radishes.

Soil: The plants have a luxuriant growth and require rich soil. Usually some stimulation is needed. An ounce or two of commercial fertilizer, such as 4–12–4, should be sufficient to work around the roots at an intermediate growing stage.

Cultivation and Care: The plants should be cultivated regularly every week or ten days to keep down weeds and break up the soil. It is advisable to work the soil up around the base of the stem so that the plants will stand up better. However, deep cultivation should be avoided since this will cut the roots, which are close to the surface, and check the plant growth.

Harvesting: Sweet peppers are picked when they are full grown, but while they are still green and before they turn red. Hot peppers, often known as chili, are usually allowed to ripen fully and to acquire their characteristic red color before picking.

Harvesting does not present any problems and is not an urgent job since the sweet type remains green for an appreciable time, while the hot type can stay on the vine without deterioration after it has become red. Picking consists merely of snapping off the hard, brittle stems.

Late in the season it is possible to pull up the plants completely and hang them so that the remaining fruits can ripen.

Uses: The principal use for green peppers by the home gardener will be for late summer and fall salads. Red peppers are used for flavoring and sauces, and both types are ingredients in various pickle recipes.

Green peppers are such a good source of vitamin A that more general use might be made of them as an appetizing and valuable food. Green peppers quartered, brushed with melted butter, and put under the broiler for a few minutes are delicious with steak. An easy way to dress up and add to the food value of canned corn is to heat it with tomatoes and chopped green pepper. Green pepper rings can be dipped in bread crumbs and French-fried in deep fat. Shrimp creole, a particularly good way to prepare shrimps, makes use of green peppers. Rice is boiled in the juice from a can of tomatoes, with finely chopped green pepper and onion added. When the rice is done, the whole tomatoes go in and the mixture is heated until it is piping hot. This is served with the shrimps.

Chopped green peppers can be added to many sandwich fillings, like cream cheese, minced ham, egg salad, lettuce, water cress. The possibilities for stuffing peppers are almost endless, but remember to parboil them to make them tender. Stuffed peppers are an economical and filling dish which can be used as a main-course dish.

20. Potatoes

(*Solanum tuberosum. Solanaceae,* nightshade family.)

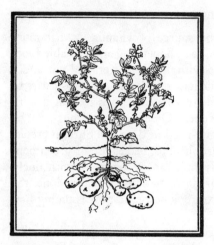

"Leek to the Welsh, to Dutchmen
butter's dear,
Of Irish swains potato is the cheer."

This verse by John Gay voices a popular conception. It is surprising, therefore, to learn that so-called Irish potatoes did not come originally from Europe or the British Isles but are native to South America, where they have been cultivated since at least the time of the Incas. Here the early explorers found potatoes in cultivation, and one of them wrote: "the skinne . . . is of earthy colour, but the inner meate thereof is very white: these are nourished in gardens . . . they are also eaten rawe and have the taste of rawe chestnuts but are somewhat sweeter." Potatoes were taken back to Spain from Peru, and there is some doubt as to whether they got to North America by way of Spain or came straight from South America through the Spanish explorers. At any rate, the early colonists of the Virginia settlement were growing them for the first time at about the same date that they were first cultivated in continental Europe.

Several people have been credited with introducing potatoes into Ireland from America, but Sir Walter Raleigh is apparently the leading contender. Following the return of the first ships he sent out, according to an English writer in 1822, "Raleigh is said to have given some potatoes to his gardener in Ireland as a fine fruit from America, and ordered them to be planted in his kitchen garden. In August the plants flowered, and in September produced the fruit; but the berries were so different from what the gardener expected, that in all ill humor he carried the potato-apples to his master. 'Is this (said he) the fine fruit from America you praised so highly?' Sir Walter either was, or pretended to be ignorant of the matter; and desired the gardener, since this was the case, to dig up the weed and throw it away. The gardener, however, soon returned with a good parcel of potatoes." This little episode took place about 1585, which is probably the date of the first introduction of potatoes into the British Isles.

But it took several hundred years before potatoes became the "rich man's luxury and the poor man's bread." As the same English writer states: "It was long, however, before potatoes were brought into general use; for by some they were reckonned not good for food, others deemed them poisonous. In Burgundy, the culture or use of the potatoe was interdicted, and it was deemed a poisonous and mischievous root. Amongst other evils, it was accused of occasioning the leprosy and dysentry." Potatoes were planted in the gardens of the nobility as a curious exotic, and in the reign of James I, in 1619, potatoes were among the articles of food provided for the Queen's household, at one shilling a pound. When the culture did get started, however, it accelerated with tremendous rapidity, as is evidenced by the potato famine in Ireland, when blight ruined the crop in 1846. In 1848 nearly a hundred varieties were exhibited by the Massachusetts Horticultural Society. The number of varieties in France increased from 60 in 1815 to 528 in 1862. Today the varieties are almost without number. The potato is by far the most common article of food of the white races, with an annual world production of six billion bushels.

Food Value: The composition of potatoes is 80 per cent water, 2 per cent protein, and 18 per cent starch. It is the high starch content that makes them such a satisfying vegetable, but they do have enough vitamin content to make them nutritious since they are a good source of vitamins B_1 and C and contain some vitamin A and G.

Culture: Potatoes take up considerable room, are not a particularly easy crop to grow, and are both inexpensive to buy in the market and available all year. Therefore, unless the home gardener has considerable space available, all that should be grown is a small planting of the early crop to provide the family with some delicious little new potatoes. They are worth growing for that reason because your own new potatoes with some of your own green peas and a chop or steak make a meal that the finest chef couldn't surpass.

Potatoes are a hardy, cool-weather crop that can stand light frosts. They grow best when the temperature is around 55°–75° F. since the tubers need both cool soil and cool air for correct formation. They are usually planted in the late winter or very early spring. The harvesting begins in Florida in February with the new potatoes (that is, immature potatoes) and moves up the coast northward, ending in Maine with a fall harvest. Very hot weather may kill the crop and always affects the production. Therefore, whenever possible, in most parts of the country, except the mild, more or less frost-free regions of the South and California, potatoes should be planted in the spring a month or so before the last frost date. In the mild regions they can be planted in the late fall and early winter. In the North where the summers are cool a second or late planting can be made for harvesting in the fall.

Potatoes require a rich soil, one that is both well fed and full of humus, since an abundant moisture supply is also one of their demands. They should be planted deep in carefully prepared soil, and they will be ready to harvest in 80–140 days, depending upon the variety.

Habits of Growth: The potato is cultivated as an annual. The part of the plant that appears above the ground consists of a branched, spreading plant growing 2–3 feet high. This bears dull green leaves, ¼ inch to 2 inches long, and clusters of variously colored flowers, which open over a span of several days. Finally there may be the fruit or seed ball, which is a small, round, green or yellowish berry about ½ inch in diameter. This is usually full of very tiny seeds. However, not many of our present-day varieties develop seed balls. The part of the plant that the gardener is interested in is what grows under the ground. The edible potato is a tuber that is actually a thickened part of the underground stem, usually the end. The white stem stops elongating and starts to thicken at the top. The result is the potato. The eyes on the potato are leaf scars which contain the buds, several in each eye, from which the sprouts arise. It is from these sprouts that new plants can grow.

The tubers begin to form about the time the first flowers arrive, which is usually 3 to 4 weeks after the plant has appeared above ground. Since all the tubers are formed at the same time, the variations in size are due to an unequal rate of growth rather than to a difference in age. Young tubers have a thin skin which can be rubbed off with the fingers. This skin is gradually replaced by a tougher one, the kind ordinarily found on old potatoes.

The temperature, as well as the length of daylight, has a decided effect on the development of the tubers. Days having a long period of daylight tend to promote excessive leaf growth, while days with less daylight tend to concentrate growth more in the tubers. Cool weather also favors tuber development.

Types and Varieties: There are many different types of potatoes; but they are not particularly well defined, they often are duplicated, and they do not mean much to the gardener. The three most important types are:

Cobbler, for early varieties.

Green Mountain, for late varieties.

Rural, for late varieties (particularly suitable for heavy soils and dry soils).

The most important early variety is *Irish Cobbler,* which is ready to harvest in about 80 days. *Pure Early Rose* is another early variety, ready for harvesting in 85 days. It has a light pink skin and excellent quality. Good late varieties are *Green Mountain* (140 days), for cool parts of the country, and *Rural Russet* or *Dibble Russet,* for any section of the country, but particularly dry, hot sections. Two new varieties, which many growers now prefer, have gained wide acceptance: *Chippewa*, an early variety which matures about the same time as or a few days later than *Irish Cobbler* and produces a very high yield; and *Katahdin*, a late variety (140 days) developed by the U. S. Department of Agriculture.

How Much to Buy:

10–15 pounds for 100 feet

To be on the safe side, you should plant 15 pounds (1 peck). Certified seed is quite expensive; a peck costs 75 cents to $2.25. On the other hand, the yield is high.

Potato seed (that is, seed potatoes for planting) must be purchased from the most reliable sources. You should buy only certified seed. Potatoes from ordinary seed tend to be badly disease ridden, and almost all the diseases are carried in the seed itself. Certified seed is grown on carefully regulated fields; the plants are practically free of disease; and, to be certified, the seed must be passed by qualified inspectors. The seed is not disease resistant but is grown under such well-controlled conditions that disease is not present. It is impossible to detect disease in an unsprouted potato; the evidence shows only in the plant. Therefore, don't just put any old spuds in the ground. The variety you plant is not nearly as important as the grade of your seed.

Planting:

Germination time: 3–4 weeks.

Depth for seed: *Early crop*, 3 inches.
Main crop, 5 inches.

Spacing of plants: 10–18 inches; 14 inches is a good distance. Cut seed can be planted closer than whole seed.

Spacing of rows: 30–36 inches.

When to Plant:

	EARLY CROP	LATE CROP
	Earliest Safe Date for Planting Seed in Garden	Latest Safe Date for Planting Seed in Garden
Zone A. Jan. 1 – Feb. 1		Sept. 15
" B. Feb. 1 – Feb. 15		Sept. 1
" C. Feb. 15 – March 1		Aug. 15
" D. March 1 – March 15		Aug. 1
" E. March 15 – April 15		July 15
" F. April 15 – May 1		July 1
" G. May 1 – June 1		June 15

(See maps at back of book showing locations of zones for spring and fall frosts. Remember that the boundaries of the spring frost zones are not the same as those of the fall frost zones, and your locality may be in different zones for the spring and fall frosts. If you live in the West outside the zones, for an approximate guide take the frost dates in your individual locality, find similar frost dates in one of the zones, and use the corresponding dates for that zone.)

Early potatoes can be planted 4–5 weeks before the date of the last killing frost in the spring. It is important to get them in the ground as soon as possible because they grow much better when the weather is cool. Delayed planting may push the harvesting into warm weather, especially in the southern and central states. If the plant has made some top growth, a frost may injure it; but, since it takes 3–4 weeks for the sprouts to appear above ground, early planting is safe. In those parts of the country where the summers are very hot, only one spring planting can be made, although a second crop of early potatoes can be sown in the fall 3 months before the first fall frost date. In the North, the first spring planting can be followed 4 to 6 weeks later by a planting of late potatoes, which will be ready for harvesting in the late summer and early fall. This is the crop to use if you intend to do any storing.

How to Plant: Potatoes are propagated in a different way from any of the other vegetables in this book. The "seeds" are either whole little potatoes or parts of larger ones; on planting, sprouts arise from the "eyes" on the potatoes. Excellent results will come from planting whole seed potatoes of 2 ounces or less in weight, with at least two good eyes. If the potato is larger, cut it up so that each piece weighs at least 1½ ounces and has one or more eyes. The accompanying illustration indicates how to go about cutting the seed potato. The size of the piece is important because if it is too small the nourishment will

Cut potato seed

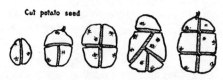

not be sufficient to get the plant off to a good start, while if it is too large there will be too many eyes and consequently too many sprouts. This limits the size of the tubers.

The seed is dropped into the hole, 3–5 inches deep, and is planted at the distance the plants stand during their growth, that is, about 14 inches apart. The planting requires no special care; simply be sure that the seed is deep enough because the fibrous roots which produce the tubers grow out from the shoot rising from the seed—and the tubers need room. And don't cut the seed until you are just ready to plant it; standing around cut does it definite harm.

Where to Plant: Potatoes need room and should be put in a part of the garden where they will not interfere with other crops, in a separate patch if you have the space. They do not use the ground all season, however. Early potatoes can be followed by any of the summer crops, such as beans, late corn, late cabbage, and so on. The main-crop varieties stay in the ground all summer, but late plantings of early varieties can be preceded by peas, early cabbage, and any of the small quick-growing crops, such as spinach, turnips, or beets.

Soil: Reams have been written about the best soil preparation and fertilizers for potatoes, but much of the information is conflicting. It is generally agreed that potatoes need a rich soil and one that is abundantly supplied with humus. This is obtained by using either well-rotted manure or a commercial fertilizer plus compost, peat moss, or some added humus, unless your soil already is well provided with it.

Dig the soil well. If possible, this should be done the previous fall, so that the backbreaking work will be over when you are ready to plant in the spring. It is difficult, if not impossible, to do much thorough digging of the hard ground at the time the early crop should be planted. Incorporate dry manure in the fall, if possible; otherwise, apply a fertilizer when you plant. If you want to be sure that you use the correct fertilizer, you should inquire from your state agricultural experiment station since the demands of soils vary considerably. In general, though, 5–8–7 is good, about 3–4 pounds per 100 feet.

The fertilizer should not come into direct contact with the seed since it injures it and the result will be a poor stand. The best way to avoid this is to put the fertilizer in bands, along the row and 2 inches away.

Cultivation and Care: The cultivation should be frequent but shallow; go over the patch every week or ten days until the tops have grown so large that cultivation is difficult and the roots so extended that you risk injuring them.

Potatoes are a moisture-loving crop and need water, especially when the weather gets warm. A few very hot days during the finishing stages of growth may even kill the plant, if it is dry.

> "The thirsty earth soaks up the rain,
> And drinks, and gapes for drink again.
> The plants suck in the rain, and are
> With constant drinking fresh and fair."

If any signs of blight appear on your potato plants, promptly supplement your routine treatment with extra sprays of Bordeaux mixture.

One of the worst pests potatoes have to contend with is the Colorado potato beetle. If they appear, and routine treatment is insufficient, use a calcium arsenate spray at once preferably after a rain, with a second dose if necessary after 2 weeks. Calcium arsenate and Bordeaux mixture can be conveniently applied as a mixed spray.

Harvesting: Potatoes are harvested both when they are immature and when they are mature.

Immature, they are called new potatoes—and they seem literally to melt in your mouth. They can be harvested soon after the plant has flowered. The best way to judge the right time is by digging around cautiously and looking. Within reason, the smaller they are the better. By starting to harvest early, you can have quite an extended period of harvesting before hot weather.

The main-crop or late potatoes are usually left to mature in the ground. They are mature when the tops have died down, and are usually dug then (or earlier if desired). In cool, dry weather they can be left in the ground for some time. They should, however, be harvested before a hard freeze.

The actual harvesting is done by digging the plant up carefully with a fork, taking plenty of earth and pulling out the potatoes by hand. Tread carefully to avoid causing injury.

Storing: Late potatoes are probably the most commonly stored vegetable. Before they are stored, they should be kept in piles for about a week at room temperature to "sweat." Potatoes keep best at a temperature of 36° F. (below this temperature they tend to get rather sweet) and require fairly moist air and little air circulation. These conditions are best found in a special cellar storage room, an outside storage room, or a storage pit (see the chapter on "Storing"). If you keep them with the root crops in a storage room, put them in the warmest corner, since the root crops keep best in a temperature somewhat below 36°. They should be placed in slatted bins or crates away from the light, since they will start sprouting if much light gets at them. The maximum storage period is 5–6 months.

Uses: Gerarde wrote a "Herball" in 1597, which is cherished by students of garden lore today and makes fascinating reading for anyone who is curious about the history of plants. In it he gives some directions for the use of potatoes, saying that they may be "rosted in the ashes, some, when they be so rosted, infuse them and sop them in wine: and others, to give them the greater grace in eating, do boile them with prunes, and so eate them; and likewise, others dress them, being first rosted with oile, vinegar, and salt, every man according to his owne taste and liking: notwithstanding, however they be dressed, they comfort, nourish, and strengthen the bodie."

Potatoes are such a common part of the daily diet that often we do not give them their due in our cooking. Boiled potatoes should not be allowed to get mushy. Baked potatoes should be rubbed with oil before they are put in the oven and pierced with a fork once or twice when they are half cooked. Mashed potatoes should be beaten long and hard, with warm cream and butter. Fried potatoes should be cooked slowly and long enough to be thoroughly done and well browned. They should be covered to get them well steamed. Little new potatoes are especially good if they are parboiled, rolled in oil and fine corn flakes, and browned in the oven. An easy dish to prepare is raw potatoes cut in thin slices and arranged in a loaf pan in layers. Each layer should be seasoned and dotted with butter. Bake for about an hour in a moderate oven until the crust is brown. This can be served directly from the pan or as a loaf if it is removed carefully. Chopped ham or thin slices of cheese inserted between the layers make this loaf a main-course luncheon dish.

Both creamed whole new potatoes and creamed, diced old potatoes are excellent baked with a covering of grated cheese or buttered bread crumbs. Or, if you have a taste for sour cream, bake parboiled sliced potatoes with sour cream instead of a cream sauce. Hashed-brown potatoes look professional and are perfect with steak. To prepare them, chop boiled potatoes very fine and put in a frying pan with bacon fat. Cook them slowly without touching them until a hard crust is formed on the bottom; then you can either turn them over and put another crust on top, or fold them over as with an omelet. Potatoes O'Brien sound elaborate, but they are simply diced, cooked potatoes sautéed gently with minced green peppers, pimento, and onion. They are good, too.

There are many other ways to use potatoes, and it behooves the meal planner in the family to dig them out and exert some originality; there should be a law against boiled potatoes one night and baked the next the year around.

21. Radishes

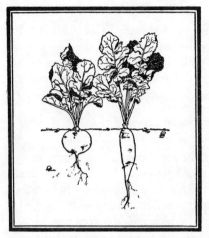

(*Raphanus sativus. Cruciferae*, mustard family.)

HISTORY: The name radish comes from the Latin, *radix*, meaning a root. The radish is one of the first recorded cultivated vegetables, dating back to earliest historical times. The actual place of origin is not known, although it is likely that it may have been China. We do know that it has been grown extensively in China, Japan, and India for centuries, as well as in western Asia and Europe. Ancients believed that if a man rubbed his hands well with either the juice of the roots or the seeds he might handle scorpions safely. They also believed if a radish were laid on one of those reptiles it would cause its death. Radishes were highly esteemed by the Egyptians at the time of the Pharaohs. When the Greeks made sacrificial offerings to Apollo, turnips were presented in lead dishes, beets in silver dishes, but radishes were served in dishes of gold. According to certain old writers the radish is called a root with justification because individual radishes have weighed as much as a hundred pounds.

Food Value: Radishes are grown and enjoyed more as an appetizer than as a nutritive food in the diet. As one writer many years ago put it, a radish "contains little beside water, woody fibre and acrid matter." Radishes are, however, an excellent source of vitamin C.

Culture: All types of radishes can be grown in any part of the country. Radishes are so easy to grow that it is almost impossible to fail in cultivating them if they are planted at the proper time. They are a hardy, quick-growing, succession crop. It is simply a matter of sowing the seed in the open ground, and the radishes will practically take care of themselves until they are ready to be eaten.

Habits of Growth: Radishes are by nature biennial, although the practice is to cultivate them as an annual crop. The plant first forms a thickened tap root and a rosette of leaves. Later, if not harvested, either in the same season or the following spring, flowers and seed appear, but the root is then inedible.

Radishes vary in shape, from globular to half-long and long varieties; they vary in size from an inch to about two feet; they vary in color, with red, white, yellow, gray, and black varieties.

The tap root is the edible part and the only one that we are ac-

customed to eat. However, a writer in 1840 said: "The plant is cultivated for its roots. Also, the seed leaves which are used as a small
salad, and even the seed pods, if picked while young and green, are
considered by some a good substitute for capers." Hence, if you are
looking for something new, try pickled radish seeds.

Types and Varieties: There are three types of radishes, the *early*,
the *summer*, and the *winter*, good varieties of which are:

Early. Early radishes are by far the most commonly grown in this
country both by home gardeners and for the market. They are small,
an inch or so in diameter, and either red, white, or a combination.
They are usually planted in the spring and mature quickly, in 3 to 6
weeks, depending upon the weather, which must be cool but not too
cold or the growth is retarded. When it gets warm, constantly above
60° F., early radishes become pithy, bitter, and tough and tend to
send up flower stalks. Early radishes also can be used for a fall crop
in any part of the country where there is a period of about 5–6 weeks
of cool but frost-free weather in the fall.

Varieties: *Early Scarlet Globe*, red, round; *French Breakfast*,
olive shaped, red with white tips; *White Icicle*, long, white.

Summer. Summer radishes are larger than the early ones (usually
about 5–6 inches long), are generally white, take 5–6 weeks to mature, will remain edible longer once they have matured, and will give
you radishes for the table in the summer when little spring ones worth
eating cannot be grown. Summer radishes are definitely tasty; but,
since the strongest part is close to the skin, if they make your eyes
water peel the skin off.

Varieties: *White Strassburg; Long White Vienna*.

Winter. Winter radishes are used in other countries much more
than they are here. In Japan the odor of black radishes pickled is as
strong in crowds as garlic odor is in Italy. They are long (12–20
inches); are red, white, or black; take about 8 weeks to mature; and,
if sown when the weather is warm and allowed to finish their growing
while it is cool, will have a crisp, delicate, mild flavor. These can be
grown both for fall eating and for winter storage. One root is sufficient for the whole family for one meal, and they are sliced for
serving.

Varieties: *Chinese Rose*, deep rose with white tips; *Long
Black Spanish*, black skinned, a very good winter keeper; *Sakura-*

jima, 20 inches long and 1 foot in diameter, white skin, unusual and well worth a try.

How Much to Buy:

1 ounce for 100 feet

An ounce will go further than this if the seed is planted between the rows of another crop (known as catch cropping), since you sow more thinly. How much to grow depends upon how much your family enjoys this sharp delicacy. Inasmuch as early radishes are not space grabbers, you can plant as much as you wish, but bear in mind that a single crop of early radishes is worth eating for only ten days or so. Hence, buy enough seed to make small plantings often.

A 20-foot row of winter radishes will give you about forty large roots.

Planting:

Germination time: 4–6 days.

Depth for seed: ½ inch.

Spacing of plants: Early, 1–1½ inches.
Summer, 2–3 inches.
Winter, 6 inches.

Spacing of rows: Early and *summer,* 5–8 inches.
Winter, 18 inches.

When to Plant:

	EARLY CROP Earliest Safe Date for Planting Seed in Garden	LATE CROP Latest Safe Date for Planting Seed in Garden
Zone A.	Jan. 1 – Feb. 1	Dec. 1
" B.	Feb. 1 – Feb. 15	Nov. 1
" C.	Feb. 15 – March 1	Oct. 15
" D.	March 1 – March 15	Oct. 1
" E.	March 15 – April 15	Sept. 15
" F.	April 15 – May 1	Sept. 1
" G.	May 1 – May 15	Aug. 15

(See maps at back of book showing locations of zones for spring and fall frosts. Remember that the boundaries of the spring frost zones are not the same as those of the fall frost zones, and your locality may be in different zones for the spring and fall frosts. If you live in the West outside the zones, for an approximate guide take the frost dates in your individual locality, find similar frost dates in one of the zones, and use the corresponding dates for that zone.)

Ordinary early radishes are a crop which can be planted any time that you are sure of 4–5 weeks of cool weather. They are very hardy and can be put in before the last frost dates in the spring. In the North a late sowing made in the fall can usually be harvested before hard frosts. In the more or less frost-free sections of the South they can be planted all during the winter.

Summer radishes can be planted when the weather turns warm. These grow more slowly than early radishes, requiring 35–40 days to mature, and can better stand the heat. For example, they should be planted around the middle of May in Zone E, for harvesting after the early radishes are finished.

Winter radishes can be planted when the weather is warm, but they should finish their growing after the weather has turned cool. They take 55–60 days to mature. Two sowings a month apart (for example, the first in July and the second in August in Zone E) will give a supply both for the table and for winter storage.

How to Plant: Sow the seed ½ inch deep out in the garden. There are no tricks or catches to this crop, and the sowing is as easy as the eating.

Where to Plant: The best plan is to use early and summer radishes as a catch crop between rows of other crops and to plant them in with other seeds that are planted early or with seeds that are slow to germinate. The tough little radish seeds are up in four or five days, break the soil for delicate seeds such as parsnips and carrots, mark the rows to facilitate cultivation, and grow so fast that they are pulled and eaten before the other plants need the room. It is foolish to give early and summer radishes a row to themselves when they are out of the way so quickly. The winter radishes stay in the ground longer and can be planted in a row already vacated by an earlier crop.

Soil: Radishes will grow in almost any soil. But if you want them perfect, they must grow rapidly. This requires the same rich, loose, sandy, well-drained soil that is best for all root crops. As with the other root crops, do not give them fresh manure. Well-rotted manure or a complete fertilizer is the best stimulus to excellence.

Cultivation and Care: Radishes grow so quickly that they do not need any care. Even weeding is not important with a crop that matures at this speed, although weeds are never the mark of a good gardener.

With the early type, the only thinning that is usually done is to pick the fastest-growing ones for eating. However, they can be thinned to stand 1–1½ inches apart if they are in a row by themselves, 2–3 inches if with another crop. While the other crop may be slow, it does require some room. Therefore, do not let the radishes take it all. The summer radishes need 2–3 inches. And the winter ones must be thinned as soon as possible to stand 6 inches apart, so that the large roots can grow properly.

Cultivation is almost nonessential. The roots are so little they are essentially surface feeders, and deep hoeing or raking does more harm than good. Radishes may be a nuisance because they have to be planted so often for a continual supply, but they make up for this trouble by not requiring any further attention once they are planted, except to be eaten.

Harvesting: Harvesting consists of merely pulling the radishes from the ground. The early ones can be harvested when they are big enough to eat, usually in about 3½ weeks. The summer radishes can be harvested in 6 to 7 weeks, and the winter ones either can be pulled in 8 weeks for immediate use or can stay in the ground until frost comes. They cannot, however, remain there all winter and be used in the spring as parsnips can.

Storing: Winter radishes can be stored under proper conditions in a cellar storage room, an outside storage room, or an outside pit (see the chapter on "Storing") in the same manner as late beets and carrots. They will keep 4–5 months.

Before you use stored winter radishes, soak them an hour or so in cold water.

Uses: Wash radishes well, peel back the red skin, dip in salt, and eat. For a special treat put a little butter on them. Boiled radishes sliced and fried in butter are a good accompaniment to chops and steaks. Raw sliced radishes make an appetizing sandwich. The summer and winter ones make a hearty main vegetable dish if they are boiled and served with a well-seasoned cream sauce. Or you can do as they did in England in 1597 and "use as a sauce with meats to procure appetite."

22. Spinach

(*Spinacia oleracea. Chenopodiaceae,*
goosefoot family.)

HISTORY: References to spinach date back to the fourteenth century. Apparently it was first cultivated by the Arabs, by whom it was introduced into North Africa and thence taken to Spain by the Moors. During the Middle Ages it was grown in monastic gardens and eaten by monks on fast days. It is curious that its name is nearly the same in many languages. In French it is *épinard*, in German *spinat*, in Italian *spinace*, in Spanish *espinaca*, in Arabic *hispane*.

The first mention of the cultivation of spinach in America was in 1806, but it has become in recent years the most widely grown potherb in the country. Its importance as a food is reflected by the increase in commercial acreage since people have become vitamin and mineral conscious. In 1919 the commercial acreage was only 13,680 but by 1937 it had jumped to 106,340.

Food Value: Spinach is an excellent source of vitamins A and C, a good source of vitamins B_1 and G, and an excellent source of iron—which puts it in the top bracket of essential items in your diet.

Culture: Spinach can be grown all over the country, but the planting must be timed so that it will have 6 or 7 weeks of reasonably cool weather. It can stand temperatures as low as 40° F. If the temperature rises above 60°–70° the plant will bolt to seed and be useless.

Spinach is an easy-to-grow, hardy, quick-maturing, cool-weather crop. It will grow satisfactorily in any good garden soil, matures in 6–7 weeks, can be grown as a succession crop, and can be intercropped. It is troubled little by disease and insects. If you happen to live in a section of the country where blight is prevalent, planting blight-resistant seed will cure that worry. The one demand spinach does make is for cool weather and the reasonably short days that accompany the cool seasons of the year. Either heat or the lengthened daylight of summer causes spinach to bolt to seed rapidly and ruins the value of the crop. Even if it does not actually bolt to seed, the quality will be very poor when the days are hot and long. *Therefore, time your planting in such a way that the crop can mature and be harvested while the weather is cool.*

Habits of Growth: Spinach is a hardy annual plant which forms a compact rosette of quite large, dark green, arrow-shaped leaves on a short stem. These leaves are the edible portion of the plant. Later the stem elongates and branches and forms a 2- or 3-foot flower stalk, which makes the plant useless as a vegetable.

It was commonly believed that warm weather was the factor that caused the plant to form a flower stalk prematurely and bolt to seed. Recent studies, however, have shown that duration of daylight may be the most influential cause, for the plant forms a seed stalk much more quickly when it is subjected to a long period of daylight than to a short one. Therefore it is not a midsummer plant even in parts of the country where the weather does not get very hot.

Types and Varieties: There are two main types of spinach, the crinkled leaf and the smooth leaf. The crinkled-leaf type has three subdivisions: savoy, long standing, and long season. It is the type most generally used by home gardeners and market growers. Commercial canners like the smooth-leaf type because dirt can be washed off easily.

There is also some variation in the seed itself. Some of it is round and some prickly. The prickly seed deserves the name and is difficult to plant for that reason. It was formerly believed that prickly seeds produced a hardier plant than the smooth seeds, but this is a mistaken notion, and there is no reason for using the prickly seeds.

There are considerable differences among round-seeded varieties; some are more disease resistant than others and some will last longer before bolting to seed, that is, they are "long standing." It pays to choose varieties carefully.

Crinkled-Leaf Type:
Savoy. Early maturing; dark green; has extremely crumpled leaves.

VARIETIES: *Long Standing Bloomsdale,* excellent for both spring and fall crops; *Virginia Blight Resistant,* goes to seed quickly; *Old Dominion,* also blight resistant, best used in a late fall sowing for an early spring crop.

Long Standing. Medium-size plants which are slow in sending up seed stalks; dark green crumpled leaves.

VARIETIES: *Victoria,* especially suitable for spring sowing; *King of Denmark,* very long standing.

Long Season. Medium-size, slow-growing plants; dark green crumpled leaves.

VARIETY: *Princess Juliana.* This name is an interesting and apt one, since a large proportion of spinach seed has up to this time been grown in Holland.

Smooth-Leaf Type:
This type has large plants; broad, smooth, medium green leaves; and is well adapted for canning.

VARIETY: *Nobel,* very large leaves; slow in going to seed.

How Much to Buy:

1 package for 25 feet
1 ounce   for 100 feet

Plant enough spinach so that some can be canned for the winter.

Planting:

Germination time: 5–9 days.

Depth for seed: ½ inch.

Spacing of plants: 4 inches.

Spacing of rows: 12–15 inches.

When to Plant:

	EARLY CROP	LATE CROP
	Earliest Safe Date for Planting Seed in Garden	*Latest Safe Date for Planting Seed in Garden*
Zone A.	Feb. 1 – Feb. 15	Nov. 1
" B.	Feb. 15 – March 1	Oct. 15
" C.	March 1 – March 15	Oct. 15
" D.	March 1 – April 1	Oct. 1
" E.	March 15 – April 15	Sept. 1
" F.	April 15 – May 1	Aug. 15
" G.	May 1 – May 15	Aug. 1

(See maps at back of book showing locations of zones for spring and fall frosts. Remember that the boundaries of the spring frost zones are not the same as those of the fall frost zones, and your locality may be in different zones for the spring and fall frosts. If you live in the West outside the zones, for an approximate guide take the frost dates in your individual locality, find similar frost dates in one of the zones, and use the corresponding dates for that zone.)

Spinach should be planted just as soon as the ground can be worked in the spring in the north and central states. It can be sown even in frozen ground. When the temperature is 40° F. or even less, the seed will germinate; the rate of germination is good at 50° or 60°. The earliest planting dates should be used for the first plantings, and successive plantings can be made about a week apart to give you a bountiful supply for the table and to can. However, it is perfectly useless to plant spinach after the later of the earliest safe planting dates given above because as soon as the days get long and the weather hot, the plants shoot to seed and cannot be eaten.

Another crop can be sown in the fall either to be harvested immediately or to be left in the ground throughout the winter for harvesting in the early spring. In the northern parts of the country the plants should be given some protection with straw or hay to prevent their being killed. Some plants may be lost anyhow, but the majority will winter over quite satisfactorily.

In the South the most satisfactory way to grow spinach is to plant from September to January or February.

How to Plant: Simply sow the seed ½ inch deep, about 2 inches apart if you are sure your seed is fresh, thicker if you are doubtful. The rate of germination drops down to 80 per cent when the seed is more than a year old, and older seed is even less viable. The seed germinates quickly, requires no care except thinning.

A good way to grow spinach if you want a considerable amount is to plant several rows very close together, 8 inches apart is enough, leaving enough space between this group of rows and the next adjoining rows of other vegetables to allow for cultivation.

Where to Plant: Spinach is a simple crop to fit into garden operations. It is in and out of the ground in 8 weeks at the most. In the North it is a spring and fall crop, and the early crop is out of the way in plenty of time for plantings of corn, tomatoes, beans, eggplant, and late cabbage in the same ground. The late crop can follow corn, beans, cauliflower, cabbage, and onions.

Soil: Although spinach will grow in any soil, a definitely superior product will be obtained if the plant makes a rapid growth in a rich soil with plenty of moisture. Light sandy soils with little organic matter produce a spindling, light green spinach of inferior quality.

Therefore have your soil well fertilized with either rotted manure or a commercial fertilizer. Since the plants require nitrogen during the growing season, give them two or three doses of nitrate of soda, about 1 ounce per square yard. Dig it into the soil and be sure that it does not touch the foliage.

Cultivation and Care: When the plants show two good-size true leaves they can be thinned to stand 4–6 inches apart. In commercial plantings thinning is seldom practiced, but in your own garden it is a wise plan to do it because, when the growth is checked or stunted later by crowding, the plants tend to run to seed much more rapidly.

The cultivation is a simple matter of a little shallow hoeing to keep down the weeds. Spinach demands little care.

Harvesting: Spinach is usually ready to be eaten about 6 or 7 weeks after planting. When the leaves are 7 or 8 inches long and there are about six of them, they can be harvested. They do not lose any flavor if they are left unpicked, but the plant is apt to shoot forth with that fatal flower stalk. The entire plant is removed by cutting the tap root just below the surface of the ground with a sharp knife or hoe. Take the largest plants first, give the smaller ones time to catch up.

Canning: Spinach is not suited for storing but it is excellent canned. For canning directions see the chapter on "Canning."

Uses: In the first place, be sure that you cook spinach properly. Don't drown out all those vitamins; simply cook it in the water that is left on the leaves after they are washed. This is ample. An onion stuck with a clove and cooked along with the spinach gives a good flavor.

Cooked, finely chopped spinach and cooked diced beets are a good combination—well seasoned, mixed with some butter, a little lemon juice, and sour cream. Creamed spinach is popular, but it is improved if the sauce is made with chicken stock instead of milk. Spinach makes a delicious soufflé (for directions see Uses in the chapter on "Turnips"). Left-over spinach is an ideal base for a cream soup. Any left-over meat can be prepared with either a cream sauce or gravy and put in a casserole over a layer of finely chopped spinach.

Edible shoot tip of
New Zealand spinach

New Zealand Spinach
(*Tetragonia expansa. Aizoaceae,* carpetweed family.)

This plant is not a true spinach, but an excellent potherb that can be used in place of spinach during the heat of the summer when the latter bolts to seed and is useless.

It is an annual, half-hardy crop which produces a large sprawling plant a foot or two tall, with numerous leaf shoots covering 4–6 feet of ground. The tips of these leaf shoots are the most tender part. They look and taste similar to small spinach leaves, although they are a little tougher. Only 3–4 inches or so of the tips are harvested. Since the buds in the axils of the leaves continue to develop new growth, you can harvest all summer until frosts kill the plant. If the plant grows properly you can get almost a peck of greens from it a week.

One of the chief merits of this crop is its capacity for withstanding and taking heat in its stride. A few plants are a simple means of assuring your table of greens throughout the summer. Swiss chard is the only other crop that provides a continual supply of summer greens.

New Zealand spinach can be grown both in the North and in the South, but in the South it is a smaller plant, usually no taller than 6–8 inches. In the extreme South it must be given some protection from the sun in the hottest summer weather.

Only one variety is available. Since a few plants will keep the family supplied, 1 package of seed should be ample.

The seed can be sown in the garden when the soil has warmed up in the late spring, for example, about May 15 in Zone E in the vicinity of New York. Inasmuch as the seed is often slow to germinate, soak it beforehand, either 24 hours in warm water or 2 hours in water at 120° F. Sow the seed 1 inch deep and thin. When the plants are established, thin them to stand 2 feet apart in rows 3–4 feet apart. Cultivation is simply a matter of keeping the weeds down until the plant has spread and completely covered the space allowed it. The soil requirements are not exacting: ordinary, good garden soil with possibly some nitrate of soda worked around the base of each plant two or three times during the summer. Do not let the soda come into contact with the stalks.

New Zealand spinach has no serious diseases and pests. It tends to self-sow and thus assure you of a crop for several years if you want it. Culture is simple, and the use of it as a summer potherb will compensate for the rather large amount of space it needs.

23. Squash

Hubbard   Buttercup

(*Cucurbita maxima. Cucurbitaceae,*
gourd or melon family.)

(NOTE: Before we consider the history of squash, a word or two about the botanical classification of the squash group seems necessary. There has been much confusion in the past, particularly in seed catalogues, between true pumpkin and true squash. What is known as summer squash is actually a pumpkin. There are three species in the general pumpkin and squash group: pumpkin (*Cucurbita moschata*); summer squash (*C. pepo*), actually pumpkin; and true squash (*C. maxima*). These crops can readily be distinguished: mature pumpkin has a hard, woody stem that is furrowed lengthwise, while mature squash has a soft, spongy stem that is not particularly furrowed.

In most home gardens there is not room to grow true pumpkins, and I have not taken up space to describe specific varieties. However, if you do try a few plants, all the information in this chapter on planting and cultural procedure applies equally well to them.)

HISTORY: The history of squash is of particular interest to us because it is one of the few vegetables that had its origin in America. The squash and pumpkin grown today were common food crops of the Indians not only when the first explorers landed in this country but, according to archeological research, for many centuries previous. Pieces of rind and seeds have been discovered in the ruins of cliff dwellings which belong to a period dating back to 1500–2000 B.C. Seeds have been found in ancient tombs and burial bowls, and the flower is the Hopi Indian emblem of fertility. The name "squash" itself has its derivation in an Indian word.

The first explorers found the Indians growing squash in such widely scattered places as Florida, New England, Virginia, the St. Lawrence Valley, the Southwest, the Dakotas, Central America, and Peru. An early Dutch writer about 1650 wrote: "The natives have another species of this vegetable peculiar to themselves, called by our people *quasiens* [squash], a name derived from the aborigines, as the plant was not known to us before our intercourse with them. It is a delightful fruit, as well to the eye on account of its fine variety of colors, as to the mouth for its agreeable taste. They do not wait for it to ripen before making use of the fruit, but only until it has attained a certain size. They gather the squashes, and immediately place them on the fire without any further trouble."

Allusions to the various members of this family, squash, pumpkin, and gourds, run all through the writings of the earliest explorers and colonists.

Food Value: Squash is an excellent source of vitamin A (especially Hubbard squash) and a fair source of vitamins B_1 and C.

Culture: Squash is a very tender, warm-weather crop that does not germinate or grow well during cool weather and is killed by frost. It is propagated by seed sown in the garden where the plant is to grow and is a relatively easy crop to raise. The plant matures in 8 to 18 weeks, depending upon the type and variety. This means that the harvest period is prolonged; and, since squash can be both stored and canned, the actual use of the crop can be made to extend from the middle of the summer throughout the entire winter.

However, squash does have two essential requirements. First, it must be sown when the ground has warmed up and the entire growing period must take place within a frost-free period. In sections of the North where this frost-free period is short the quick-maturing summer squash rather than the slow-maturing winter variety should be planted. Second, it must have a rich soil. All the members of this large family make a widespread, lush growth and need nutrients to further it. That necessitates some special feeding. The lush growth also means that the trailing type of squash takes up a considerable amount of room. This need not necessarily be vegetable garden space, since the plant can be seeded alongside your flower garden and the vines can trail over the edge of your lawn, or they can be trained to grow along a fence.

Habits of Growth: There are two kinds of squash plants, the bush and the vining. Both are very tender annuals with large leaves; the flowers produce fruits which are the edible portion of the plant.

Three to eight lateral branches arise close to the base of the main stem. In the bush kind the stems are fairly short and half erect, but they tend to spread; in the vining kind the stems are so long and trailing that attention is required to keep them within bounds. The stems produce tendrils, and the vining kind will climb if you give it the opportunity. The flowering period lasts several weeks. Only certain flowers, however, form fruits. In the bush kind, which is quick maturing, the plant may set half a dozen or more fruits, which are harvested when they are tender skinned and immature and weigh 1–2 pounds. The vining kind sets two or three large fruits which may weigh up to 50 pounds but which usually are considerably smaller. These fruits should grow to maturity and be harvested when the rind is hard.

The surface of the fruit is sometimes smooth, sometimes furrowed, sometimes warty. There is a great difference in both size and color between varieties.

Types and Varieties: Only the two generally grown types of squash will be described, the so-called summer squash and winter squash, ignoring pumpkins. There are numerous divisions of the two main types.

Summer or *bush* squash. This is quick-maturing squash for the table and includes some universally liked varieties. The old crookneck squash has been replaced by straightneck varieties, which are the same except for the shape.

VARIETIES: *Early Yellow Prolific* is a recent and excellent dwarf variety. The fruit is about 14 inches long, smooth, straight and a bright lemon-yellow color. The plant matures in 50–60 days and is a prolific producer. A larger variety of the same order is *Giant Summer Straightneck*. The fruit is the same color but about 19 inches long, thicker and warted. *Early Bush Scallop*, Patty Pan, or "Cymling" (maturity, 55 days), gives a fruit shaped like a saucer with scalloped edges. It is about 7–8 inches in diameter and is available in either white or yellow varieties. *Cocozelle*, or *Italian Vegetable Marrow*, has an elliptical fruit about 12–14 inches long and 4–5 inches in diameter. The skin is smooth and dark green, with lighter green and yellow marbling. This has a delicate and delicious flavor and is highly recommended. It takes over 60–65 days to mature.

Another intermediate type of early squash, one of the best tasting of all but little known and appreciated here, is the *English Vegetable Marrow*. The plant is of the vining kind, but the fruit can be used when it is half grown, as with most summer squash, and it can be harvested in about 60 days. The plant is a prolific producer. (In fact, in England, my father-in-law had 39 fruit from one plant and wrote to me that the end wasn't at hand then.) If you don't know these marrows, grow at least one or two plants as an experiment.

Winter or *vine* squash. This type has large fruit with a richer, heartier, and some people think a better, flavor than the bush type. This type is usually suitable for storing and canning.

VARIETIES: The *Hubbard* varieties of winter squash are the old standard and still good. The fruit is hard skinned and heavily warted, weighs 12–14 pounds, and usually has a dark bronze-green tough rind; and the flesh is orange-yellow, dry, sweet, and rich. Hubbard varieties are very good keepers and should stay in good condition all winter. It takes about 16–17 weeks for the various Hubbard varieties to mature. *Golden Delicious* is one of the best varieties of winter squash for canning because of the very dry flesh. It is also good for table use. The fruit is shaped like a top, has orange skin and flesh, weighs about 7 pounds, and matures in 14–15 weeks. *Boston Marrow* resembles the Hubbard squash but is smaller (weighing 6–9 pounds), matures quite early (requiring only 14 weeks), and has an orange skin and an excellent taste, which makes it well liked at the table and very popular with canners. *Buttercup* (maturity, about 15 weeks) is a new variety which has proved a worthy addition to the list of good winter squash. The fruit is small, 4–5 pounds, with an unusual shape, and the flesh is dry and sweet. *Table Queen* (*Des Moines* or *Little Acorn*) is a winter squash variety which is deservedly very popular for baking. The fruit is shaped like an acorn, and has a thick, dark green, ribbed rind and a yellow flesh. These little squashes are about 7 inches long and 3–4 inches thick. When split and baked with some butter, they taste very much like yams. They mature in about 11–12 weeks. They are usually grown to be harvested in the fall and are suitable for storing. Also they can be planted for summer harvesting. The vines are runners and very prolific.

If you have the room and the curiosity, grow a vine or two of a squash called *Vegetable Spaghetti*. The fruit is about 10 inches long and 5 inches in diameter and is ready to be picked in 8½ weeks. When it is cooked it presents quite a surprise because the center is filled with a pulp very much like spaghetti, long and stringlike. It has a fine taste after it has been seasoned properly.

How Much to Buy:

Summer, 1 package for   8–10 hills
          1 ounce   for 25–30 hills
Winter, 1 package for   3– 4 hills
          1 ounce   for   15 hills

The average small garden does not have much room for many squash plants, but if possible a few hills of different varieties should be grown. The Hubbard squash belongs more on farms and estates because of the size of the plant. A small garden could have 2 or 3 hills of Cocozelle or Patty Pan, 1 hill of Vegetable Marrow and

1 or 2 hills of Acorn trailing over the lawn. Whatever your choice, get 2 or 3 packages of various types, even if you only have 1 hill of each—packages of seed do not cost much, and even with a single hill you will more than get your money back.

Planting:

Germination time: 8–10 days.

Depth for seed: 1 inch.

Spacing: Squash is commonly grown in "hills," which are squares of ground that may be raised up a foot or so in the center where the seeds are planted. The bush or vine is allowed to spread in all directions. The size of the hill for bush varieties should be 4 feet square, and for trailing varieties from 8 to 10 feet square. Bush varieties can also be grown in rows 4 feet apart, with the plants spaced 3 feet apart in the rows.

When to Plant:

	EARLY CROP	LATE CROP
	Earliest Safe Date for Planting Seed in Garden	*Latest Safe Date for Planting Seed in Garden*
Zone A.	March 1 – March 15	Summer type – Oct. 1
		Winter " – —
" B.	March 15 – April 1	Summer " – Sept. 1
		Winter " – —
" C.	April 1 – April 15	Summer " – Aug. 15
		Winter " – July 15
" D.	April 15 – May 1	Summer " – Aug. 1
		Winter " – July 1
" E.	May 1 – June 1	Summer " – July 15
		Winter " – June 15
" F.	June 1 – June 15	Summer " – July 1
		Winter " – June 15
" G.	June 1 – June 15	Summer " – June 15
		Winter " – June 15

(See maps at back of book showing locations of zones for spring and fall frosts. Remember that the boundaries of the spring frost zones are not the same as those of the fall frost zones, and your locality may be in different zones for the spring and fall frosts. If you live in the West outside the zones, for an approximate guide take the frost dates in your individual locality, find similar frost dates in one of the zones, and use the corresponding dates for that zone.)

Squash must not be planted until the weather is settled and the ground is warm. The seed will rot in cold soil, and it germinates best at quite a high temperature. Summer and winter squash can both be planted at the same time in the spring on the early-crop planting dates given above. Summer squash will mature in the summer, while the winter squash will mature in the fall in time to be harvested for storing. In the South a fall crop of summer squash can be planted for a harvest before frost; and, in all states where the frost-free season is long enough, a second planting of summer squash can be made in the late summer for harvesting before frost. Generally speaking, though, in most parts of the country squash is regarded as a one-season crop.

How to Plant: A small amount of commercial fertilizer or a shovelful of well-rotted manure should be put into the center of each hill, preferably a week or so before planting, and covered with 3-4 inches of earth. Then 10 or 12 seeds should be planted in this earth, in a circle 12 inches in diameter, and covered with an inch of dirt. When the plants are well along and you are quite sure that the beetles are not going to do your thinning for you, thin to 1 plant per hill for the bush varieties and 2 for the trailing varieties. If the bush varieties are planted in rows, sow the seed thickly and then thin so that the plants stand 3 feet apart in rows that are about 4 feet apart.

If an especially early crop is desired, seed can be started a month earlier than the above outdoor planting dates either in a hotbed, in a greenhouse, or in the house. Squash plants do not take kindly to transplanting, and if the roots are disturbed in any way, or if the earth is removed from around them, the plant probably will either not survive or will not set fruit properly. Therefore, the seed must be sown in some form of container which will hold the roots in a solid mass that can be transplanted together with a considerable amount of soil. Six-inch flower pots or strawberry baskets are good. Sow 5 or 6 seeds and before they get too crowded thin to 1 plant. This special seeding is not necessary and is usually attempted only by truck gardeners who can get a high price for early fruit, or by extremely ambitious gardeners who have a greenhouse for special seedings.

Where to Plant: Care has to be exercised in choosing a spot for squash, especially the trailing kind, because the growth is often so rampant that it may overpower small vegetables near by. If there is room, the trailing crop should be planted outside the garden proper. Pumpkin and squash are often grown between rows of corn. This is a good place for them in a large garden. If they cannot be segregated, put them in a corner or along the edge of the main garden so that they can trail over your lawn instead of your carrots. The bush varieties stay within decent limits and are respectable members of the garden proper. The trailing varieties occupy the land for the remainder of the season once they are planted, but an early crop of spinach or lettuce could be grown before they are planted. The same crops could precede the bush varieties, and there might be time after harvesting for a quick crop of spinach or radishes.

Soil: Squash will grow in any type of soil, but it grows best in a well-drained but moist, warm, rich soil containing plenty of humus. So with all vine crops, they should make a rapid continuous growth; and two or three forkfuls of well-rotted manure used to be considered a prime necessity for feeding the plant during growth. It still is good if you can get it and can afford it, but satisfactory results can be obtained from the use of a commercial fertilizer worked into the soil around the roots in the center of the hill when the plant is well along.

Cultivation and Care: Cultivation should begin soon after the plants have shown above the ground and continue until the vines start covering the ground. The root system is large and grows rapidly, filling in the upper 6 or 8 inches of soil. The cultivation therefore should be shallow; and, as the plant grows, weed removal is all that is necessary. When the vines start to run well, all you can do is hand-weed the big ones.

The only special care the plants need is protection from the attacks of striped cucumber beetles. If routine treatment is not sufficient, try a calcium arsenate spray after rain, or the special method described on page 101 for cucumbers.

Harvesting: The harvesting of both types of squash is the same and is simply a matter of pulling the fruit from the vines, making sure that you have left a piece of the stem attached. This stem is important because if it is removed a scar is left in the fruit through which decay can penetrate. Decay also starts from any injury or bruise; hence, great care must be used in all handling of squash, particularly if it is to be stored.

The harvesting of summer and winter types of squash is not done at the same period of development. The summer squash is harvested when it is young and small, the seeds inside have not hardened, and the rind is so tender that it can readily be punctured by a thumbnail. Usually this is when the fruit is about half grown. When the fruit is once set, it grows rapidly and will be ready to harvest in 3 to 5 days. Therefore, watch it and harvest regularly and often. Winter squash, on the other hand, is allowed to stay in the field until the rind is hard and thick, the plant is fully mature, and the vines have been killed by a light frost, but before hard frost can affect the fruit. The sugar content increases as the fruit becomes thoroughly ripe and the squash will keep much better.

Storing: Winter squash is quite an easy crop to store. It will keep for five or six months if stored at a temperature of 40°–50° F. and with a low humidity of 30–50 per cent. Any warm, dry, well-ventilated place will do—a shelf in the cellar or a heated attic. There should be a good circulation of air, and it is best if the squashes are in a single layer not touching one another. Store only squashes that are free from bruises and that have been ripened for several days after harvesting either in the garden, if the weather is warm and sunny, or in a well-heated, dry room. This ripening hardens the shell.

Canning: Winter squash can also be canned, primarily for use in pies. For canning directions see the chapter on "Canning."

Uses: In general, summer squash can be eaten either boiled or fried. When they are very young and tender, as they are when you pick your own directly from the bush, they can be boiled whole without even paring the skin and served with butter, salt, and pepper. If the fruit is too large to be boiled whole, slice without paring, and then boil. It is customary to mash the squash if it is not served whole. A few tablespoonfuls of cream make a good dish perfect. To fry, merely cut the squash into slices about ½ inch in size, dip the slices into flour, shake off any surplus, and fry in butter until browned. Italian squash is often cooked in Italian style by frying in olive oil. This can be served sprinkled with some freshly grated Parmesan cheese.

Summer squash can also be baked in a casserole. Cut the squash into slices; cover with salt, pepper, and cream; top with buttered bread crumbs; and bake until browned.

Vegetable Marrow is cut into pieces, boiled, and served either with plain butter or with a cream sauce. Both the marrow and the large summer squash make a hearty main-course luncheon dish when they are stuffed. The fruit is split in half lengthwise, the seeds and membrane are removed, and it is parboiled for five minutes. Heat 2 tablespoonfuls of butter in a saucepan, and add a minced onion, about 2 cupfuls of bread crumbs, some chopped parsley, and half a cup of ground cooked ham. Bind it with a beaten egg, season and fill the shells with the mixture, and bake until browned. Or the center can be filled with any creamed left-over vegetables, such as carrots, peas, or onions.

The large winter squash is cut up in pieces, the seeds and stringy center are removed, and the pieces are either boiled or steamed. Or they can be seasoned and spread with melted butter and baked. A little brown sugar adds to the flavor. Bacon or thin slices of cooked ham can be spread over the squash. Acorn squash is simply split and baked, with a little sugar, seasoning, and a lump of butter.

24. Tomatoes

(*Lycopersicon esculentum. Solanaceae,*
nightshade family.)

HISTORY: Tomatoes seem to have originated in Central or South America. The name itself comes from an Aztec word, *Zitomate*. The plant was grown by Indians in Mexico and Peru long before the time of Columbus. It was taken from Peru to Italy, where it met with favor. There it was called "golden apple" and "love apple," but by 1695 the name "tomato" had come into general use. When the cultivation of the plant first started in northern Europe, the fruit was considered poisonous and was grown more for curiosity and ornament than for use. The English herbalist Gerarde wrote in 1595 that "love apples" were eaten abroad, prepared and boiled with pepper, salt, and oil and also as a sauce, but he reported that they "yield very little nourishment to the bodie, and the same naught and corrupt."

The first written mention of tomatoes in the United States was made by Thomas Jefferson in 1781, but they were not grown commonly for use even then. Some time later, the secretary of the Connecticut Board of Agriculture wrote: "We raised our first tomatoes about 1832 as a curiosity, made no use of them, though we had heard that the French ate them. They were called love apples." By about 1835 culinary use had become more general, although many people still considered them poisonous,

This attitude is particularly interesting in view of the enormous popularity that tomatoes enjoy today. They are the third leading truck crop, exceeded only by potatoes and sweet potatoes and are the most important canning crop in the country and the most generally grown home-garden vegetable. Two million tons are used annually simply by the canneries. In view of the importance of tomatoes in the diet, they should be an indispensable crop in every home garden.

———————◆•◆———————

Food Value: Red tomatoes are an excellent source of vitamins A and C and a good source of vitamin B_1. Yellow tomatoes are an excellent source of vitamin C and a good source of vitamins A and B_1. It should be noted that canning does not affect the vitamin content of tomatoes, so that both canned tomatoes and canned tomato juice are as valuable in the diet as fresh tomatoes are.

Culture: Tomatoes are a tender, warm-season, long-maturing crop. The plants thrive best when the temperature is about 65°–85° F., and they can stand higher temperatures, although the fruit will not be quite so red as usual. When young they fare very badly in cool, damp weather, and they may be so retarded that they will fail to set fruit properly. A temperature below freezing will usually kill them at any stage of their growth.

Tomato plants require 4–5 months to produce mature fruit from the first seedings. Once the first fruit is set, the plant should continue producing until killed by frost in the North, even for another 2–3 months where the frost-free season is very long. Outdoor seed planting in most parts of the country is either impossible or not feasible because it drastically limits the potential crop. Tomatoes are a special seedbed crop requiring either hotbed, indoor, or cold-frame planting.

This special seeding means that tomatoes cannot be rightly classed as an easy crop to grow because special seeding always demands some skill. But once the plants are set in the garden, their culture is very simple since they grow readily and produce abundantly. And the problem of providing sound plants can always be solved by buying them from a commercial grower; the market is usually flooded with plants in the spring. They are quite inexpensive; 20 or 25 cents should buy a dozen good plants of a named variety.

Habits of Growth: The plant produces a main stem which grows erect until it is a foot or two tall and then falls over unless staked. Many lateral stems form in every leaf axil, although they do not all necessarily develop. Since these lateral stems have secondary laterals, the plant is finally very branched and leafy. The leaves are 5 to 18 inches long; the foliage is a grayish green and has a strong characteristic scent. The stems are round, soft, and brittle at first; but as the plant becomes old the stems get hard and woody.

The flowers are followed by the fruit, which is a red or yellow berry and is usually nearly round, solid, and smooth. Tomatoes in former days used to be ribbed; but plant breeders have been working diligently, with the result that most tomatoes today have a completely smooth skin. The plant, if left to its own devices, produces fruit from many of its lateral stems, and picking the fruit regularly stimulates further production.

Types and Varieties: The two main types of modern tomatoes are the regular large size, of which most of the varieties are red, and the small novelty tomatoes, both red and yellow, which resemble in size and shape the fruits they are named for (cherry, pear, and so on).

Large-fruited type:

The number of good, recommended varieties today is small, 10 or 15 at most; but formerly there were a staggering number listed by seedsmen. Many of them were synonymous and the choice was correspondingly difficult. In 1902, for instance, seedsmen listed 327 varieties.

This type is divided into three groups, the *early*, the *second early* or *midseason*, and the *late*.

Early. The early varieties are the smallest and the quickest to mature.

VARIETIES: *Bonny Best* and *Earliana* are the two leading red varieties; and *June Pink*, the best pink. They mature in 65 to 70 days after the plants are set in the field and should be used if early fruit is wanted. The quality and size of the fruit are below those of the later varieties. Of the three, Bonny Best is the preferred variety.

Midseason. The midseason group includes some of the best tomatoes grown.

VARIETIES: *Marglobe* (75 days) is undoubtedly one of the finest tomatoes on the market, and the new variety *Rutgers* (85 days) is proving excellent. *Pritchard* (75 days) is another good choice.

Late. The late varieties include *Stone Certified* (85 days), a very popular variety for canning; *Greater Baltimore Certified* (80 days), a good canning variety for the South and Middle West because of its resistance to extreme heat and drought; and *Ponderosa* (85 days), a huge beefsteak-type tomato. The standard large yellow tomato is *Golden Queen*, which matures in about 85 days.

Small-fruited type:

These tiny tomatoes are interesting to grow for salads and preserves, for pickling, and simply for curiosity and pleasure. The fruits are an inch or so in diameter, are borne in clusters, and are very prolific.

All varieties are equally good. Your choice depends upon the shape you prefer: *Red Cherry, Yellow Cherry-Red, Yellow Pear, Red Plum, Yellow Plum, Red Currant, Yellow Peach.* They require 70–75 days to mature.

How Much to Buy:

1 package for 100 plants
1 ounce for 1000 plants

Tomatoes are a vital part of the diet. Either oranges or tomatoes should be eaten every day for their vitamin C content. Since the home gardener can grow tomatoes and can't grow oranges (except in a very few states), the family should be served tomatoes in some form at least three or four times a week. Various agricultural experiment stations recommend 18–25 plants for each member of the family for a year's supply, including table, canning, and tomato juice. The major part of the crop should be a first-class variety, such as *Marglobe* or *Rutgers,* and some of a good canning variety, such as *Stone Certified.* To vary salads and meals in summer, a few plants of *Golden Queen* and one plant of the small-fruited type can be grown.

Planting:

Germination time: 8–10 days.

Depth for seed: ¼ inch.

Spacing of plants: 18 inches to 4 feet, depending upon method of growing. (See Cultivation and Care.)

Spacing of rows: *Early,* 3 feet.
Late, 4 feet.

When to Plant:

	EARLY CROP	LATE CROP
	Earliest Safe Date for Setting Plants in Garden	*Latest Safe Date for Setting Plants in Garden*
Zone A.	March 1 – March 15	Oct. 1
" B.	March 15 – April 1	Sept. 1
" C.	April 1 – April 15	Aug. 15
" D.	April 15 – May 1	July 15
" E.	May 1 – June 1	July 1
" F.	June 1 – June 15	June 15
" G.	June 15 – June 30	–

(See maps at back of book showing locations of zones for spring and fall frosts. Remember that the boundaries of the spring frost zones are not the same as those of the fall frost zones, and your locality may be in different zones for the spring and fall frosts. If you live in the West outside the zones, for an approximate guide take the frost dates in your individual locality, find similar frost dates in one of the zones, and use the corresponding dates for that zone.)

Tomatoes are a one-season crop. It takes this plant 4–5 months from the date of seed sowing to produce fruit, and harvesting lasts for several months after the production of fruit has once started. This lengthy season precludes more than one crop except in the South, where a late fall planting can be made for a canning supply. In general, tomatoes are seeded in a hotbed, in a cold frame, or in the house 8–10 weeks before the date for outdoor planting; and they are not planted outdoors until the weather has warmed up. Nothing is to be gained by setting the plants out when the weather is still cool because they will do little growing then. On the other hand, do not delay outdoor planting unduly because late planting shortens the season. As soon as the chances of a frost are past and the nights are warm, plant your tomatoes, as close to the earliest safe planting date as possible.

In the few frost-free sections of the country, tomatoes can be grown during the winter.

How to Plant: If you grow your own plants, the seed must be sown in a special seedbed, preferably 6–8 weeks before the date for outdoor planting. The easiest way for the home gardener to handle the seed is to plant it indoors in a flat. If your indoor facilities are limited but you want to try your luck on some seed, tomatoes are probably the best ones to experiment with. Almost everyone has a sunny window where a flat can go, and the heat usually found in modern homes, which is fatal to many other seedling plants, is good for tomatoes.

Sow the seed in rows 2 inches apart in a flat, or 6 inches apart if you are using a hotbed. When the seedlings show their first true leaves, transplant. The simplest method is to transplant only once, either in flats, to stand 4 inches apart, or in individual pots, paper containers, or tin cans. Some growers transplant twice, the first time to 2 inches apart both ways, the second to the distances given above. But this intermediate transplanting is necessary only if you do not have room for the additional flats or individual containers.

The plants should never be allowed to become crowded and pot bound. If the leaves start to turn yellow and some of the lower leaves drop and fall, the plant will get woody and will probably not be much good when it is set in the garden. A good plant will be stocky and about as broad as it is long, and it will have a faint purplish tinge. The best height at which plants should be set out is about 6–10 inches.

If your plants grow any taller than this indoors, pinch out the terminal bud.

When you are setting the plants in the garden, plant them deep, up to the first pair of leaves. If the plant looks leggy and spindly, remove two or three pairs of leaves, and set the plant up to the remaining leaves; it will form roots along the stem portion that is under the ground, and deep planting means more roots and therefore a stronger plant.

If you buy plants, be sure that you get a named variety from a reliable source and that the plants are stocky, a healthy color, and not too tall.

Where to Plant: Tomatoes require much space, no matter how you grow them, and occupy the land the whole season. For these reasons they should be put in a section of the garden where they can grow at will without interfering with other garden activities, either at one end or with the other all-season, space-consuming vegetables.

Soil: Tomatoes will produce fruit of some sort on almost any kind of soil, but ideally they need a soil that is dug deep because they have quite a large root system. They also need some fertilizer, but not so much that the plant will tend to grow rampant vines and fail to set fruit. Well-rotted manure is good, fresh manure is not. A not too generous application of a complete fertilizer stimulates the plant into satisfactory production. The application of 3 or 4 pounds per 100 square feet either can be made all at once a week or ten days before planting or can be divided into four doses: one, a week or ten days before planting; one, a month after setting the plants out; one, when the plants have been in the ground for two months and are blooming and setting fruit; and the last when the plants are bearing fruit.

Cultivation and Care: The cultivation should be regular and shallow. Keep the weeds down and the soil loose. But, since the roots grow close to the surface, the cultivation must not go deep enough to harm them. Weed control is the prime requirement in cultivation.

Tomatoes will sprawl if not supported. There is much controversy in garden circles as to whether the plants should be allowed to grow at will or whether they should be curbed and restrained. Many growers, especially canners who sell tomatoes for $10 to $15 a ton and have no money to waste on extra labor, let their plants grow unpruned and unstaked. Time and labor are saved, and the plants produce abundantly even if the fruit is inclined to be small.

To protect the fruit, conserve space, and ensure larger fruit, home gardeners had better stake their plants. This can be done either by driving a single pole into the ground for each plant before planting (after planting there is danger of damage to roots) or by putting posts in the ground every 15 feet in the row and stringing two wires between them, one close to the top and one about 6 feet from the ground. Heavy twine should be strung perpendicularly between the wires. When single stakes are used, the plant is simply tied with raffia or soft twine, tight enough to support the branches but not so tight that they will be unable to grow or will be cut. When wire and twine are used, the stems are wrapped around the twine and tied in a few places to secure their position.

Staked tomato plants should be pruned. The severest type of pruning consists of limiting the plant to one central stem. All the side shoots are pinched out when two leaves have been formed; and, since there is little branch and leaf production, all the strength of the plant can go into the fruit. The fruit will be earlier than on unstaked plants, and much larger. There will also be much less fruit. This severe type of pruning is recommended only if you want very early and especially large fruit for a particular purpose. This method is often used by commercial growers because the early bird catches the biggest price. But home gardeners would do well to confine their pruning to cutting out the suckers (the productive axillary shoots between the stems and the leaves) and, in extreme cases, to limiting the plant to two or three stems.

The advantages of staking are that the fruit is larger and easier to spray and that the plants can be close together. Plants pruned to single stems need only 18 inches of space each. Also, since the sun reaches the fruit easily, the fruit matures more quickly and will not decay easily.

Either method of planting will give you plenty of fruit. Both have advantages and disadvantages. For the home gardener, I should advise staking and pruning of suckers (with severe pruning only if you go in for exhibitions).

If your tomatoes are attacked by corn-ear worms, pick them off if there are not too many, or spray or dust with calcium arsenate.

Harvesting: Harvesting simply consists of picking the fruit from the vine when it is fully ripe. Do not take any of the stem with the fruit because the stubs may puncture other tomatoes in the harvesting basket. Many tomatoes bought in the market are picked green and ripened later, but the flavor is much better when the fruit ripens on the vine. Once the fruit is red and ripe, though, it does not remain firm very long, especially in hot weather. So the harvesting should not be delayed.

Storing: Ripe tomatoes do not keep well, 10 days at most if the temperature is around 40° F.

But there are several ways of saving green tomatoes that have not ripened before frost. In the first place, in the North there is often one early frost in the fall, followed by three or four weeks before there is any more nipping weather. Therefore, if a frost threatens, cover your tomato plants with burlap and thus you may be able to keep them for a few weeks longer.

If you decide that the early frost is going to be a hard one that marks the definite end of mild weather, you can pick the remaining green fruit and store it at 50°–60° F. for at least a month, probably longer. Go over the fruit every 2 or 3 days and use the ones that have ripened.

Or you can pull up the whole plant with the green fruit on it and hang it upside down from the rafters in the attic. The fruit gets some nourishment from the plant and keeps on maturing.

Canning: Canning is the chief way of preserving tomatoes for the winter table. If possible, an ample supply should be canned of both whole tomatoes and tomato juice. For canning directions see the chapter on "Canning."

Uses: Every housewife probably believes that she knows enough ways to prepare tomatoes and needs no further instruction. And yet a writer in 1840 mentions these culinary freaks: "Beside the various modes of preparing this delicious vegetable for the table, it may be preserved in sugar and used either as a dessert, or on the tea-table, or as a substitute for peaches or other sweet meats. It also makes exquisite pies and tarts."

A pamphlet issued by Tuskegee Institute lists 115 ways of preparing tomatoes. There are without doubt many other recipes; so any sort of detailed discussion would be beyond the limits of this book. We shall merely include two recipes for rather unusual ways of preserving tomatoes for winter use.

Peel and quarter ½ bushel of ripe tomatoes. Chop fine 18 carrots, 2 heads of cabbage, 12 small white onions, 4 green peppers, 4 sweet red peppers, and 4 hot red peppers. Cut 4 quarts of string beans into thin slices and boil for 5 minutes. Also cook a dozen ears of corn for 5 minutes and cut the corn from the cob. Mix all these vegetables and add 1¼ cupfuls of salt. Cook the entire mixture until it reaches the boiling point; pack it into sterilized pint jars; partially seal and cook in a pressure cooker at 10 pounds pressure for 70 minutes. This is good as a vegetable course, in soups, or in stews.

Put 1 peck of green tomatoes and 6 seeded lemons through your food chopper. Add 7 pounds of sugar and let it simmer for about 4 hours. Put into hot jars and seal. This is called "tomato marmalade" and is delicious and unusual—and a good way to use up green tomatoes in the fall.

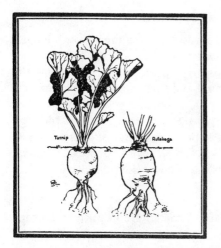

Turnip   Rutabaga

25.
Turnips and Rutabagas

(Brassica rapa; Brassica napobrassica. Cruciferae, mustard family.)

HISTORY: The turnip has been in cultivation for hundreds of years and it grows wild in Europe from the Baltic Sea to the Caucasus. In A.D. 42 a writer stated that this vegetable was eaten by both men and animals; Pliny mentioned five different kinds of turnips and said that one root weighed 40 pounds. (This great weight, however, has often been equaled and exceeded in modern times; in California in 1850 there is a record of a root of 100 pounds weight.) Turnips are mentioned frequently in the writings of herbalists in Europe and England. In England this vegetable was used in armorial bearings to represent a kind-dispositioned person who relieved the poor. The cultivation of turnips in this country dates back to the seventeenth century, and in 1612 the first settlers in Virginia suffered from scurvy until they were able to get relief from the turnip crop they cultivated.

Rutabagas (Swedish turnips or Lapland turnips) were first introduced into England toward the end of the eighteenth century and in American gardens in 1806. Its name implies an origin either in Sweden itself or in some part of northern Europe.

———

Food Value: Turnip tops or greens are one of the richest vegetable sources of health-building vitamins and minerals. They are an excellent source of vitamins A, C, and G, and a good source of vitamin B_1. They are also an excellent source of iron and calcium.

Turnips themselves (that is, the roots) are an excellent source of vitamin C, a fair source of vitamin B_1, and a good source of calcium.

Rutabagas are an excellent source of vitamin C and a good source of calcium.

Culture: Both turnips and rutabagas are of very simple culture. They belong to the same genus, *Brassica*, and have the same general requirements and appearance, differing only in minor matters of root shape and leaf structure.

They are both hardy, cool-weather, partial-season root crops. They will grow in any soil, are seeded in the garden where they are to stand, germinate and grow with speed, and require very little care.

Turnips mature in about 2 months, rutabagas require a month longer. They are the most generally grown of all the root crops. Many people are inclined to disparage them, often condemning the taste as bitter and strong. Sometimes old roots bought in the markets justify that assertion, but fresh roots from the garden have a most succulent and appealing flavor. Any one who eats a bought rutabaga covered with the wax often used to preserve them just does not know what the vegetable really tastes like. These vegetables are economical on space and extremely good to eat. They belong in every garden, even small ones.

Habits of Growth: These two vegetables are biennial root crops which produce both leaves and enlarged tap roots during the first year and flowers and seeds the second year. Both the roots and the tops, or "greens," of turnips can be eaten. (Rutabaga tops are not very palatable.) Young tops are best. The shape of the root may be conical or round. The major part of it may be either white or yellow fleshed, while the top of the root may be white, yellow, green, or purple. The roots vary in size from about 4 inches across to 8 or 12 inches. They will grow larger, but they are usually harvested before they get too big.

Turnips are smaller in size than rutabagas and mature more quickly; they have dark green, somewhat hairy leaves. Rutabagas are oval shaped and generally longer than turnips. They have a thick, elongated neck and greenish-blue, smooth foliage. The flesh is deep yellow, firm, generally richer and more succulent than turnips.

Types and Varieties: The main distinction between varieties of these vegetables is in the color of the top of the root. Since these differences are relatively unimportant from the point of growing the roots, it is not worth elaborating them. The varieties are few. Two are outstanding. *Purple Top White Globe* is the best turnip, *American Purple Top Yellow* the best rutabaga. *Snowball* is a pure-white turnip of attractive appearance and fine quality. *Seven Top* is the best variety of turnip to use if you are interested in greens because it produces abundant foliage and tiny roots.

How Much to Buy:

        1 package for   50 feet
        1 ounce   for 200 feet

If possible, every garden should have at least one row of turnips in the spring and one in the fall, with a planting of rutabagas for fall harvesting. They are so hardy that they can stay in the ground until hard frosts are due and can therefore keep the table supplied late into the fall.

Planting:

Germination time: 4–7 days.

Depth for seed: ½ inch.

Spacing of plants: *Early turnips,* 3 inches.
Late turnips, 4–8 inches, depending upon whether you are going to eat them young or let them grow large for storage.
Rutabagas, 8–12 inches.

Spacing of rows: *Turnips,* 12 inches.
Rutabagas, 20 inches.

When to Plant:

	EARLY CROP	LATE CROP
	Earliest Safe Date for Planting Seed in Garden	*Latest Safe Date for Planting Seed in Garden*
Zone A.	Jan. 1 – Feb. 1	Nov. 15
" B.	Feb. 1 – Feb. 15	Nov. 1
" C.	Feb. 15 – March 1	Oct. 15
" D.	March 1 – March 15	Sept. 1
" E.	March 15 – April 15	Aug. 1
" F.	April 15 – May 1	July 15
" G.	May 1 – May 15	July 1

(See maps at back of book showing locations of zones for spring and fall frosts. Remember that the boundaries of the spring frost zones are not the same as those of the fall frost zones, and your locality may be in different zones for the spring and fall frosts. If you live in the West outside the zones, for an approximate guide take the frost dates in your individual locality, find similar frost dates in one of the zones, and use the corresponding dates for that zone.)

It should always be remembered, when planting dates for these crops are being figured out, that they are both cool-season crops and that rutabagas require a month longer than turnips to mature. In the South they are both usually planted in the fall for winter and early spring harvesting. Late winter plantings may give turnips time to mature while the weather is still cool, but rutabagas are a risky gamble. In the North turnips should be planted in the spring, just as early as the soil can be worked. Delayed planting may mean harvesting when the weather has turned warm, and hot weather makes turnips tough and bitter. Don't worry about the frost, do worry about letting the heat catch up with them. Rutabagas do not have time in the spring to reach an eating stage before the weather gets warm. Therefore they are generally planted in the summer, as late as possible, because brisk cool nights make them sweet. But they should be given the three months they need to reach maturity before frost. They will stand a light frost, but they should be harvested before hard frost. The crop can be eaten or stored.

Another crop of turnips can be sown in the fall, 2 or 2½ months before the first frost dates, for a late eating supply and a supply for storage. In sections of the North where the summers stay cool, you can plant every two weeks for a continual supply.

The latest dates for planting given above are right for turnips, but put your rutabagas in a month or six weeks earlier.

How to Plant: The seed is sown ½ inch deep in the row where it is to mature. The seed should be sown thin, and thinned out soon and drastically.

The thinning is usually done when the young plants are big enough to cook as greens. They are good used this way, especially if a piece of bacon or salt pork is put in the water they are cooked in. Don't wait until the plants are so crowded that they push one another out of shape and place. The early turnips need only about 3 inches apiece, the late ones 4–8 inches, depending upon whether you are going to eat them when they are still quite small or allow them to grow large for storage. Rutabagas, being considerably larger, need 8–12 inches.

Where to Plant: Both are short-season crops which can be fitted very well into succession plantings. The early turnips can be followed by any of the late crops, such as beets, cabbage, carrots, or potatoes. The late plantings of rutabagas and turnips can be preceded by lettuce, spinach, beets, carrots, or early cabbage.

Soil: Turnips and rutabagas need to grow quickly to be good. That means a light, sandy, well-drained soil, the sort in which all root crops thrive best. The soil should be well pulverized, and there should be sufficient moisture. Everything should be made easy for the plants to get a good, speedy growth. They do not require an especially rich soil, so you can let them follow another crop without any additional fertilizing.

Cultivation and Care: Cultivation consists of nothing more than ordinary garden routine—weeding and hoeing. The tops grow rampant, and even routine cultivation is eliminated once the tops have covered the ground. The only special care required is to thin out the seedlings properly.

Turnips and rutabagas may be attacked by cabbage worms, but these usually do not warrant any special measures since the plants will not suffer if a few of the abundant leaves are destroyed.

Harvesting: As with all fast-growing vegetables, turnips and rutabagas should be harvested promptly, or the peak of their flavor and sweetness is lost and you are faced with a definitely inferior product, which wipes out all the point of raising your own crop.

Early turnips are pulled when they are about 3 inches in diameter. The fall crop matures when the weather is cool, and it can stay in the ground a longer time. Turnips either can be harvested when they have been in the ground for 2 months or can be left until just before the hard frosts. Rutabagas are usually allowed to stay in the ground until there has been a light frost, but they should be harvested before the ground is frozen hard.

All the harvesting is done by pulling the roots out by hand.

Storing: Late turnips and rutabagas can be successfully stored during the winter under proper conditions. However, they keep best at freezing temperature or slightly lower, but alternate freezing and thawing ruin them. They can be stored the same way as beets and carrots in a cellar storage room if the temperature stays around freezing. However, they are better adapted for keeping in an outside storage room or pit (see the chapter on "Storing"), particularly since they tend to give off odors which might penetrate into the house from an inside storage room.

Late turnips and rutabagas for storage should be dug up when the soil is dry, and should be of medium size. Examine them carefully and discard any with flaws. The tops should be cut off 1 inch or less above the crowns. Cover with straw in a storage pit, or place in crates if kept in a storage room.

The maximum storage period for turnips and rutabagas is 3–4

months. Rutabagas retain their taste somewhat better than turnips. The Montana Agricultural Experiment Station made some interesting tests on the storage of turnips. Two lots of turnips were stored under different conditions. One lot was kept in a cool, damp place, with the temperature varying from 37° to 49° F., the humidity from 81 to 96 per cent. At the end of 6 months the turnips in this lot were still firm, crisp, tender, and sweet, and required the same time to cook that they had taken 6 months before, about 20 minutes. The other lot was kept in an ordinary basement, in slightly damp sand. The temperature range was higher, 41°–69° F., the humidity lower, 19–63 per cent. There was a high percentage of spoilage; the turnips that remained were rather flabby, tough, fibrous, and strong or bitter in taste; and they required a longer cooking time. They were edible but not very palatable.

The results of this experiment would be likely to apply to any of the root vegetables. Beets, carrots, radishes, and turnips should all be kept cool and moist. Another conclusion from the same experiment was that the winter storage had no marked effect upon either the vitamin B_1 and C content or its potency.

Canning: Turnip tops are well worth canning in view of their high vitamin and mineral content. For canning directions see the chapter on "Canning."

Uses: Both these vegetables are commonly diced and boiled, and then either mashed or served still diced. Southerners cook young turnips and greens with a good piece of salt pork—the greens in the bottom layer, the whole baby turnips on top. Another method of preparing rutabagas is to parboil them whole until tender but not mushy, and then scoop out the centers and serve them filled with peas; they can be filled with the mashed centers bound with a beaten egg, topped with peas. Cooked diced turnips and peas are a good combination blended with a cream sauce. Cooked diced rutabagas can be baked in a casserole, the pieces dotted with butter and brown sugar, the whole dish cooked until it is brown.

Parboiled rutabagas can be added to a roast half an hour before it is done, and browned along with the usual potatoes. And for a very special dish make a soufflé. (This can also be made with other vegetables that can be mashed or chopped very fine—carrots, spinach, onions, and so on.) About a pound of the vegetable is needed, cooked, and in as fine a state as possible. Make a cream sauce with 4 tablespoonfuls of butter and ¾ cupful of liquid (either all rich milk or half cream and half the water the vegetable was cooked in). Add the vegetable, heat but do not boil, season with salt and pepper, and add 4 egg yolks well beaten. Let it cool slightly while you beat the whites of the 4 eggs stiff; then fold in the whites; put it in a buttered baking dish; and cook in a moderate oven, 375° F., for a very puffy soufflé, or 325° F. for a more solid soufflé. The time depends upon the temperature, about 20 or 30 minutes, but watch it. Do not open the door of the oven until the soufflé has cooked at least 20 minutes, from then on a few peeks are the best test. And eat it the second it's served. A soufflé of this sort with some cold meat or a tossed salad makes a perfect summer luncheon.

Frost-Zone Maps

In the eastern and middle western states there is a reasonably uniform progression in the frost dates from south to north that makes division into zones possible. In each of the two accompanying maps, seven zones are shown, marked A to G. The zones are not identical in the two maps since spring and fall frost dates are not separated by the same time interval in different parts of the country. Also, below are given two tables summarizing the average dates of spring and fall frosts for each zone.

		Map 1 *Average Dates of Latest Spring Frosts*	Map 2 *Average Dates of Earliest Fall Frosts*
Zone	A.	Feb. 15 – March 1	No frost
"	B.	March 1 – March 15	Nov. 25 – Dec. 10
"	C.	March 15 – April 1	Nov. 10 – Nov. 25
"	D.	April 1 – April 15	Oct. 25 – Nov. 10
"	E.	April 15 – May 1	Oct. 15 – Oct. 25
"	F.	May 1 – May 15	Oct. 1 – Oct. 15
"	G.	May 15 – June 1	Sept. 15 – Oct. 1

It is a simple matter to find your own zone on these two maps. The planting dates corresponding to the zones are given in the individual chapters. If your location is borderline, split the difference between the planting dates for the adjacent zones.

In the western states there is no uniformity in the frost dates, owing to the effect of the Rockies and Sierra Nevadas on climate conditions. Sample dates are given in the two maps illustrating some of the extreme variations. Planting dates must therefore depend on local conditions. You can obtain your actual spring and fall frost dates from your state agriculture department if you do not know them accurately. From these dates ascertain which zone you would be in if you lived in the Middle West or East, and use the corresponding planting dates for this zone.

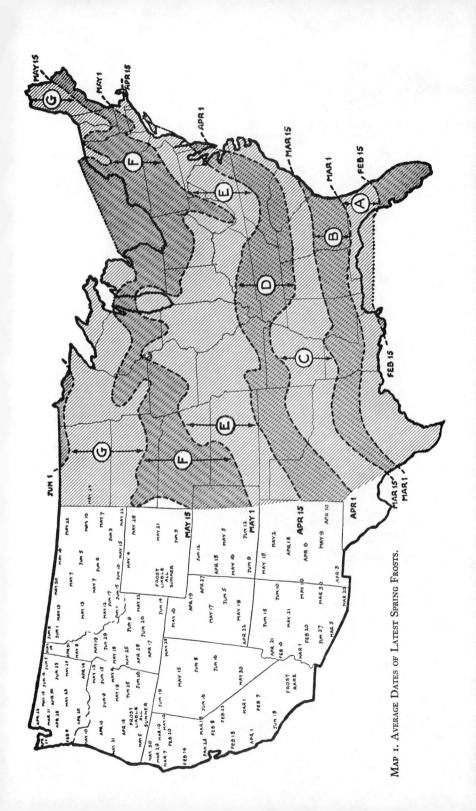

Map 1. Average Dates of Latest Spring Frosts.

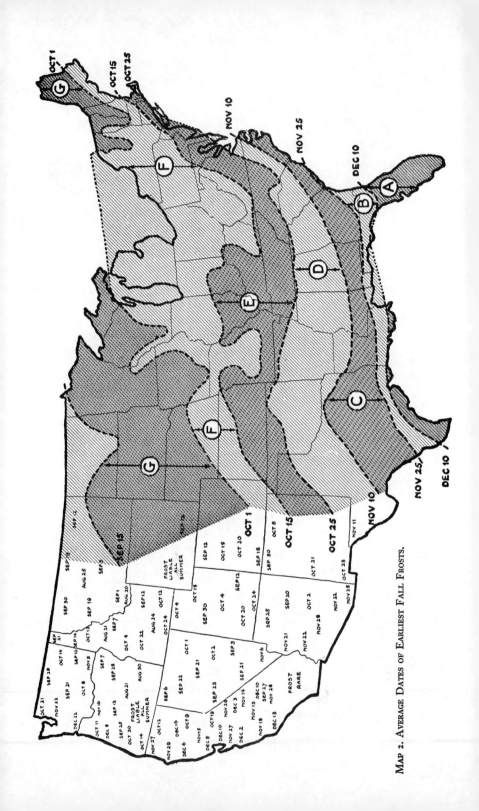

MAP 2. AVERAGE DATES OF EARLIEST FALL FROSTS.

Vegetable-Garden Plans

An important part of your preliminary work consists in designing the layout for economical use of the space you have available, ahead of time, and choosing crops and the proper amounts to grow to meet the needs and tastes of your own family.

It must be remembered that vegetables need room to grow, and that a small garden will not produce miraculous yields of all crops.

A back-yard plot of about 1000 square feet, 20 by 50 feet, will not normally supply every vegetable needed throughout the year by a small family unit of two or three people. However, it will produce enough to make a major dent in your usual summer vegetable bills if the right crops are grown, though there will not be much left over for storing and canning for the winter. You will have to use selection in such a small plot and not attempt to grow all the twenty-five vegetables described in the previous chapters; otherwise you will have samples rather than real crops.

At the other end of the scale, half an acre, or about 100 by 200 feet, should provide everything needed by a family of five or so, including storing and canning for the winter. This size verges on a regular farm vegetable garden, which is almost too much for a single individual to handle without a horse-drawn or mechanical cultivator.

The size of the average home vegetable garden will probably range between the small 20 by 50–foot, and the medium 75 by 150–foot plot.

I am giving only two typical plans. But I would emphasize that, while the experience of others can help you, your own experience in successive years will probably be the best guide.

Before I describe these plans, a few general comments are necessary. Certain of the following ideal requirements may be slightly conflicting:

Rows should run N-S to receive equal sunlight.
On sloping ground, rows should run across the slope and not up and down, to provide proper drainage.

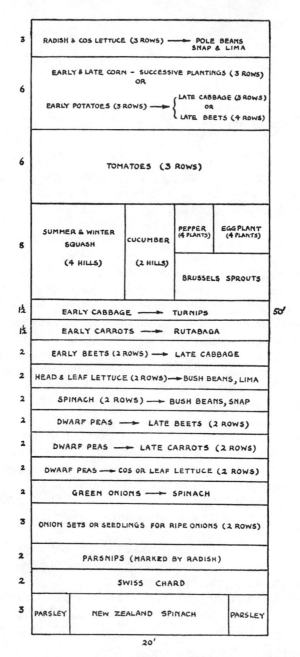

3	RADISH & COS LETTUCE (3 ROWS) ——► POLE BEANS SNAP & LIMA
6	EARLY & LATE CORN - SUCCESSIVE PLANTINGS (3 ROWS) OR EARLY POTATOES (3 ROWS) ——► { LATE CABBAGE (3 ROWS) OR LATE BEETS (4 ROWS)
6	TOMATOES (3 ROWS)
8	SUMMER & WINTER SQUASH (4 HILLS) / CUCUMBER (2 HILLS) / PEPPER (4 PLANTS) / EGGPLANT (4 PLANTS) / BRUSSELS SPROUTS
1½	EARLY CABBAGE ——► TURNIPS
1½	EARLY CARROTS ——► RUTABAGA
2	EARLY BEETS (2 ROWS) ——► LATE CABBAGE
2	HEAD & LEAF LETTUCE (2 ROWS) ——► BUSH BEANS, LIMA
2	SPINACH (2 ROWS) ——► BUSH BEANS, SNAP
2	DWARF PEAS ——► LATE BEETS (2 ROWS)
2	DWARF PEAS ——► LATE CARROTS (2 ROWS)
2	DWARF PEAS ——► COS OR LEAF LETTUCE (2 ROWS)
2	GREEN ONIONS ——► SPINACH
3	ONION SETS OR SEEDLINGS FOR RIPE ONIONS (2 ROWS)
2	PARSNIPS (MARKED BY RADISH)
2	SWISS CHARD
3	PARSLEY / NEW ZEALAND SPINACH / PARSLEY

50'

20'

PLAN 1. SMALL-SIZE VEGETABLE GARDEN.
(The symbol → means "followed by.")

8	**ASPARAGUS (2 ROWS)** PERMANENT BED
3	SWISS CHARD / NEW ZEALAND SPINACH
4	PARSNIPS (2 ROWS MARKED BY RADISH)
2	CELERY / PARSLEY
2	CARROTS — SUCCESSIVE PLANTINGS
2	BEETS — SUCCESSIVE PLANTINGS
2	ONION SETS OR SEEDLINGS — FOR RIPE ONIONS
20	EARLY POTATOES (8 ROWS) → TURNIPS (2 ROWS) / RUTABAGA (2 ROWS) / LATE BEETS (2 ROWS) / LATE CABBAGE (2 ROWS)
3	EARLY CABBAGE → WINTER RADISH
3	CAULIFLOWER / BRUSSELS SPROUTS
3	BROCCOLI
2	GREEN ONIONS → SPINACH
2	SPINACH → COS LETTUCE
2	HEAD & LEAF LETTUCE → BUSH BEANS, LIMA
4	EARLY & LATE PEAS (2 ROWS) → BUSH BEANS, SNAP
6	POLE BEANS, SNAP & LIMA (2 ROWS)
24	EARLY & LATE CORN - SUCCESSIVE PLANTINGS (8 ROWS)
8	SUMMER & WINTER SQUASH (15 HILLS) / CUCUMBER (10 HILLS)
4	PEPPER (20 PLANTS) / EGGPLANT (20 PLANTS)
16	TOMATOES (4 ROWS)
30	LATE POTATOES (10 ROWS)

150'

75'

PLAN 2. MEDIUM-SIZE VEGETABLE GARDEN.
(The symbol → means "followed by.")

Crops of the same general types should be located near one another to facilitate pest control.

Tall-growing crops should be placed to the north of low-growing crops so that the latter will not be shaded.

Rows should be as long as possible to facilitate cultivation—but short rows are a psychological advantage to the home gardener.

Plan 1 is for a small-size 20 by 50–foot plot. The space is utilized to maximum advantage by succession crops. Certain of the more difficult crops, such as celery, cauliflower, and broccoli, are not included. The yield from the area proposed for corn will be quite small; hence, the alternative of a few delicious early potatoes followed by late cabbage or late beets might be preferable. The space does not justify an asparagus bed (which is a permanent fixture) or a planting of late potatoes. The tall crops are at one end, the root and leafy crops in the middle, and the all-season crops at the other end. The space devoted to peppers, eggplant, and Brussels sprouts is small and can be regarded as experimental; these are a little tricky and may present difficulties your first year, unless you purchase plants. If you have any side space available, the squash and cucumber could be grown there, and more root crops or tomatoes could be grown in the garden proper. You may have enough harvest to can some tomatoes and chard, pickle some cucumbers, and store or can some beets and carrots.

Plan 2 is for a medium-size 75 by 150–foot plot. It includes all the twenty-five vegetables described in the previous chapters, including rutabagas as an ally of turnips and New Zealand spinach as a variant of regular spinach. Ample spacing for the rows is indicated to facilitate cultivation. The all-season crops and the root and leafy crops are at one end. The fall crops and vines are in the center, and a large patch of late potatoes is at the other end. Certain succession crops are indicated, though this problem is not so vital as in a small garden. Obviously the space devoted to beans, corn, tomatoes, and late potatoes can be varied to suit the predilections of your family. From this layout, a family of five should get sufficient table vegetables from spring to fall, with Swiss chard and New Zealand spinach filling in as potherbs in the hot summer months. And the harvest should yield enough to can tomatoes, corn, beans, beets, carrots, and spinach, and possibly some green peas; to pickle cucumbers; and to store potatoes, onions, beets, turnips, rutabagas, and cabbage.

Plan 2 can be expanded sideways and lengthwise for a large 100 by 200–foot plot. However, it would then be better to have long 200-

foot rows to make cultivation simpler, or alternatively to divide the garden into two, with corn, squash, cucumbers, tomatoes, and late potatoes together, and separated from the other crops. From such an enlarged plot, your winter larder should be filled to overflowing.

Storing

The vegetables considered as storable in this book from the point of view of the home gardener are:

Group 1
1. The root crops: beets, carrots, turnips and rutabagas, parsnips, and winter radishes
2. Potatoes
3. Cabbage
4. Celery

Group 2
5. Onions
6. Winter squash
7. Eggplant
8. Parsley
9. Brussels sprouts
10. Tomatoes (for a brief time)

The vegetables of group 2 are miscellaneous; the storage requirements are all different and are described in the individual chapters. Winter squash and tomatoes are more satisfactorily preserved by canning; parsley is easily kept; and eggplant can be regarded as an experiment. Therefore the only ones in this group of which you will probably wish to store much are onions particularly and Brussels sprouts.

Winter storage of the group 1 vegetables with ordinary home facilities is not in general a simple or casual matter. It is essentially a job that should be done properly or not at all. The whole purpose of storage is to keep the vegetables as far as possible in their pristine harvested state; if proper conditions of temperature, moisture, and ventilation are not maintained, decay will set in.

The temperature should preferably be kept around freezing and should never go above 40° F.; the air must remain quite moist; and there should be little air circulation. These requirements can be taken care of only in a specially constructed cellar storage room, an outside storage room, or an outside storage pit. If you do decide to store the group 1 vegetables, I strongly recommend that you first write to your state agriculture department or to the U. S. Department of

Agriculture in Washington for their numerous and excellent pamphlets on home vegetable storage. You are practically certain to find suggestions and plans that will aid you in building a storage room or pit suitable for your individual house and garden.

All these vegetables can be stored inside or outside, though control of the necessary conditions is obviously easier in a cellar storage room. However, cabbage, turnips, and rutabagas tend to give off odors which may penetrate into the house; therefore, if considerable quantities are to be stored, an outside pit would be better.

The following hints may be helpful:

1. A cellar storage room can be constructed by carefully boarding off a corner of the cellar as far from the furnace as possible. The

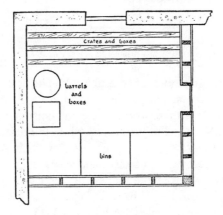

FIGURE I. CELLAR STORAGE ROOM.

boarding should be double thickness with a dead air space between, and it should be covered with insulating paper. A window to the outside air is essential so that the temperature can be controlled and moist air from outside can enter. Make sure that as little as possible of the dry air from the main cellar gets in. (See Figure 1.) A duct, with a damper, leading down from the window is helpful. Hang a thermometer on the wall. You should watch the temperature every day and open or close the window to keep the temperature as uniform as possible.

2. An outdoor storage room in states where the winters are cold should be partly below ground. Concrete, brick, or tile construction is preferable to wood for long life, though a dirt floor is advisable to

maintain proper moisture conditions. The roof should be covered over with earth and sod. An air intake and outlet are necessary for ventilation. (See Figure 2.)

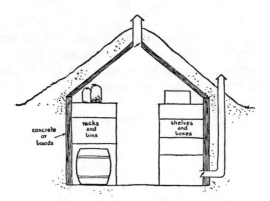

FIGURE 2. OUTSIDE STORAGE ROOM.

3. Outside storage pits are of several kinds. The best is probably the trench type. Dig a trench about 3 feet deep and 3 feet wide and as long as you require up to 10 feet or so. Cover the bottom and sides with a good thickness of straw. Put in the vegetables in burlap bags or small crates. Cover with straw and a 6-inch layer of earth. As the weather gets colder, add more layers of earth and straw. Dig a small drainage trench around the edges of the mound. A ventilating pipe should be inserted, such as an old length of stove pipe pierced with holes at the bottom, with a cover on top. (See Figure 3.) The vegetables should be arranged in assorted groups along the trench, in such a way that

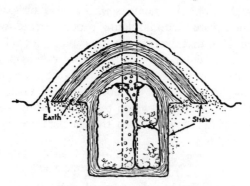

FIGURE 3. OUTSIDE STORAGE PIT.

you can remove them as required from one end. It is better to fill in
the trench as you take them out. Where the winters are very cold, you
may need a pick to get in. In such regions several small square pits
should be used, so that you can take out all the contents of one at one
time, without disturbing the others.

It is worth remembering that apples can be successfully stored all
winter, along with vegetables, in a storage room or pit—and many
people say that storage actually improves the taste of apples.

Canning

As the old saying goes—"eat what you can and can what you can't."

If a vegetable is both cannable and storable, I strongly advise canning. Canning is now a very simple proposition for the home vegetable grower—or for his wife.

The purpose of canning is to kill or sterilize the various organisms which cause food to spoil. Research has shown that certain organisms are heat resistant and are not killed at ordinary boiling temperature, 212° F., even after several hours, in a nonacid environment. Since practically all vegetables (except tomatoes) are nonacid, the only canning method recommended is pressure cooking—using steam under pressure at high temperatures which kills off practically all organisms with reasonable certainty.

It is true that in the past many people have used the so-called hot-water and oven-canning methods for vegetables without any dire results. However, neither is now regarded as wholly safe or satisfactory for nonacid vegetables by the U. S. Department of Agriculture, and other authorities, since the temperatures involved will not kill off all harmful organisms and the canned vegetables may spoil or be harmful to health.

Therefore, only the pressure-cooking method of canning vegetables will be described here. This method is suitable for tomatoes also, and it has the additional advantage of preserving the real fresh vegetable taste much better than the other methods.

The only major items of equipment required are: (1) A *pressure cooker*, which incidentally should be a standard kitchen utensil in use throughout the year for ordinary cooking of vegetables, and meats too. There are a number of excellent pressure cookers now on the market. These are simple and safe to use if elementary precautions are taken. Full directions for use come with every new cooker. (2) *Glass jars with seal tops* (the term "canning" is rather a misnomer, since glass jars are far more practicable than tin cans for the home gardener, whose ambitions will probably be satisfied by a few hundred jars at most). Many standard types of pint and quart jars are available, with screw-down or clamp glass or metal lids and a rubber ring or gasket between the top of the jar and the lid. The clamp glass-lid type is very simple to use. There are also special so-called self-sealing jars.

Canning is essentially a matter of planning, patience, and cleanliness. If you have worked out your planting dates carefully with harvesting in mind, you will be able to harvest a number of crops simultaneously and have a canning session. As a preparation, the glass jars and tops should be sterilized in the pressure cooker. Invert the jars in an inch or so of water in the cooker; place the top on the cooker; and steam for about ten minutes at the standard recommended pressure, usually about 15 pounds. Remove and place the jars on a rack to cool, and handle them as little as possible before use.

Naturally, only sound ripe roots, fruits, or leaves should be selected for canning, and they should be thoroughly washed to remove all dirt. Preliminary cooking by boiling or steaming is highly advisable if not essential. The precooked vegetables should be packed while hot in the sterilized jars. Do not pack too densely (particularly corn, peas, and beans). The water in which they have been precooked is usually added. A small amount of salt should be put in each jar for most vegetables. The level of the water should not be higher than ½ inch from the top of the jar. If you see any air bubbles, work them out with a wooden spoon. Wipe the top of the jar, place the rubber sealing ring in position, and *lightly* clamp or screw down the lid. Place the jars in the pressure cooker, and steam the required time (for details see following table). After releasing pressure from the cooker, remove the jars and at once seal them *tightly*. Let the jars cool upright, and then label them.

Store the jars in a cool, dry closet or storage rack in the cellar, away from direct light. Do not disturb the lids before using.

Properly canned vegetables will keep almost indefinitely, but they should preferably be used within a year of canning.

Canning Directions for Use of Pressure Cooker: In the following table the cooking time in the pressure cooker is given for pint jars; if you use quart jars, increase the time by five minutes.

"Liquid" means the liquid in which the vegetables are precooked.

"Pack" means to place the vegetables while still hot from precooking into the sterilized jars, which preferably should be warmed. The packing should be reasonably loose; do not squeeze or push the vegetables in. Leave ¼ to ½ inch at the top of the jar.

"Add salt" means to put in ½ teaspoonful of salt for pint jars and twice this amount for quart jars.

Vegetable	Preparation and Precooking	Pressure (in pounds)	Time (in minutes)
Asparagus.......	Cut into lengths to fit jar. Boil 3 minutes. Pack, add salt, cover with liquid.	10	35
Beans (snap).....	Cut up as for table use, in either long or short lengths. Pack, add salt, cover with liquid.	10	35
Beans (lima).....	Shell. Boil until skins of beans are loose. Peel. Pack, add salt, cover with liquid.	10	55
Beets...........	Use young beets. Cut off tops. Boil 15 minutes. Remove skins. Pack, add salt, cover with fresh boiling water.	10	35
Carrots.........	Use young carrots. Cut off tops leaving ½ inch of stem. Slice or dice if desired. Boil 15 minutes. Pack, add salt, cover with liquid.	10	35
Cauliflower.....	Separate head into clusters. Soak in salt water 1 hour. Remove and boil 3 minutes in fresh water. Pack, add salt (and a little sugar, if desired), cover with fresh boiling water.	10	35
Corn	Use young corn (i.e., the inside of the kernels must still be milky). Cut raw from cob. Boil 5 minutes. Pack, add salt (and a little sugar, if desired). Cover with liquid.	10	75

Vegetable	Preparation and Precooking	Pressure (in pounds)	Time (in minutes)
Greens .... (spinach, beet and turnip tops, chard)	Trim leaves. Boil 5 minutes or less in small amount of water, till stems wilt. Pack, but cut across pack. Add salt. Cover with liquid.	15	60
Peas (green).....	Use young peas, shelled. Boil 5 minutes. Pack, add salt. Cover with liquid.	10	45
Squash (winter)..	Cut into sections. Boil until flesh can be easily removed from rind. Pack pulp, add salt.	15	75
Tomatoes........	Scald till skin breaks. Peel and remove any skin portion. Pack whole or cut into pieces. Add salt. If desired, the pack can be covered with tomato juice.	5	10
Tomato Juice....	Crush cold tomatoes, and put through a press or sieve to remove juice. Pour into jar. Add salt. (Alternatively, the tomatoes can be boiled till soft before straining, but this does not retain all the vitamin content).	5	10

Index

A CATALOGUE OF SELECTED DOVER BOOKS
IN ALL FIELDS OF INTEREST

A CATALOGUE OF SELECTED DOVER BOOKS
IN ALL FIELDS OF INTEREST

AMERICA'S OLD MASTERS, James T. Flexner. Four men emerged unexpectedly from provincial 18th century America to leadership in European art: Benjamin West, J. S. Copley, C. R. Peale, Gilbert Stuart. Brilliant coverage of lives and contributions. Revised, 1967 edition. 69 plates. 365pp. of text.

21806-6 Paperbound $3.00

FIRST FLOWERS OF OUR WILDERNESS: AMERICAN PAINTING, THE COLONIAL PERIOD, James T. Flexner. Painters, and regional painting traditions from earliest Colonial times up to the emergence of Copley, West and Peale Sr., Foster, Gustavus Hesselius, Feke, John Smibert and many anonymous painters in the primitive manner. Engaging presentation, with 162 illustrations. xxii + 368pp.

22180-6 Paperbound $3.50

THE LIGHT OF DISTANT SKIES: AMERICAN PAINTING, 1760-1835, James T. Flexner. The great generation of early American painters goes to Europe to learn and to teach: West, Copley, Gilbert Stuart and others. Allston, Trumbull, Morse; also contemporary American painters—primitives, derivatives, academics—who remained in America. 102 illustrations. xiii + 306pp.

22179-2 Paperbound $3.50

A HISTORY OF THE RISE AND PROGRESS OF THE ARTS OF DESIGN IN THE UNITED STATES, William Dunlap. Much the richest mine of information on early American painters, sculptors, architects, engravers, miniaturists, etc. The only source of information for scores of artists, the major primary source for many others. Unabridged reprint of rare original 1834 edition, with new introduction by James T. Flexner, and 394 new illustrations. Edited by Rita Weiss. 6⅝ x 9⅝.

21695-0, 21696-9, 21697-7 Three volumes, Paperbound $13.50

EPOCHS OF CHINESE AND JAPANESE ART, Ernest F. Fenollosa. From primitive Chinese art to the 20th century, thorough history, explanation of every important art period and form, including Japanese woodcuts; main stress on China and Japan, but Tibet, Korea also included. Still unexcelled for its detailed, rich coverage of cultural background, aesthetic elements, diffusion studies, particularly of the historical period. 2nd, 1913 edition. 242 illustrations. lii + 439pp. of text.

20364-6, 20365-4 Two volumes, Paperbound $6.00

THE GENTLE ART OF MAKING ENEMIES, James A. M. Whistler. Greatest wit of his day deflates Oscar Wilde, Ruskin, Swinburne; strikes back at inane critics, exhibitions, art journalism; aesthetics of impressionist revolution in most striking form. Highly readable classic by great painter. Reproduction of edition designed by Whistler. Introduction by Alfred Werner. xxxvi + 334pp.

21875-9 Paperbound $3.00

VISUAL ILLUSIONS: THEIR CAUSES, CHARACTERISTICS, AND APPLICATIONS, Matthew Luckiesh. Thorough description and discussion of optical illusion, geometric and perspective, particularly; size and shape distortions, illusions of color, of motion; natural illusions; use of illusion in art and magic, industry, etc. Most useful today with op art, also for classical art. Scores of effects illustrated. Introduction by William H. Ittleson. 100 illustrations. xxi + 252pp.

21530-X Paperbound $2.00

A HANDBOOK OF ANATOMY FOR ART STUDENTS, Arthur Thomson. Thorough, virtually exhaustive coverage of skeletal structure, musculature, etc. Full text, supplemented by anatomical diagrams and drawings and by photographs of undraped figures. Unique in its comparison of male and female forms, pointing out differences of contour, texture, form. 211 figures, 40 drawings, 86 photographs. xx + 459pp. 5⅜ x 8⅜.

21163-0 Paperbound $3.50

150 MASTERPIECES OF DRAWING, Selected by Anthony Toney. Full page reproductions of drawings from the early 16th to the end of the 18th century, all beautifully reproduced: Rembrandt, Michelangelo, Dürer, Fragonard, Urs, Graf, Wouwerman, many others. First-rate browsing book, model book for artists. xviii + 150pp. 8⅜ x 11¼.

21032-4 Paperbound $2.50

THE LATER WORK OF AUBREY BEARDSLEY, Aubrey Beardsley. Exotic, erotic, ironic masterpieces in full maturity: Comedy Ballet, Venus and Tannhauser, Pierrot, Lysistrata, Rape of the Lock, Savoy material, Ali Baba, Volpone, etc. This material revolutionized the art world, and is still powerful, fresh, brilliant. With *The Early Work*, all Beardsley's finest work. 174 plates, 2 in color. xiv + 176pp. 8⅛ x 11.

21817-1 Paperbound $3.00

DRAWINGS OF REMBRANDT, Rembrandt van Rijn. Complete reproduction of fabulously rare edition by Lippmann and Hofstede de Groot, completely reedited, updated, improved by Prof. Seymour Slive, Fogg Museum. Portraits, Biblical sketches, landscapes, Oriental types, nudes, episodes from classical mythology—All Rembrandt's fertile genius. Also selection of drawings by his pupils and followers. "Stunning volumes," *Saturday Review*. 550 illustrations. lxxviii + 552pp. 9⅛ x 12¼.

21485-0, 21486-9 Two volumes, Paperbound $10.00

THE DISASTERS OF WAR, Francisco Goya. One of the masterpieces of Western civilization—83 etchings that record Goya's shattering, bitter reaction to the Napoleonic war that swept through Spain after the insurrection of 1808 and to war in general. Reprint of the first edition, with three additional plates from Boston's Museum of Fine Arts. All plates facsimile size. Introduction by Philip Hofer, Fogg Museum. v + 97pp. 9⅜ x 8¼.

21872-4 Paperbound $2.00

GRAPHIC WORKS OF ODILON REDON. Largest collection of Redon's graphic works ever assembled: 172 lithographs, 28 etchings and engravings, 9 drawings. These include some of his most famous works. All the plates from *Odilon Redon: oeuvre graphique complet,* plus additional plates. New introduction and caption translations by Alfred Werner. 209 illustrations. xxvii + 209pp. 9⅛ x 12¼.

21966-8 Paperbound $4.50

DESIGN BY ACCIDENT; A BOOK OF "ACCIDENTAL EFFECTS" FOR ARTISTS AND DESIGNERS, James F. O'Brien. Create your own unique, striking, imaginative effects by "controlled accident" interaction of materials: paints and lacquers, oil and water based paints, splatter, crackling materials, shatter, similar items. Everything you do will be different; first book on this limitless art, so useful to both fine artist and commercial artist. Full instructions. 192 plates showing "accidents," 8 in color. viii + 215pp. 8⅜ x 11¼. 21942-9 Paperbound $3.50

THE BOOK OF SIGNS, Rudolf Koch. Famed German type designer draws 493 beautiful symbols: religious, mystical, alchemical, imperial, property marks, runes, etc. Remarkable fusion of traditional and modern. Good for suggestions of timelessness, smartness, modernity. Text. vi + 104pp. 6⅛ x 9¼. 20162-7 Paperbound $1.25

HISTORY OF INDIAN AND INDONESIAN ART, Ananda K. Coomaraswamy. An unabridged republication of one of the finest books by a great scholar in Eastern art. Rich in descriptive material, history, social backgrounds; Sunga reliefs, Rajput paintings, Gupta temples, Burmese frescoes, textiles, jewelry, sculpture, etc. 400 photos. viii + 423pp. 6⅜ x 9¾. 21436-2 Paperbound $5.00

PRIMITIVE ART, Franz Boas. America's foremost anthropologist surveys textiles, ceramics, woodcarving, basketry, metalwork, etc.; patterns, technology, creation of symbols, style origins. All areas of world, but very full on Northwest Coast Indians. More than 350 illustrations of baskets, boxes, totem poles, weapons, etc. 378 pp. 20025-6 Paperbound $3.00

THE GENTLEMAN AND CABINET MAKER'S DIRECTOR, Thomas Chippendale. Full reprint (third edition, 1762) of most influential furniture book of all time, by master cabinetmaker. 200 plates, illustrating chairs, sofas, mirrors, tables, cabinets, plus 24 photographs of surviving pieces. Biographical introduction by N. Bienenstock. vi + 249pp. 9⅞ x 12¾. 21601-2 Paperbound $4.00

AMERICAN ANTIQUE FURNITURE, Edgar G. Miller, Jr. The basic coverage of all American furniture before 1840. Individual chapters cover type of furniture—clocks, tables, sideboards, etc.—chronologically, with inexhaustible wealth of data. More than 2100 photographs, all identified, commented on. Essential to all early American collectors. Introduction by H. E. Keyes. vi + 1106pp. 7⅞ x 10¾. 21599-7, 21600-4 Two volumes, Paperbound $11.00

PENNSYLVANIA DUTCH AMERICAN FOLK ART, Henry J. Kauffman. 279 photos, 28 drawings of tulipware, Fraktur script, painted tinware, toys, flowered furniture, quilts, samplers, hex signs, house interiors, etc. Full descriptive text. Excellent for tourist, rewarding for designer, collector. Map. 146pp. 7⅞ x 10¾. 21205-X Paperbound $2.50

EARLY NEW ENGLAND GRAVESTONE RUBBINGS, Edmund V. Gillon, Jr. 43 photographs, 226 carefully reproduced rubbings show heavily symbolic, sometimes macabre early gravestones, up to early 19th century. Remarkable early American primitive art, occasionally strikingly beautiful; always powerful. Text. xxvi + 207pp. 8⅜ x 11¼. 21380-3 Paperbound $3.50

ALPHABETS AND ORNAMENTS, Ernst Lehner. Well-known pictorial source for decorative alphabets, script examples, cartouches, frames, decorative title pages, calligraphic initials, borders, similar material. 14th to 19th century, mostly European. Useful in almost any graphic arts designing, varied styles. 750 illustrations. 256pp. 7 x 10. 21905-4 Paperbound $4.00

PAINTING: A CREATIVE APPROACH, Norman Colquhoun. For the beginner simple guide provides an instructive approach to painting: major stumbling blocks for beginner; overcoming them, technical points; paints and pigments; oil painting; watercolor and other media and color. New section on "plastic" paints. Glossary. Formerly *Paint Your Own Pictures.* 221pp. 22000-1 Paperbound $1.75

THE ENJOYMENT AND USE OF COLOR, Walter Sargent. Explanation of the relations between colors themselves and between colors in nature and art, including hundreds of little-known facts about color values, intensities, effects of high and low illumination, complementary colors. Many practical hints for painters, references to great masters. 7 color plates, 29 illustrations. x + 274pp.
20944-X Paperbound $2.75

THE NOTEBOOKS OF LEONARDO DA VINCI, compiled and edited by Jean Paul Richter. 1566 extracts from original manuscripts reveal the full range of Leonardo's versatile genius: all his writings on painting, sculpture, architecture, anatomy, astronomy, geography, topography, physiology, mining, music, etc., in both Italian and English, with 186 plates of manuscript pages and more than 500 additional drawings. Includes studies for the Last Supper, the lost Sforza monument, and other works. Total of xlvii + 866pp. 7⅞ x 10¾.
22572-0, 22573-9 Two volumes, Paperbound $10.00

MONTGOMERY WARD CATALOGUE OF 1895. Tea gowns, yards of flannel and pillow-case lace, stereoscopes, books of gospel hymns, the New Improved Singer Sewing Machine, side saddles, milk skimmers, straight-edged razors, high-button shoes, spittoons, and on and on . . . listing some 25,000 items, practically all illustrated. Essential to the shoppers of the 1890's, it is our truest record of the spirit of the period. Unaltered reprint of Issue No. 57, Spring and Summer 1895. Introduction by Boris Emmet. Innumerable illustrations. xiii + 624pp. 8½ x 11⅝.
22377-9 Paperbound $6.95

THE CRYSTAL PALACE EXHIBITION ILLUSTRATED CATALOGUE (LONDON, 1851). One of the wonders of the modern world—the Crystal Palace Exhibition in which all the nations of the civilized world exhibited their achievements in the arts and sciences—presented in an equally important illustrated catalogue. More than 1700 items pictured with accompanying text—ceramics, textiles, cast-iron work, carpets, pianos, sleds, razors, wall-papers, billiard tables, beehives, silverware and hundreds of other artifacts—represent the focal point of Victorian culture in the Western World. Probably the largest collection of Victorian decorative art ever assembled—indispensable for antiquarians and designers. Unabridged republication of the Art-Journal Catalogue of the Great Exhibition of 1851, with all terminal essays. New introduction by John Gloag, F.S.A. xxxiv + 426pp. 9 x 12.
22503-8 Paperbound $5.00

A HISTORY OF COSTUME, Carl Köhler. Definitive history, based on surviving pieces of clothing primarily, and paintings, statues, etc. secondarily. Highly readable text, supplemented by 594 illustrations of costumes of the ancient Mediterranean peoples, Greece and Rome, the Teutonic prehistoric period; costumes of the Middle Ages, Renaissance, Baroque, 18th and 19th centuries. Clear, measured patterns are provided for many clothing articles. Approach is practical throughout. Enlarged by Emma von Sichart. 464pp. 21030-8 Paperbound $3.50.

ORIENTAL RUGS, ANTIQUE AND MODERN, Walter A. Hawley. A complete and authoritative treatise on the Oriental rug—where they are made, by whom and how, designs and symbols, characteristics in detail of the six major groups, how to distinguish them and how to buy them. Detailed technical data is provided on periods, weaves, warps, wefts, textures, sides, ends and knots, although no technical background is required for an understanding. 11 color plates, 80 halftones, 4 maps. vi + 320pp. 6⅛ x 9⅛. 22366-3 Paperbound $5.00

TEN BOOKS ON ARCHITECTURE, Vitruvius. By any standards the most important book on architecture ever written. Early Roman discussion of aesthetics of building, construction methods, orders, sites, and every other aspect of architecture has inspired, instructed architecture for about 2,000 years. Stands behind Palladio, Michelangelo, Bramante, Wren, countless others. Definitive Morris H. Morgan translation. 68 illustrations. xii + 331pp. 20645-9 Paperbound $3.00

THE FOUR BOOKS OF ARCHITECTURE, Andrea Palladio. Translated into every major Western European language in the two centuries following its publication in 1570, this has been one of the most influential books in the history of architecture. Complete reprint of the 1738 Isaac Ware edition. New introduction by Adolf Placzek, Columbia Univ. 216 plates. xxii + 110pp. of text. 9½ x 12¾. 21308-0 Clothbound $12.50

STICKS AND STONES: A STUDY OF AMERICAN ARCHITECTURE AND CIVILIZATION, Lewis Mumford.One of the great classics of American cultural history. American architecture from the medieval-inspired earliest forms to the early 20th century; evolution of structure and style, and reciprocal influences on environment. 21 photographic illustrations. 238pp. 20202-X Paperbound $2.00

THE AMERICAN BUILDER'S COMPANION, Asher Benjamin. The most widely used early 19th century architectural style and source book, for colonial up into Greek Revival periods. Extensive development of geometry of carpentering, construction of sashes, frames, doors, stairs; plans and elevations of domestic and other buildings. Hundreds of thousands of houses were built according to this book, now invaluable to historians, architects, restorers, etc. 1827 edition. 59 plates. 114pp. 7⅞ x 10¾. 22236-5 Paperbound $3.50

DUTCH HOUSES IN THE HUDSON VALLEY BEFORE 1776, Helen Wilkinson Reynolds. The standard survey of the Dutch colonial house and outbuildings, with constructional features, decoration, and local history associated with individual homesteads. Introduction by Franklin D. Roosevelt. Map. 150 illustrations. 469pp. 6⅝ x 9¼. 21469-9 Paperbound $5.00

THE ARCHITECTURE OF COUNTRY HOUSES, Andrew J. Downing. Together with Vaux's *Villas and Cottages* this is the basic book for Hudson River Gothic architecture of the middle Victorian period. Full, sound discussions of general aspects of housing, architecture, style, decoration, furnishing, together with scores of detailed house plans, illustrations of specific buildings, accompanied by full text. Perhaps the most influential single American architectural book. 1850 edition. Introduction by J. Stewart Johnson. 321 figures, 34 architectural designs. xvi + 560pp.

22003-6 Paperbound $4.00

LOST EXAMPLES OF COLONIAL ARCHITECTURE, John Mead Howells. Full-page photographs of buildings that have disappeared or been so altered as to be denatured, including many designed by major early American architects. 245 plates. xvii + 248pp. 7⅞ x 10¾. 21143-6 Paperbound $3.50

DOMESTIC ARCHITECTURE OF THE AMERICAN COLONIES AND OF THE EARLY REPUBLIC, Fiske Kimball. Foremost architect and restorer of Williamsburg and Monticello covers nearly 200 homes between 1620-1825. Architectural details, construction, style features, special fixtures, floor plans, etc. Generally considered finest work in its area. 219 illustrations of houses, doorways, windows, capital mantels. xx + 314pp. 7⅞ x 10¾. 21743-4 Paperbound $4.00

EARLY AMERICAN ROOMS: 1650-1858, edited by Russell Hawes Kettell. Tour of 12 rooms, each representative of a different era in American history and each furnished, decorated, designed and occupied in the style of the era. 72 plans and elevations, 8-page color section, etc., show fabrics, wall papers, arrangements, etc. Full descriptive text. xvii + 200pp. of text. 8⅜ x 11¼. 21633-0 Paperbound $5.00

THE FITZWILLIAM VIRGINAL BOOK, edited by J. Fuller Maitland and W. B. Squire. Full modern printing of famous early 17th-century ms. volume of 300 works by Morley, Byrd, Bull, Gibbons, etc. For piano or other modern keyboard instrument; easy to read format. xxxvi + 938pp. 8⅜ x 11. 21068-5, 21069-3 Two volumes, Paperbound $10.00

KEYBOARD MUSIC, Johann Sebastian Bach. Bach Gesellschaft edition. A rich selection of Bach's masterpieces for the harpsichord: the six English Suites, six French Suites, the six Partitas (Clavierübung part I), the Goldberg Variations (Clavierübung part IV), the fifteen Two-Part Inventions and the fifteen Three-Part Sinfonias. Clearly reproduced on large sheets with ample margins; eminently playable. vi + 312pp. 8⅛ x 11. 22360-4 Paperbound $5.00

THE MUSIC OF BACH: AN INTRODUCTION, Charles Sanford Terry. A fine, nontechnical introduction to Bach's music, both instrumental and vocal. Covers organ music, chamber music, passion music, other types. Analyzes themes, developments, innovations. x + 114pp. 21075-8 Paperbound $1.50

BEETHOVEN AND HIS NINE SYMPHONIES, Sir George Grove. Noted British musicologist provides best history, analysis, commentary on symphonies. Very thorough, rigorously accurate; necessary to both advanced student and amateur music lover. 436 musical passages. vii + 407 pp. 20334-4 Paperbound $2.75

CATALOGUE OF DOVER BOOKS

JOHANN SEBASTIAN BACH, Philipp Spitta. One of the great classics of musicology, this definitive analysis of Bach's music (and life) has never been surpassed. Lucid, nontechnical analyses of hundreds of pieces (30 pages devoted to St. Matthew Passion, 26 to B Minor Mass). Also includes major analysis of 18th-century music. 450 musical examples. 40-page musical supplement. Total of xx + 1799pp.
(EUK) 22278-0, 22279-9 Two volumes, Clothbound $17.50

MOZART AND HIS PIANO CONCERTOS, Cuthbert Girdlestone. The only full-length study of an important area of Mozart's creativity. Provides detailed analyses of all 23 concertos, traces inspirational sources. 417 musical examples. Second edition. 509pp.
21271-8 Paperbound $3.50

THE PERFECT WAGNERITE: A COMMENTARY ON THE NIBLUNG'S RING, George Bernard Shaw. Brilliant and still relevant criticism in remarkable essays on Wagner's Ring cycle, Shaw's ideas on political and social ideology behind the plots, role of Leitmotifs, vocal requisites, etc. Prefaces. xxi + 136pp.
(USO) 21707-8 Paperbound $1.50

DON GIOVANNI, W. A. Mozart. Complete libretto, modern English translation; biographies of composer and librettist; accounts of early performances and critical reaction. Lavishly illustrated. All the material you need to understand and appreciate this great work. Dover Opera Guide and Libretto Series; translated and introduced by Ellen Bleiler. 92 illustrations. 209pp.
21134-7 Paperbound $2.00

BASIC ELECTRICITY, U. S. Bureau of Naval Personel. Originally a training course, best non-technical coverage of basic theory of electricity and its applications. Fundamental concepts, batteries, circuits, conductors and wiring techniques, AC and DC, inductance and capacitance, generators, motors, transformers, magnetic amplifiers, synchros, servomechanisms, etc. Also covers blue-prints, electrical diagrams, etc. Many questions, with answers. 349 illustrations. x + 448pp. 6½ x 9¼.
20973-3 Paperbound $3.50

REPRODUCTION OF SOUND, Edgar Villchur. Thorough coverage for laymen of high fidelity systems, reproducing systems in general, needles, amplifiers, preamps, loudspeakers, feedback, explaining physical background. "A rare talent for making technicalities vividly comprehensible," R. Darrell, *High Fidelity*. 69 figures. iv + 92pp.
21515-6 Paperbound $1.25

HEAR ME TALKIN' TO YA: THE STORY OF JAZZ AS TOLD BY THE MEN WHO MADE IT, Nat Shapiro and Nat Hentoff. Louis Armstrong, Fats Waller, Jo Jones, Clarence Williams, Billy Holiday, Duke Ellington, Jelly Roll Morton and dozens of other jazz greats tell how it was in Chicago's South Side, New Orleans, depression Harlem and the modern West Coast as jazz was born and grew. xvi + 429pp.
21726-4 Paperbound $3.00

FABLES OF AESOP, translated by Sir Roger L'Estrange. A reproduction of the very rare 1931 Paris edition; a selection of the most interesting fables, together with 50 imaginative drawings by Alexander Calder. v + 128pp. 6½x9¼.
21780-9 Paperbound $1.50

AGAINST THE GRAIN (A REBOURS), Joris K. Huysmans. Filled with weird images, evidences of a bizarre imagination, exotic experiments with hallucinatory drugs, rich tastes and smells and the diversions of its sybarite hero Duc Jean des Esseintes, this classic novel pushed 19th-century literary decadence to its limits. Full unabridged edition. Do not confuse this with abridged editions generally sold. Introduction by Havelock Ellis. xlix + 206pp. 22190-3 Paperbound $2.00

VARIORUM SHAKESPEARE: HAMLET. Edited by Horace H. Furness; a landmark of American scholarship. Exhaustive footnotes and appendices treat all doubtful words and phrases, as well as suggested critical emendations throughout the play's history. First volume contains editor's own text, collated with all Quartos and Folios. Second volume contains full first Quarto, translations of Shakespeare's sources (Belleforest, and Saxo Grammaticus), Der Bestrafte Brudermord, and many essays on critical and historical points of interest by major authorities of past and present. Includes details of staging and costuming over the years. By far the best edition available for serious students of Shakespeare. Total of xx + 905pp. 21004-9, 21005-7, 2 volumes, Paperbound $7.00

A LIFE OF WILLIAM SHAKESPEARE, Sir Sidney Lee. This is the standard life of Shakespeare, summarizing everything known about Shakespeare and his plays. Incredibly rich in material, broad in coverage, clear and judicious, it has served thousands as the best introduction to Shakespeare. 1931 edition. 9 plates. xxix + 792pp. (USO) 21967-4 Paperbound $3.75

MASTERS OF THE DRAMA, John Gassner. Most comprehensive history of the drama in print, covering every tradition from Greeks to modern Europe and America, including India, Far East, etc. Covers more than 800 dramatists, 2000 plays, with biographical material, plot summaries, theatre history, criticism, etc. "Best of its kind in English," *New Republic*. 77 illustrations. xxii + 890pp. 20100-7 Clothbound $8.50

THE EVOLUTION OF THE ENGLISH LANGUAGE, George McKnight. The growth of English, from the 14th century to the present. Unusual, non-technical account presents basic information in very interesting form: sound shifts, change in grammar and syntax, vocabulary growth, similar topics. Abundantly illustrated with quotations. Formerly *Modern English in the Making*. xii + 590pp. 21932-1 Paperbound $3.50

AN ETYMOLOGICAL DICTIONARY OF MODERN ENGLISH, Ernest Weekley. Fullest, richest work of its sort, by foremost British lexicographer. Detailed word histories, including many colloquial and archaic words; extensive quotations. Do not confuse this with the Concise Etymological Dictionary, which is much abridged. Total of xxvii + 830pp. 6½ x 9¼. 21873-2, 21874-0 Two volumes, Paperbound $7.90

FLATLAND: A ROMANCE OF MANY DIMENSIONS, E. A. Abbott. Classic of science-fiction explores ramifications of life in a two-dimensional world, and what happens when a three-dimensional being intrudes. Amusing reading, but also useful as introduction to thought about hyperspace. Introduction by Banesh Hoffmann. 16 illustrations. xx + 103pp. 20001-9 Paperbound $1.00

POEMS OF ANNE BRADSTREET, edited with an introduction by Robert Hutchinson. A new selection of poems by America's first poet and perhaps the first significant woman poet in the English language. 48 poems display her development in works of considerable variety—love poems, domestic poems, religious meditations, formal elegies, "quaternions," etc. Notes, bibliography. viii + 222pp.

22160-1 Paperbound $2.50

THREE GOTHIC NOVELS: THE CASTLE OF OTRANTO BY HORACE WALPOLE; VATHEK BY WILLIAM BECKFORD; THE VAMPYRE BY JOHN POLIDORI, WITH FRAGMENT OF A NOVEL BY LORD BYRON, edited by E. F. Bleiler. The first Gothic novel, by Walpole; the finest Oriental tale in English, by Beckford; powerful Romantic supernatural story in versions by Polidori and Byron. All extremely important in history of literature; all still exciting, packed with supernatural thrills, ghosts, haunted castles, magic, etc. xl + 291pp.

21232-7 Paperbound $2.50

THE BEST TALES OF HOFFMANN, E. T. A. Hoffmann. 10 of Hoffmann's most important stories, in modern re-editings of standard translations: Nutcracker and the King of Mice, Signor Formica, Automata, The Sandman, Rath Krespel, The Golden Flowerpot, Master Martin the Cooper, The Mines of Falun, The King's Betrothed, A New Year's Eve Adventure. 7 illustrations by Hoffmann. Edited by E. F. Bleiler. xxxix + 419pp. 21793-0 Paperbound $3.00

GHOST AND HORROR STORIES OF AMBROSE BIERCE, Ambrose Bierce. 23 strikingly modern stories of the horrors latent in the human mind: The Eyes of the Panther, The Damned Thing, An Occurrence at Owl Creek Bridge, An Inhabitant of Carcosa, etc., plus the dream-essay, Visions of the Night. Edited by E. F. Bleiler. xxii + 199pp. 20767-6 Paperbound $1.50

BEST GHOST STORIES OF J. S. LEFANU, J. Sheridan LeFanu. Finest stories by Victorian master often considered greatest supernatural writer of all. Carmilla, Green Tea, The Haunted Baronet, The Familiar, and 12 others. Most never before available in the U. S. A. Edited by E. F. Bleiler. 8 illustrations from Victorian publications. xvii + 467pp. 20415-4 Paperbound $3.00

MATHEMATICAL FOUNDATIONS OF INFORMATION THEORY, A. I. Khinchin. Comprehensive introduction to work of Shannon, McMillan, Feinstein and Khinchin, placing these investigations on a rigorous mathematical basis. Covers entropy concept in probability theory, uniqueness theorem, Shannon's inequality, ergodic sources, the E property, martingale concept, noise, Feinstein's fundamental lemma, Shanon's first and second theorems. Translated by R. A. Silverman and M. D. Friedman. iii + 120pp. 60434-9 Paperbound $2.00

SEVEN SCIENCE FICTION NOVELS, H. G. Wells. The standard collection of the great novels. Complete, unabridged. *First Men in the Moon, Island of Dr. Moreau, War of the Worlds, Food of the Gods, Invisible Man, Time Machine, In the Days of the Comet.* Not only science fiction fans, but every educated person owes it to himself to read these novels. 1015pp. (USO) 20264-X Clothbound $6.00

LAST AND FIRST MEN AND STAR MAKER, TWO SCIENCE FICTION NOVELS, Olaf Stapledon. Greatest future histories in science fiction. In the first, human intelligence is the "hero," through strange paths of evolution, interplanetary invasions, incredible technologies, near extinctions and reemergences. Star Maker describes the quest of a band of star rovers for intelligence itself, through time and space: weird inhuman civilizations, crustacean minds, symbiotic worlds, etc. Complete, unabridged. v + 438pp. (USO) 21962-3 Paperbound $2.50

THREE PROPHETIC NOVELS, H. G. WELLS. Stages of a consistently planned future for mankind. *When the Sleeper Wakes,* and *A Story of the Days to Come,* anticipate *Brave New World* and *1984,* in the 21st Century; *The Time Machine,* only complete version in print, shows farther future and the end of mankind. All show Wells's greatest gifts as storyteller and novelist. Edited by E. F. Bleiler. x + 335pp. (USO) 20605-X Paperbound $2.50

THE DEVIL'S DICTIONARY, Ambrose Bierce. America's own Oscar Wilde— Ambrose Bierce—offers his barbed iconoclastic wisdom in over 1,000 definitions hailed by H. L. Mencken as "some of the most gorgeous witticisms in the English language." 145pp. 20487-1 Paperbound $1.25

MAX AND MORITZ, Wilhelm Busch. Great children's classic, father of comic strip, of two bad boys, Max and Moritz. Also Ker and Plunk (Plisch und Plumm), Cat and Mouse, Deceitful Henry, Ice-Peter, The Boy and the Pipe, and five other pieces. Original German, with English translation. Edited by H. Arthur Klein; translations by various hands and H. Arthur Klein. vi + 216pp.
20181-3 Paperbound $2.00

PIGS IS PIGS AND OTHER FAVORITES, Ellis Parker Butler. The title story is one of the best humor short stories, as Mike Flannery obfuscates biology and English. Also included, That Pup of Murchison's, The Great American Pie Company, and Perkins of Portland. 14 illustrations. v + 109pp. 21532-6 Paperbound $1.25

THE PETERKIN PAPERS, Lucretia P. Hale. It takes genius to be as stupidly mad as the Peterkins, as they decide to become wise, celebrate the "Fourth," keep a cow, and otherwise strain the resources of the Lady from Philadelphia. Basic book of American humor. 153 illustrations. 219pp. 20794-3 Paperbound $1.50

PERRAULT'S FAIRY TALES, translated by A. E. Johnson and S. R. Littlewood, with 34 full-page illustrations by Gustave Doré. All the original Perrault stories— Cinderella, Sleeping Beauty, Bluebeard, Little Red Riding Hood, Puss in Boots, Tom Thumb, etc.—with their witty verse morals and the magnificent illustrations of Doré. One of the five or six great books of European fairy tales. viii + 117pp. 8⅛ x 11. 22311-6 Paperbound $2.00

OLD HUNGARIAN FAIRY TALES, Baroness Orczy. Favorites translated and adapted by author of the *Scarlet Pimpernel.* Eight fairy tales include "The Suitors of Princess Fire-Fly," "The Twin Hunchbacks," "Mr. Cuttlefish's Love Story," and "The Enchanted Cat." This little volume of magic and adventure will captivate children as it has for generations. 90 drawings by Montagu Barstow. 96pp.
22293-4 Paperbound $1.95

THE RED FAIRY BOOK, Andrew Lang. Lang's color fairy books have long been children's favorites. This volume includes Rapunzel, Jack and the Bean-stalk and 35 other stories, familiar and unfamiliar. 4 plates, 93 illustrations x + 367pp.
21673-X Paperbound $2.50

THE BLUE FAIRY BOOK, Andrew Lang. Lang's tales come from all countries and all times. Here are 37 tales from Grimm, the Arabian Nights, Greek Mythology, and other fascinating sources. 8 plates, 130 illustrations. xi + 390pp.
21437-0 Paperbound $2.50

HOUSEHOLD STORIES BY THE BROTHERS GRIMM. Classic English-language edition of the well-known tales — Rumpelstiltskin, Snow White, Hansel and Gretel, The Twelve Brothers, Faithful John, Rapunzel, Tom Thumb (52 stories in all). Translated into simple, straightforward English by Lucy Crane. Ornamented with head-pieces, vignettes, elaborate decorative initials and a dozen full-page illustrations by Walter Crane. x + 269pp.
21080-4 Paperbound **$2.00**

THE MERRY ADVENTURES OF ROBIN HOOD, Howard Pyle. The finest modern versions of the traditional ballads and tales about the great English outlaw. Howard Pyle's complete prose version, with every word, every illustration of the first edition. Do not confuse this facsimile of the original (1883) with modern editions that change text or illustrations. 23 plates plus many page decorations. xxii + 296pp.
22043-5 Paperbound $2.50

THE STORY OF KING ARTHUR AND HIS KNIGHTS, Howard Pyle. The finest children's version of the life of King Arthur; brilliantly retold by Pyle, with 48 of his most imaginative illustrations. xviii + 313pp. 6⅛ x 9¼.
21445-1 Paperbound $2.50

THE WONDERFUL WIZARD OF OZ, L. Frank Baum. America's finest children's book in facsimile of first edition with all Denslow illustrations in full color. The edition a child should have. Introduction by Martin Gardner. 23 color plates, scores of drawings. iv + 267pp.
20691-2 Paperbound $2.50

THE MARVELOUS LAND OF OZ, L. Frank Baum. The second Oz book, every bit as imaginative as the Wizard. The hero is a boy named Tip, but the Scarecrow and the Tin Woodman are back, as is the Oz magic. 16 color plates, 120 drawings by John R. Neill. 287pp.
20692-0 Paperbound $2.50

THE MAGICAL MONARCH OF MO, L. Frank Baum. Remarkable adventures in a land even stranger than Oz. The best of Baum's books not in the Oz series. 15 color plates and dozens of drawings by Frank Verbeck. xviii + 237pp.
21892-9 Paperbound $2.25

THE BAD CHILD'S BOOK OF BEASTS, MORE BEASTS FOR WORSE CHILDREN, A MORAL ALPHABET, Hilaire Belloc. Three complete humor classics in one volume. Be kind to the frog, and do not call him names . . . and 28 other whimsical animals. Familiar favorites and some not so well known. Illustrated by Basil Blackwell.
156pp. (USO) 20749-8 Paperbound $1.50

EAST O' THE SUN AND WEST O' THE MOON, George W. Dasent. Considered the best of all translations of these Norwegian folk tales, this collection has been enjoyed by generations of children (and folklorists too). Includes True and Untrue, Why the Sea is Salt, East O' the Sun and West O' the Moon, Why the Bear is Stumpy-Tailed, Boots and the Troll, The Cock and the Hen, Rich Peter the Pedlar, and 52 more. The only edition with all 59 tales. 77 illustrations by Erik Werenskiold and Theodor Kittelsen. xv + 418pp. 22521-6 Paperbound $3.50

GOOPS AND HOW TO BE THEM, Gelett Burgess. Classic of tongue-in-cheek humor, masquerading as etiquette book. 87 verses, twice as many cartoons, show mischievous Goops as they demonstrate to children virtues of table manners, neatness, courtesy, etc. Favorite for generations. viii + 88pp. $6\frac{1}{2}$ x $9\frac{1}{4}$.
22233-0 Paperbound $1.25

ALICE'S ADVENTURES UNDER GROUND, Lewis Carroll. The first version, quite different from the final *Alice in Wonderland*, printed out by Carroll himself with his own illustrations. Complete facsimile of the "million dollar" manuscript Carroll gave to Alice Liddell in 1864. Introduction by Martin Gardner. viii + 96pp. Title and dedication pages in color. 21482-6 Paperbound $1.25

THE BROWNIES, THEIR BOOK, Palmer Cox. Small as mice, cunning as foxes, exuberant and full of mischief, the Brownies go to the zoo, toy shop, seashore, circus, etc., in 24 verse adventures and 266 illustrations. Long a favorite, since their first appearance in St. Nicholas Magazine. xi + 144pp. $6\frac{5}{8}$ x $9\frac{1}{4}$.
21265-3 Paperbound $1.75

SONGS OF CHILDHOOD, Walter De La Mare. Published (under the pseudonym Walter Ramal) when De La Mare was only 29, this charming collection has long been a favorite children's book. A facsimile of the first edition in paper, the 47 poems capture the simplicity of the nursery rhyme and the ballad, including such lyrics as I Met Eve, Tartary, The Silver Penny. vii + 106pp. (USO) 21972-0 Paperbound $1.25

THE COMPLETE NONSENSE OF EDWARD LEAR, Edward Lear. The finest 19th-century humorist-cartoonist in full: all nonsense limericks, zany alphabets, Owl and Pussycat, songs, nonsense botany, and more than 500 illustrations by Lear himself. Edited by Holbrook Jackson. xxix + 287pp. (USO) 20167-8 Paperbound $2.00

BILLY WHISKERS: THE AUTOBIOGRAPHY OF A GOAT, Frances Trego Montgomery. A favorite of children since the early 20th century, here are the escapades of that rambunctious, irresistible and mischievous goat—Billy Whiskers. Much in the spirit of *Peck's Bad Boy,* this is a book that children never tire of reading or hearing. All the original familiar illustrations by W. H. Fry are included: 6 color plates, 18 black and white drawings. 159pp. 22345-0 Paperbound $2.00

MOTHER GOOSE MELODIES. Faithful republication of the fabulously rare Munroe and Francis "copyright 1833" Boston edition—the most important Mother Goose collection, usually referred to as the "original." Familiar rhymes plus many rare ones, with wonderful old woodcut illustrations. Edited by E. F. Bleiler. 128pp. $4\frac{1}{2}$ x $6\frac{3}{8}$. 22577-1 Paperbound $1.00

Two Little Savages; Being the Adventures of Two Boys Who Lived as Indians and What They Learned, Ernest Thompson Seton. Great classic of nature and boyhood provides a vast range of woodlore in most palatable form, a genuinely entertaining story. Two farm boys build a teepee in woods and live in it for a month, working out Indian solutions to living problems, star lore, birds and animals, plants, etc. 293 illustrations. vii + 286pp.

20985-7 Paperbound $2.50

Peter Piper's Practical Principles of Plain & Perfect Pronunciation. Alliterative jingles and tongue-twisters of surprising charm, that made their first appearance in America about 1830. Republished in full with the spirited woodcut illustrations from this earliest American edition. 32pp. 4½ x 6⅜.

22560-7 Paperbound $1.00

Science Experiments and Amusements for Children, Charles Vivian. 73 easy experiments, requiring only materials found at home or easily available, such as candles, coins, steel wool, etc.; illustrate basic phenomena like vacuum, simple chemical reaction, etc. All safe. Modern, well-planned. Formerly *Science Games for Children*. 102 photos, numerous drawings. 96pp. 6⅛ x 9¼.

21856-2 Paperbound $1.25

An Introduction to Chess Moves and Tactics Simply Explained, Leonard Barden. Informal intermediate introduction, quite strong in explaining reasons for moves. Covers basic material, tactics, important openings, traps, positional play in middle game, end game. Attempts to isolate patterns and recurrent configurations. Formerly *Chess*. 58 figures. 102pp. (USO) 21210-6 Paperbound $1.25

Lasker's Manual of Chess, Dr. Emanuel Lasker. Lasker was not only one of the five great World Champions, he was also one of the ablest expositors, theorists, and analysts. In many ways, his Manual, permeated with his philosophy of battle, filled with keen insights, is one of the greatest works ever written on chess. Filled with analyzed games by the great players. A single-volume library that will profit almost any chess player, beginner or master. 308 diagrams. xli x 349pp.

20640-8 Paperbound $2.75

The Master Book of Mathematical Recreations, Fred Schuh. In opinion of many the finest work ever prepared on mathematical puzzles, stunts, recreations; exhaustively thorough explanations of mathematics involved, analysis of effects, citation of puzzles and games. Mathematics involved is elementary. Translated bv F. Göbel. 194 figures. xxiv + 430pp.

22134-2 Paperbound $3.50

Mathematics, Magic and Mystery, Martin Gardner. Puzzle editor for Scientific American explains mathematics behind various mystifying tricks: card tricks, stage "mind reading," coin and match tricks, counting out games, geometric dissections, etc. Probability sets, theory of numbers clearly explained. Also provides more than 400 tricks, guaranteed to work, that you can do. 135 illustrations. xii + 176pp.

20335-2 Paperbound $1.75

CATALOGUE OF DOVER BOOKS

MATHEMATICAL PUZZLES FOR BEGINNERS AND ENTHUSIASTS, Geoffrey Mott-Smith. 189 puzzles from easy to difficult—involving arithmetic, logic, algebra, properties of digits, probability, etc.—for enjoyment and mental stimulus. Explanation of mathematical principles behind the puzzles. 135 illustrations. viii + 248pp.
20198-8 Paperbound $1.75

PAPER FOLDING FOR BEGINNERS, William D. Murray and Francis J. Rigney. Easiest book on the market, clearest instructions on making interesting, beautiful origami. Sail boats, cups, roosters, frogs that move legs, bonbon boxes, standing birds, etc. 40 projects; more than 275 diagrams and photographs. 94pp.
20713-7 Paperbound $1.00

TRICKS AND GAMES ON THE POOL TABLE, Fred Herrmann. 79 tricks and games—some solitaires, some for two or more players, some competitive games—to entertain you between formal games. Mystifying shots and throws, unusual caroms, tricks involving such props as cork, coins, a hat, etc. Formerly *Fun on the Pool Table*. 77 figures. 95pp.
21814-7 Paperbound $1.00

HAND SHADOWS TO BE THROWN UPON THE WALL: A SERIES OF NOVEL AND AMUSING FIGURES FORMED BY THE HAND, Henry Bursill. Delightful picturebook from great-grandfather's day shows how to make 18 different hand shadows: a bird that flies, duck that quacks, dog that wags his tail, camel, goose, deer, boy, turtle, etc. Only book of its sort. vi + 33pp. 6½ x 9¼. 21779-5 Paperbound $1.00

WHITTLING AND WOODCARVING, E. J. Tangerman. 18th printing of best book on market. "If you can cut a potato you can carve" toys and puzzles, chains, chessmen, caricatures, masks, frames, woodcut blocks, surface patterns, much more. Information on tools, woods, techniques. Also goes into serious wood sculpture from Middle Ages to present, East and West. 464 photos, figures. x + 293pp.
20965-2 Paperbound $2.00

HISTORY OF PHILOSOPHY, Julián Marias. Possibly the clearest, most easily followed, best planned, most useful one-volume history of philosophy on the market; neither skimpy nor overfull. Full details on system of every major philosopher and dozens of less important thinkers from pre-Socratics up to Existentialism and later. Strong on many European figures usually omitted. Has gone through dozens of editions in Europe. 1966 edition, translated by Stanley Appelbaum and Clarence Strowbridge. xviii + 505pp. 21739-6 Paperbound $3.50

YOGA: A SCIENTIFIC EVALUATION, Kovoor T. Behanan. Scientific but non-technical study of physiological results of yoga exercises; done under auspices of Yale U. Relations to Indian thought, to psychoanalysis, etc. 16 photos. xxiii + 270pp.
20505-3 Paperbound $2.50

Prices subject to change without notice.
Available at your book dealer or write for free catalogue to Dept. GI, Dover Publications, Inc., 180 Varick St., N. Y., N. Y. 10014. Dover publishes more than 150 books each year on science, elementary and advanced mathematics, biology, music, art, literary history, social sciences and other areas.